WALKIN'
PREACHER
OF THE
OZARKS

"In the beginning was the Word."

WALKIN'
PREACHER
OF THE
OZARKS

By

GUY HOWARD

HARPER & BROTHERS
New York and London

To MARY LOUISE

CONTENTS

FOREWORD

THIS IS THE MODERN SAGA OF A COUNTRY PREACHER who has, literally, walked into the lives of countless Ozark-backhills people. It is of necessity (and in truth) the intimate revelation of their physical and spiritual existence. Many were good lives; some were bad.

Therefore, in deference to those lives which are revealed where all may see, in the crisp black type of these pages, the actual names and places are not always given. The records of some have already been entered in the Great Book, but lest the living fear identification, it is not presumed that this narrative could prejudice the text of their final Record.

THE AUTHOR

ACKNOWLEDGMENT

The author wishes to thank May Kennedy McCord, Mary Elizabeth Mahnkey, Dr. Fred S. Robison, Perry J. Mason, Thomas Elmore Lucy, and the late Gordon Hudelson for their timely suggestions and kind assistance in the writing of this book.

The author especially desires to express his appreciation to his friends Townsend and Helen Godsey for help received in the preparation of the manuscript and their kindness in making available illustrations which appear herein.

WALKIN'
PREACHER
OF THE
OZARKS

CHAPTER 1

The Corn Grows Tall

THE CREAKING CULTIVATOR DROPPED INTO LAGGING tempo and the halting movements of the mules warned of nearness to the fence. One more trip completed. One more row nearer harvest.

Corn grows tall in Iowa—after it is cultivated. And before the sun's downing, irrespective of the importance of a Memorial Day speech, all the grayish earth between rows of greening blades must reveal the rich black of fresh-turned loam.

Tomorrow would be Memorial Sunday, and there remained so little time to do so many things. Important things they were too, for farms do not run themselves and become successful, even in Lucas County. And I, the district schoolteacher, wanted more than anything else in the world to be a successful farmer; was willing to slave for the necessary capital with a singleness of purpose in diligent industry—aided, of course, by the span of mules borrowed from Uncle Doras Baker.

A violent yellow jacket, mischief bent, circled uncomfortably near the mules. Kate shook her long ears vehemently, and vibrations rippled the length of her sleek brown body, rattling the chains at snaffle and cockeye. The jack heeded the warning and buzzed off into the fragrant air.

Jinny and Kate calmly bent down to nuzzle the bluestem that fringed the fence. Suddenly Jinny foxed her ears. A quail whirred out of the plum thicket in yon draw. I sat and watched the bird fly off, pondering how

I had taught my spring pupils at Strahan School that every creature had its place in God's plan. The neighborly Bobwhite and his humble works were a demonstration of how unassuming creatures of the fields and woodlands help the farmer—help him in his ceaseless warfare against an evil that would destroy his crops. For upon humble things the success of a great thing often depends.

"Gee," I called, and we swung about for a fresh turn at the limitless expanse of field that spread out in a gray-green pattern.

Then the mules stopped. Quite abruptly! It is better to believe theirs was a mulish rebellion at so much unfinished work, rather than brutish objection to the verbal punishment that was being inflicted upon them by the repetitious practice of my speech.

I hadn't wanted to accept the invitation to give the principal Memorial Day address, knowing full well it would require time for preparation. The graybeard lawyer who in years past had furnished the oratory for the county had moved to Des Moines, and the committee had sought a substitute. There was no preacher in the community so the next best choice had been to seek out the schoolteacher, who, like the preacher, is called upon to serve in so many capacities. It always seems the easiest alternative in any rural community just "to ask the preacher or the teacher," neither of whom can ever seem to find an acceptable excuse.

I was jealous of every precious moment of my summer vacation and wanted it uninterrupted for farming so that when harvest was in there might be money—perhaps even enough to make it unnecessary for me to teach school next year. Then I could work hard all winter, and come spring Madge would be graduated and we could be married. (I hadn't asked her yet lest it give the gossips something succulent to mouth as they do fresh green onions, chewing the tender portions, tossing aside the green tops and having a bad taste left in their palates.)

Often a rural teacher married one of the pupils, even before school was out. There was no question of any big difference in age, for frequently, as in my own case, the teacher was a high-school graduate who had taken an examination for a limited certificate, and many of the older pupils would be near his age.

Such was life in a day and age when one could muster a squad of Civil War veterans for a Memorial Day parade.

"Giddap," I called, almost angrily, and the mules sulked their way down the corn rows.

When we married, would the lives of Madge, myself and all our kinsfolk be complicated, as had been the lives of my parents, by the fact that her people were Calvinists and I was from a Methodist family? These two sects were bitter rivals in Lucas County.

But Madge would be at the services to hear the speech— I'd best get my thoughts back to it; I must make good, if only for her.

As the cultivator blades furrowed the soil, so I plowed the furrows of my memory to turn from a famous essay or novel I had read some phrases which I might effectively use. I tried repeating many quotations with every variety of inflection, shading and timing them with dramatic endeavor. Old Judge Barnes had always been eloquent and had used impressive Latin phrases. Folk would expect as much from the schoolteacher. But my eloquence wasn't convincing, even to the mules, who finally became so frustrated that I realized something must be done. Mine were vain repetitions, lacking in honest simplicity.

Then I remembered. . . . Hadn't that fellow (hardly anyone can ever remember his name) orated more than two hours before Abraham Lincoln made his ageless two-minute speech? Why not forget about trying to impress folk—even Madge?

I saw it all no longer "through a glass, darkly," but then as clearly and simply as the white-barked sycamore is reflected in a woodland pool.

"In the annals of the history of all civilized nations certain days are set apart to commemorate historical events. Christmas Day is universally observed to glorify the birth of the Son of God; the Fourth of July is celebrated to laud the birth of our nation; Thanksgiving is proclaimed that we may commemorate the birth of our consciousness of the bounties that God has bestowed upon us. Memorial Day is set aside, not to honor a birth, but that we may stand with bowed heads in tribute to the thousands of noble soldiers—men who died that you and I as citizens of this great nation might today enjoy an undenied freedom.

"Let us turn back the pages of history to 1861 and 1898. What do we see? A great host of American manhood giving up their business prospects, their chances for an education, their right to a home, love, peace and contentment, for a great ideal.

"That ideal was the ideal of country. It will ever be thus in this nation of free men, so long as it is free. . . ."

I was not conscious of reaching the end of the field. The mules must have voluntarily turned and headed back; for when I again became aware of them out in front, their heads bobbed rhythmically as they plodded on to turn another row.

CHAPTER 2

A Day of Memories

IT WOULD HAVE BEEN PLEASANT TO ACCOMPANY MADGE and her family to the Memorial Day service at Union Chapel, but there was no one to help me with my chores and no time to spare for going early. As I gave my boots a coat of blacking that mingled an oily odor of tallow and chimney soot with other strange smells of the back stoop, I could see folk trailing down the sunlit road toward the church and its God's Acre across the way. The Gaillard Catbird sang from the Osage Orange hedge. On such a glorious late spring day a large crowd could be expected for the services.

Many would come for the worship and speaking. Others would return from wanderings in distant places to bring stiff store-boughten sprays or waxy-leaved wreaths for the family grave plots. A few would bring dried floral wreaths encased in glass-topped boxes. These expensive offerings would appear cheap beside the bountiful red and white peonies or yellow roses gathered from farmyards round about.

Mother had gathered her flowers before the dew left them and had taken a basketful for the "decorating." She and father took much pride in the old burial ground and assumed their share of responsibility to the dead interred there.

Beneath a carved sandstone marker bearing the inscription "Reverend Joseph Benjamin Howard" the bones of my great-grandfather mingled with the soil. A pioneer in the windswept prairies, he had organized the first

5

church and Sunday school and had preached the first sermon in Lucas County. He had conducted services in his sod house for more than a year, until a sawmill moved on the creek and its operator made his peace with God by sawing the lumber for a rude church house.

So complete had been Mother's harvest there wasn't a single blossom left in the yard when I sought one for my coat lapel. However, one yellow dandelion had escaped her spring green gathering and it made a colorful boutonniere. Alone, I walked to church.

Out over the rolling green countryside the church bell exhorted the stragglers and those still decorating in the cemetery to hasten to the chapel. Having laid in place the last blossom, having stuck into the good earth the pine staff of the last starched, red-white-and-blue flag, the rural folk of the Iowa prairie community trailed into the church.

As I entered, old Dr. Thomas, seated just inside the door, tried to slide down the bench to make room for me. But the line wouldn't budge. He peered out across the laps to see who was ignoring his nudgings. It was the wooden end of the bench that wouldn't give and there were no empty seats nearby. I turned to lean against the doorjamb but the committee chairman beckoned me down in front to a vacant chair on the platform. I smiled wryly to the old doctor and walked down the aisle toward the seat of honor.

It was only a few steps from the rear of the church to the platform in front, but in traversing that distance I passed several generations of county history. The gay young bucks and their girls were seated at the back; in the next benches were folk who seldom showed their faces inside a church excepting for funerals or special holiday services; the substantial and insubstantial farmers of the region and the regular churchgoers in their order filled the center; on the front rows were war veterans, wives and widows of veterans and a group of small children.

It was only after the chairman had shaken my hand and escorted me to the vacant seat on the platform that I had a chance to look for Madge. She was with her family a few seats behind the rows of veterans. Her smile was as reassuring as the one sent by Mother, but I looked away from both of them lest I become distracted. They expected so much of me.

The row of old men on the benches held my attention so completely that I barely heard the preliminary remarks. I caught myself looking at these old warriors over the top of my hymnal. They were sixteen in number. Most of them wore faded blue coats and each wore a campaign medal. One, sprightlier than the others, displayed on his coat front a half-dozen variously shaped and beribboned badges, souvenirs of state and national reunions. The wives of some of them sat at their sides, but on the seat behind, widows of other veterans sat alone with folded hands. Through the early part of the service, the old men sat in erect, soldierly attitude; as the program wore on some sagged against a neighbor, others scrunched in their seats or leaned heavily upon their canes. Old Uncle Joel was struggling with his quid of soggy weed and trying to dispose of it in a great red handkerchief lest his daughter across the aisle see him and reprimand him later. And then I heard my name spoken . . . the time had come. . . .

My knees alone applauded the presentation. There was a hushed silence just as there had always been before Judge Barnes began to speak. It seemed almost an eternity before, in the hushed quiet, the words came.

"In the annals of history . . . Christmas . . . Fourth of July . . . Thanksgiving . . . Decoration Day . . . sacrifice . . . for freedom . . ."

It all seemed so brief that when the closing hymn was sung I wondered if I had spoken at all. Then, as I stepped from the platform the extended gnarled hands of the veterans, the smiles and nods of their children and the audible whisperings of others bespoke approval. I looked for Madge. Was it a knowing wink of approval I saw crowning her smile? Mother obviously approved. Members of her quilting circle hovered about, but she pushed her frail way through silks and twill to my side.

"It was so good, Guy.... Your father is going home with Grandma Howard. Mrs. Thomas wants us to go to dinner with her."

Everyone knew the doctor's wife set a good table.

After dinner the good doctor and I carried rockers to the porch, and while the women crumbed the table and "redded up" the dishes we sat and talked.

"Guy," he began, "you did right well today—might have been one of your ancestors preaching. Though the Lord knows you didn't get messed up in the whys and wherefores of religion like some of your kinfolk used to."

"I've heard a few tales," I said, "about my grandparents' warring over church. Some of them must be true for they're always at outs."

The doctor didn't answer for a minute. There was a disconcerted rattle of his dentures. "Dang these things, Guy! They're fine for a man's pride but they sure aren't any help to his appetite." After a moment of plagued silence he went on. "A fellow doesn't often get to know much about his borning, but yours started such a scrap you ought to know about it."

"Mother and father always got along well," I defended. "Does this quarreling of their families date back to my birth?"

"I reckon it went back farther than when you were born but that was the first I knew much about it." The doctor fished a pipe from one coat pocket, a pinch of tobacco from another, and wedded the two. Taking a match from his unbuttoned vest he kindled a flame that sent wreaths of smoke about his venerable head.

"There's been lots of layings-in and deliveries I wouldn't remember about," he resumed. "But I'll never forget the night I delivered your mother. She'd been laboring about two days and was mighty weak when your paw came and got me. Your Grandma Howard and Grandma Baker were both there.

" 'She sure wants a girl this time,' one of the grand-mothers said as I walked into the house.

"Well it wasn't long after that 'til you were born, Guy. Long about twilight as the sun went over the rim of Nicollet's Bowl, I handed you over to your grandmothers. While I was attending your mother, above the wailin' I heard one of 'em say, 'It's another boy.' Then your Grand-ma Howard says, 'We'll call him Samuel Johnathan after his two grandpas.'

"I was too busy to notice much, but your mother was listenin' and spoke up, 'Oh no we won't. His name is Guy Wesley.'

" 'That's it,' says Grandma Baker. Of course she would, being a Methodist from way back. Your Grandma Howard had a different notion. 'Humph! If I was naming him after a church man,' she snapped, 'it wouldn't be a Wesley. Calvin'd be a heap prettier name and then maybe he'd be a preacher and keep up the Howard family ways.' "

"Where was my father all this time?" I asked as I handed the doctor another match.

"Oh, he was standing right there in the bedroom door-way, just as helpless as any other new father," he chuckled. "But your Grandma Howard didn't stop for anything and she lit right in on him. 'George,' she says, 'It's bad enough for you to join Cora's church without you standing there and naming this baby after a Meth-odist.'

"Finally I had to put a stop to it for your mother's sake. 'The idea of quarreling over church when this little mother needs quiet and rest after all this labor,' I said to them, just like that.

"Your father stiffened in the doorway and spoke up. 'That's right! Cora has stood all the pain and suffering. She can name this baby whatever she pleases.'"

Dr. Thomas turned and looked at me over his spectacles. "Your father don't speak often, Guy, but when he does he means what he says."

I nodded in agreement.

Then the doctor continued. "I can see it all, right now. Grandma Howard began loosening the two long strips of cloth that had been tied to the posts at the foot of the bed for your mother to use while she was in labor. That was a common practice used by old doctors and midwives. (It still works sometimes.) They figured the labor could be hurried by letting the mother pull herself to a halfway sitting position. Anyway, Grandma Howard sure showed she was put out by the way she yanked that cloth from the bedpost.

"Well I figured that wasn't the end of the argument, but Cora had had a hard time and needed rest and quiet so I called your father aside and told him we'd better wait a few days to file the birth certificate and give the women folks a little time to thrash out the name. Your father just said for me to do it however Cora wanted it— church or no church. And so I registered you Guy Wesley Howard."

"And that's why the religious ruckus hasn't ever died down," I grinned.

"Partly," he nodded. "I remember after I had my say your grandmas lit out home, both of 'em mad as wet hens. In the little house everything was quiet. As I went out your father was sitting in a chair near the heating stove. He'd put an old envelope between the lamp flue and the prong that held it on, to shade the light from your mother's eyes though she had dropped off to sleep.

"'Course I'd known your folks a long time. George and Cora had grown up in the same community and they'd gone to spellin' matches and literary and debatin' societies together. George told me, when we were making out the birth certificate, that after he and Cora were married they each had insisted on joining the other's church.

"There were just three churches in Newbern, the nearest trading town. They hated each other like poison but they had their meetings on alternate Sundays. The first Sunday after your folks were married, they went to church. It happened the services were with the Methodists and George joined. That was your mother's church."

"And then," I said, "they were approved by the Methodists and damned by the Presbyterians! Mother told me that much; and how my father's brother, at a theological school back East, had written and condemned him for letting his wife lead him astray and bringing everlasting shame upon the family."

"Well I didn't know about that part of it," said the doctor, "but after I got home that night you was born, Martha and I talked about the row between your grandparents. Martha always waited up for me when I was out nights and had me something hot to drink when I got in. She was never one to quiz me about my patients but she was always interested in the babies—never had any ourselves; always too busy gettin' somebody else's.

"When I told Martha about your grandmas' argument she nigh blew up. 'Calvinism! Methodism!' she cried. 'Each one renders good Christian service to the world, but around here they defeat themselves by their everlasting fighting. Poor little tyke,' she added sadly.

" 'Might make a preacher,' I said as she set a steaming poached egg in front of me—just to see what she'd say.

" 'Preacher—humph!' She snorted. 'The child'll get a

good Christian training and his pa and ma aren't so set in their ways. But both their families being hotheaded about religion, all the little fellow will hear from his grand-parents will be predestination and backsliding and sprinkling and such.'"

The doctor pulled his pipe from between his teeth and cradled it in his hands.

"Well, my job," he said, "has been to bring babies into the world. I leave getting them into heaven to the preach-ers. I told Martha, though, that if that little boy had as hard a time being born again as he had the first time, he sure stood a good chance of being lost."

Dr. Thomas knocked out his pipe and refilled it. He turned to face me quizzically: "Guy," he squinted as he packed the tobacco firmly in the bowl, "it seems to me that those who officiate at the second birth don't agree on correct procedure as well as we who have been trained to attend the first borning."

"Doctor, the greatest Teacher of all times taught them the way," I said. "He gave the world a Book of rules so plain that 'a wayfaring man, though a fool, shall not err therein.'"

"Now you're preaching, Guy. I was thinking at the services today that maybe I was right years ago, when I told Martha you might be a preacher. Maybe you ought to try it. If you could rise above the petty prejudices of this community . . . yes, maybe you ought to."

"I don't want to be a preacher," I rebelled. "I want to be a farmer. I want to make money and have things. I'm going to be a success."

"There's nothing wrong with farming, Guy," the doctor answered. "But there's a lot to life besides making money. The most that's wrong with half the bellyachin' patients I've had the last twenty years has been pains from having too much or from worrying over not having something they wanted. Success isn't things, Guy—it's a feeling. Lord knows it's even possible to be a successful preacher."

I wanted to argue further but the flypapers on the screen door rattled and the women folk came out. If Mother heard what we were saying, she'd want to argue too—on the side of the doctor.

CHAPTER 3

To Man's Estate

IT IS REMARKABLE HOW NATURE RESPONDS TO MAN'S simple kindnesses, even to the cultivating of a cornfield. The green spires that rowed the countryside back of our farmhouse had made the most of the growing weather. In so short a space of time—from Saturday to Monday— the corn had assumed new importance to the quiet landscape. Today it gave promise of a worthy stand and, once past the swelter of July's heat, a bountiful harvest. Oh glorious world!

The old doctor could speak of preachers! He could, from the acquired comfort of his broad, freshly painted veranda, speak of opportunities, and talent, and success in terms of country preachers. He'd made his mark and wanted not for comfort: he had his bed, his board and shelter—more and to spare. He had his Martha. The doctor had labored diligently and wrestled with life and death many times over to achieve this measure of success which, in the graying years, was now his. Couldn't a farmer likewise engage the forces of good and evil—good seasons and bad, good land and foul, fertility and its opposite—in husbandry to attain success? Preaching had its advantages, I was sure, but none of the Howards nor any preacher I knew had ever waxed more affluent than the proverbial church mouse.

I had returned Uncle Doras' mules to the shelter of their own barn Saturday night, but there was still the unfulfilled obligation for their use. For that, I must spend the day riding the cultivator. As I walked through the dewy grasses to Uncle's farm, the admonition of the doctor mingled with the confusion of praises remembered from Sunday's minor success.

Riding a cultivator gives a man ample time to think, as any farm-reared lad knows well. I had been busy through the lesser years growing in stature, and in superficial wisdom, and in Sunday favor with God. There had been little time and less reason to ponder my existence: I had always taken ME for granted. With the Memorial Day speaking had come a consciousness of a desire for favor with men.

Perhaps it is a mark of growth in a man when he takes stock of himself and the episodes of life that make him what he is. At least I liked to believe that was the case as I took inventory of my growing years on this morning when I turned my eyes from my own cornfield and aimed the mules down the rows of Uncle Doras' field.

There had been some pleasantness in my life but the hardships of the early years had left a deep impress. When I was four years old, a baby brother was born. Chester was a frail infant and for long months required almost constant attention of my parents and the endless stream of relatives and neighbors who came to help care for him. The medicine and prepared foods needed consumed most of my father's income. There was too little margin between eleven-cent corn and five-cents-a-dozen eggs and our expenses to permit more than the simplest kind of living. The years of '93, '94 and '95 were bitter ones with crop failures and an economic depression in their history.

Then in '96 we had a good season and all Lucas County blossomed. Everyone had an abundance of grain, feed, vegetables and fruit. The gallon glass Horlick's Malted Milk jars of Chester's baby days were filled with vegetables and fruit against the winter months to come.

Mother dried large quantities of some fruits and vegetables in the warm fall sunshine. Great rings of yellow pumpkin were hung on pegs to dry. Peaches were quartered and dried on a clean cloth spread on the sloping roof of the lean-to kitchen.

Apple drying was quite an interesting chore for my older brother and me. The pippins were peeled and divided into small sections. We strung them on long white cords and festooned them between parallel rows of poles which ran across the back yard. The strings of drying fruit curved in perfect symmetry the full length of this improvised drying rack.

Each evening before sundown the apples were brought into the house to protect them from the night dampness. Each morning it was Hugh's and my job to stand on chairs and help tie the strings to the drying poles. Sometimes when Mother had a busy evening in the house Hugh and I would untie the drying fruit and take it to the kitchen. One evening we discovered that if a string of apples was lowered to the proper jumping height we could have a perfect hurdle race. What a merry time we had until Mother discovered our track.

Our little forty-acre farm was none too productive, and while there was always enough plain, wholesome food and no one went hungry, there was little variety. There were three or four cows and a few hogs and Mother had a large flock of Plymouth Rock chickens. These supplied us with meat, lard, butter, milk, eggs and an occasional fried or baked chicken. Surplus eggs and butter were sold to buy coffee, sugar, kerosene and such necessities not produced on the farm. Each summer a large garden furnished beans, cabbage, tomatoes, potatoes and squashes, the surplus of which was properly stored to use throughout the winter months. We always made a barrel of sauerkraut. An uncle once gave us boys a pup. Watch became a fine squirrel dog and, aside from the joy of the hunt, he was valuable in providing further variety to our meat diet.

A meal was never eaten at our house until some member of the family thanked God for the food even though it might be plain and meager. Almost as soon as we could talk, Mother taught each of us grace, which we took turns repeating before a meal. "Our Heavenly Father, we thank Thee for this food and Thy love. We pray that Thou wilt always keep us and watch over us. Amen."

Our parents were firm believers in everyone having a share in the work, so Hugh and I had regular chores and duties. When there was hoeing to be done, Father would count the rows and give each of us an equal number. Also it was one of my regular duties to find the hens' nests that were hidden out in the brush. Hugh was obedient and more industrious than I. He quickly did his work and then I would bribe him to help me get my share done. One summer I collected twenty-four Arbuckle coffee wrappers from neighbors and got a Barlow knife as a premium. How I loved to whittle with it! Once I promised to carve a bird out of a piece of soft pine if Hugh would hoe my last seven rows of cane. The plan worked perfectly until Father caught us. He had his notions about a man doing his own work, and he was willing to thrash when necessary, to make his point.

Each spring we planted a large patch of sorghum cane and come fall we had the cane made into molasses "on the shares" at Mason's Mill. How I hated those days after the first frost when Father kept us home from school to strip cane. We would work up and down the long rows from daylight until dark, knocking off the leaves with a short paddle. One year we evolved a game which made the distasteful task somewhat easier. We were soldiers with stripping-paddle "swords." The rows of cane stalks were the enemy in battle formation. We backed up ten feet from the end of a row, held our swords aloft,

and at a called "Charge!" rushed the enemy. Each strove
to win the battle by being the first to strip every enemy
clean. A blade left on the stalk was an enemy soldier
missed and a point toward defeat. Leaves flew.

The leaves were tied into bundles with elm-bark string
and saved for winter stock feed. Father cut the canes,
chopped off the seedy heads and hauled the long stalks
to the sorghum mill. The seedy heads were placed in the
loft of the poultry house for chicken feed. Mother
laughed when I suggested we use a threshing machine on
the cane. "Pay money to thresh it? How foolish that
would be! The chickens thresh it for nothing and it's a
good thing for laying hens to have to scratch for their
living.

"People are the same way, son," she continued. "Those
who have to work hard, plan, skimp, save and depend
on the Lord, are far better off than those who have things
too easy." A warm, yeasty odor pervaded the kitchen as
Mother turned and pulled four great brown loaves of
bread from the oven. "You'll learn, Guy," she continued
her sermonette, "that if you are a successful man, you'll
have to scratch for most of the things you get. It's like
that lesson you were reading this morning in McGuffey's
Reader: 'Idleness is the Devil's Workshop.' That means
that people who don't have enough to do get into
trouble." She brushed a wisp of hair from her forehead
and straightened her apron. "We all get very, very tired
sometimes when we work hard, Guy; but it rests our
souls and minds to know that God gives us strength to
help ourselves—and other people, too."

Father often supplemented the meager family income
by helping more prosperous neighbors during threshing,
corn-cutting and corn-shucking seasons.

My older brother and I often walked the two miles to
Newbern with a bucket of eggs. These we bartered for
household supplies. Mother would give us a list of things

to bring home and there was seldom any credit left after making the purchases. Yet these trips to the general merchandise store, which was operated by Mother's brother-in-law, were red-letter days for us boys. Uncle Fred always seemed to know just what little boys wanted. He would dip his hand into the glass candy jar on the counter and say: 'You boys help me out trading here for your mother so I'll give you a barber pole.' Then he would hand each of us a large stick of red-striped candy. Sometimes his gift was a handful of dried raisins or a stick of the much-coveted licorice. Occasionally it was a generous lump of brown sugar.

When Hugh was eleven and I was ten we had another bad year. Crops had been poor the season before and we had little to sell. One of our horses was killed by lightning and the other one died in foaling. Father worked out for a neighbor but the top wages of twenty dollars a month must needs be carefully saved to purchase another team. Hugh and I worried about the prospects of the Fourth of July celebration.

"Why don't you boys earn some money of your own?" Mother suggested. "There are a lot of wild gooseberries this year and they're extra large. If you pick and stem some, I believe you could sell them." Thirty minutes later we were on our way to the woods, and for four days we worked diligently with only time out to go home and eat, sleep and do our chores. Late evening of the fourth day we had four gallons of the shiny green berries sorted and stemmed and ready for the market. Early next morning we carried our wealth to Newbern. We solicited every house in the little town but couldn't sell a berry.

"Let's quit and go home," fretted Hugh.

"No," I said, "I'm going out to Aunt Martha's."

"Gosh, Guy," he groaned, "it's a mile and a half out there and there won't be any teams going that way."

"Then we'll walk," I insisted.

We arrived at kind Aunt Martha's tired and sweaty. It was far past noon but she insisted on giving us some dinner. When she learned of our unsuccessful berry venture, she kept the berries and tied a new half-dollar in a corner of our handkerchiefs. That was a veritable fortune for boys who had never before had more than fifteen cents.

We were proud of those half-dollars! Joyous hours were filled with planning what to buy at the Fourth of July celebration. Hugh spent twenty cents of his wealth when the great day came, but I so hated to break my shiny new coin that it was still secure in its knot when we wearily returned home after the celebration.

That fall, at Mother's suggestion, we gathered and hulled hazelnuts. Two bushel baskets held our wealth, which sold for three dollars a bushel. Mother had always made our shirts and overalls, doing the work by hand; now with the nut money we each bought our first pair of factory-made denim overalls and a pair of overshoes.

Every Lord's Day through the years, regardless of the weather, we drove the two miles to Newbern to church. Sunday school was held at the Methodist Church at ten o'clock and at the Presbyterian Church at three o'clock in the afternoon. Preaching came one Sunday a month at each church. The United Brethren Church, a third place of worship in the little town, had no Sunday school but had preaching once each month. Our family seldom missed a service at any of the churches.

Revival meetings were frequent and members of all the churches made the pretense of uniting in the activity. In the heat of spiritual emotion the service took rather an impromptu form. An hour of singing, testifying and shouting often preceded the regular preaching service. One winter old Brother Matheeney held a nine weeks' revival at the Methodist Church. His revival ended with two hundred and twenty-five converts. Less than two years later, Brother Heardman held a revival for six weeks in the Presbyterian Church with about the same number of converts. And there were fewer than five hundred persons in the whole community! This tempo of religious fervor promoted a deeply righteous environment.

Hugh and I were always sent to Sunday services even when my baby brother was at his worst and our parents couldn't attend. Either Mother or Father would take us a mile across the fields to Mother's old home and Grandpa and Grandma Baker would take us on to the services.

Aunt Lizzie, Mother's sister, took us to church one Sunday when Grandma was ill. My, with what religious vigor she washed my ears that day. She believed that "cleanliness is next to Godliness" and did not intend to be found short.

"Hurry now and black your shoes and get your stockings and shoes on," she blustered. There was a place in my right shoe about the size of a dime where my little toe had worn through. I discovered, after dressing the foot, that the stocking had a hole too, and that it corresponded with the hole in the shoe. The toe was in noticeable contrast to the freshly blackened boot. Rather than change the stocking to the other foot I got the polish bottle and blacked the offending toe. Sunday school classmates laughed heartily at my subterfuge. So, proud of my ingenuity, I displayed the paint job to Aunt Lizzie; whereupon she added one more vigorous spanking to the hundreds acquired in my rearing. From my early home training I acquired the concept that worship and chastisement are very necessary parts of life.

Religion sometimes brought on situations I could not understand and which only added to the confusion resulting from my attendance at churches of different denominations. The old doctor's tale of how my birth had served to alienate my parents from their kinsmen was easily understood for I had seen how hair-splitting differences wrecked whole churches and congregations. They even quarreled over the question of what musical instruments could be piously played within a church.

The Strawn boys had a pretty cousin who used to come out from the city for summer visits. One summer Miss Abernathy brought along a friend who sang well, and on Sunday morning she sang a solo for church. Miss Abernathy accompanied her with the violin. She must have known how to play the violin mighty well for even as a boy I was stirred by the beauty of the music she made. The young ladies had barely resumed their seats when, before the pastor could speak, Grandma Graves rose as if ascending into her own private heaven and in a high-pitched voice of self-righteous indignation exhorted:

"Brethern and Sisters! Are we so spiritually weak that we're afeared to speak out in the Lord's house? We ought to be like Joshua and Caleb. They weren't afeared to speak out and neither am I. Maybe I'll have to stand alone, but there ain't any Graveses afeared to stand up for the Lord. The Bible may say for wimmen to keep still in church but somebody's got to speak out, and it ain't likely the menfolks'll take a stand. Lord have mercy that I should live to see the day that arch instrument of the devil, that dancin' fiddle of sin an' shame, should be brought into the Lord's house. I beseech you let us kneel and pray...."

Thus spoken, she turned to kneel on the bench, leaning over the back, thus maintaining a dominating position over the others, who knelt humbly on the floor. She covered her upraised face with her left hand blinding only one eye that she might survey the flock as a divine cyclops. She raised a pontifical fist high above her black bonnet and began.

"Ohoooooooooo God. Fergive us sinners and especially that that brought disgrace to your pure house...." Her petition continued, rising and falling in an emotional cadence.

Careful lest Grandma Graves find me with her all-seeing eye, I glanced at Miss Abernathy, who had knelt with the others. The knuckles on her dainty bow hand whitened as she gripped the bench. Her teeth bit into her lower lip. Then the cyclops found me and I was aware only of a knot in the floor. The sun had lengthened its shadow across two planks before Grandma Graves's voice trailed off into an unintelligible mumble that ended suddenly with a loud "Amen."

The congregation readjusted itself in the pews. The organist quickly led off into a hymn almost before Grandma Graves could finish rubbing the numbness from her knees. Miss Abernathy opened her hymnal to the proper page and looked at it very hard, but no song came forth. When the service was over Grandma Graves rustled to the front of the church and the pastor. Miss Abernathy carefully laid her violin in its case and tucked it away under her arm. She raised her chin proudly and she and her friend and the cousins went quickly out of the door. I would have been surprised to hear that any member of the group ever again entered a church.

The rural school where Hugh and I began our studies in the same year was two miles from home. Mother drove us over in the wagon and left us. School was in session when we arrived. Hugh, seven, and one year my senior, did the talking. He gave our names and ages and his birthday correctly but he couldn't remember my birthday. "He was borned in corn-shuckin'," he said to the merriment of the pupils. When the primer class was called I went forward but was afraid to recite. At the first recess they nicknamed me "Geyser," punning my name (and rightly so, for a placid lake was located under my seat).

Miss Margaret Smith was a kind and gentle teacher—too kind for the welfare of the school perhaps, for there were twelve or fourteen big boys and girls who needed rigid discipline. Discipline was a major problem in those schools, which many big boys and girls attended. It was no time or place to spare the rod and spoil the child. The teacher who did not rule with the rod was counted a failure. He who whipped everyone for everything was a success.

Pupils of this era were classified according to the McGuffey Readers, and education was complete when one had thoroughly mastered McGuffey's Fifth Reader, Ray's Third Part Arithmetic and Webster's blue-backed speller. The three R's, Readin', 'Ritin' and 'Rithmetic, were the all-important subjects. Geography, history and English grammar were taught, being commonly rated in the order named although patrons generally did not want teachers to deviate from the three R's. There were high schools in a few of the county seat towns but tuition and board were almost prohibitive for rural children.

The school session came in three terms. There was a two-months fall term followed by a two-weeks vacation for corn-shucking. The winter term usually lasted three months with a four- to six-weeks spring vacation. Spring term followed that and ended the last of May or mid-June. Usually the older boys and girls did not attend the fall and spring terms for they were expected to remain on the farms and work. When there was little work on the farms except care of the stock, schools often had sixty or more pupils during the three months of the winter term. The big boys always tried to run the school or the teacher and made life miserable for the very young pupils.

One cold winter's evening when the snow-filled wind spanked us on our way home from school, three of the older boys made cigarettes out of corn silks. I threatened to "tell the teacher," whereupon they caught me, stripped me of all my clothes and tied them into hard knots. It was a bitter mile I ran shivering down the road.

We smaller boys breathed a sigh of relief when the winter term closed and plowing time saved us from the tormenting and bullying of the older boys.

Fifteen harvests had been gathered off our Iowa farm since the day of my birth. That spring I won a county-wide scholarship to Blackburn Seminary. This was a co-operative boarding school where each student worked in the kitchen or about the farm or dairy to help pay expenses. The same basic subjects of the present-day high school were taught.

For the first time in my life, I was away from home. I was teased, tormented and picked on by the upper-classmen. This continual razzing prolonged an acute homesickness, but it had to be endured patiently for the good reason that I was small for my age and could not adequately defend myself.

Then one evening I was called into Dean Blackburn's office and questioned regarding a reported breach of discipline by upperclassmen who roomed on the same floor with me. I pleaded with the dean, "Please don't make me tell."

"I haven't done nothin' bad," I declared, "but I don't want to tell on nobody."

"Anybody," he corrected. "Very well, that's all. And my boy," said the old dean administering a kindly pat on my shoulder, "loyalty is a wonderful thing. Any boy who learns a deep loyalty to his God, to himself and to his fellow man will go far in the world. Never forget that."

The four culprits were awaiting my return. One sat in the only chair in my room; the other three sprawled on my cot.

"Tell us," one said threateningly, "what didja blab to

the dean?" We hadn't noticed the door opening quietly. Dean Blackburn stepped into the room.

"He wouldn't tell me anything," he said. "I should punish you four boys, but I think I won't this time. Perhaps we can all learn a lesson in loyalty from what has happened. You mistreated Guy and he repaid you by loyal silence. I shall do likewise." He smiled hopefully and walked from the room.

The largest boy arose and extended his hand toward me. "Shake," he said, "and this goes for everyone in this school; whoever mistreats Runt will have me to whip." Their persecution ceased and I was accepted as one of the group. Now that I was a true member of the fraternity my year at Blackburn Seminary became a happy one.

However, its glories ended abruptly a month before commencement when the boys' dormitory burned. Fire broke out one evening while we were in the dining room and the white pine building burned like excelsior. I lost my books, bedding and the only complete suit I possessed. (Though his own property loss was heavy, Dean Blackburn bought me another suit.) The dean and his wife had invested everything in the school and had the buildings and equipment only lightly insured. Classrooms and the school library had been located on the ground floor of the old dormitory and there was not enough room in the two buildings left standing to house the school. They made heroic efforts to raise money for rebuilding but were unsuccessful.

I returned to our humble farm home deeply disappointed for I felt sure my chances of an education had been consumed in the fire. Towns where public high schools were located took no interest in providing work for country students. I made many inquiries but always received the same reply: "Sorry, sonny, but there's a lot of the home town boys looking for work, too, and we have to help them first." To pay tuition, room and board and buy the necessary books would cost a hundred twenty-five dollars. This sum was more than I could ever hope to earn in one summer.

A neighboring farmer hired me that spring. My pay was fifteen dollars a dry month plus board, room and washing. A dry month consisted of twenty-six days of weather that permitted work. If a week of rain kept us out of the fields we got room and board but no salary for those days. I worked there for a year. In that time I drew cash to the amount of fifteen dollars for clothing, two dollars for the Fourth of July and five dollars for Christmas. When the year of work had ended the farmer paid me one hundred fifty-eight dollars in currency.

Fifteen dollars I spent for a blue serge suit and a few additional "Sunday clothes." Ninety dollars was spent at a farm sale for a pair of colts. (It was worth the price just to be able to lead them home in public view.) The remainder of the money I gave to Father to buy feed for the colts.

The following summer I went to work for an uncle. He paid me twenty-five dollars a month plus the usual board, room and laundry. He was one of the most spiritual men I have ever known and as I look back across the years I realize just how much his beautiful daily Christian life influenced mine.

That summer a group of public-spirited business men started a high school in Oakley, a little town five and a half miles from home. Tuition was fifty dollars for the nine months and I figured that if I could board at home I would have enough money to attend. My uncle gladly released me when he learned of my desire to continue my education.

So September first found me again in school. I walked the eleven miles daily, cross-country as the crow flies. A large creek ran between our home and Oakley and along its banks during the freezing months I set sixty steel traps. The income derived from this trapping more than paid my tuition, bought my books, clothes and noon-day lunch.

Soon some of the other boys attending the academy learned of my trapping and promptly began to call me "Civet Cat" and "Daniel Boone." I didn't mind much for Daniel Boone had always been an idol of mine and in my imagination I, too, was being a pioneer.

About a week before Christmas some schoolmates saw me walking up the railroad track with a sack of furs. One boy yelled, "Let's go see Daniel Boone trade his furs for bacon and beans." There were ten or twelve boys all teasing and taunting by the time we reached the fur buyer's. Wonderful, yet comical to behold, was the trans-formation in their attitudes and faces when the fur buyer counted out fifty-eight dollars for me.

One of the boys grinned and said, "Say, Guy, sorry we've called you Daniel Boone. Give us a treat and we won't do it no more."

"Come on, it's Christmas," another boy joined in.

"It's been okay with me," I said. "In fact, I liked it." I hesitated a moment and then went on, "Well, here's three dollars; go fill up on candy."

That left me fifty-five dollars, and fifty was all I'd expected for the furs anyway.

After graduating from Oakley Academy I passed county examinations and was awarded a teaching certif-icate; but I went back to work for my uncle during the summer. One day in July while we were threshing, a Mr. Cowan came and offered me the Strahan school (about three miles from home). The district board had set the wages for the eight-months' term at three hundred two dollars and fifty cents—thirty-five dollars a month for five months and forty-two dollars and fifty cents for each of the three winter months. I accepted, and began teaching September 16, 1912. Thirty-two fine country children were enrolled in the school.

The joys of teaching this first year were heightened by the presence of a quiet, co-operative, blue-eyed pupil. She was almost as old as I and could be counted on to help with the small pupils and keep peace among the older ones. She was most satisfactory as a student, too, and none could spell her down. I took her to spelling matches against the champions of many other schools and she was never defeated. I "saw her home," with her parents' consent, more and more frequently. When spring came, I knew that I loved Madge.

School ended in May with a program by the pupils. Patrons and friends came from miles around to enjoy the big Last Day. Much of the talk concerned plans for Memorial Sunday. A committeeman argued that I was the one to make the address. He said finally, "If you're willing to try, we're willing to listen," and there wasn't much else for me to say.

Yes, Grandfather Howard had probably been a great force for good in the day when pioneers were spreading their fence rails across the prairies. Yet all the time he was too busy with the Lord's work to attend his own. And what did it profit the man? An extra bunch of peonies laid on his plot on Decoration Day. Not an attractive future for a young man who wanted more of the things of the flesh than of the spirit. Dr. Thomas meant well, but he wasn't young. . . .

Out ahead Jinny and Kate plodded down the corn rows.

CHAPTER 4

Gray Days and the Dark Angel

MY HARVEST WAS GOOD AND THE COLTS GREW INTO A team; there was a contract for another term at Strahan school. And I was a man. So Madge and I were married and together we sought to achieve the success that may come to an Iowa farmer. I continued teaching and bought a small farm.

It took little effort in the year 1915 to borrow a thousand dollars at the county seat bank. It meant mortgaging my school contract and chattels but I was impatient. We put borrowed money into more and more stock and equipment as Madge and I envisioned how it all would increase and we would prosper.

Those first three years of married life were busy ones with schoolteaching, stock feeding and crop raising. They became increasingly busy when two sons, Albert and Clayton, were born in successive years. Now we were four and I buried myself deeper in work.

Work, work, work! And the glow of success and prosperity ever less bright. After Dr. Thomas delivered Clayton he reopened that old question of my future. He had followed our struggles silently but now again he sought to advise me.

He turned to Madge and said gently, "I've always told Guy that he should be a preacher." Then, wiping his spectacles with a snow-white handkerchief: "He can speak right convincingly."

"He convinced me," Madge smiled up at both of us.

Dr. Thomas put his handkerchief back into his pocket

and adjusted his glasses on his nose. "Remember that Memorial Day address three years ago?" He looked up to where I was standing near the head of the bed.

"I do," Madge said quickly.

"Guy is no farmer, Doctor, no matter how hard he works. I've always felt he could preach." There was a glow of pride in her voice. "And every day I pray God to open the way for him." She said this softly as her hand stole from under the covers to pat my own rough, calloused one.

"I don't mind the work," I replied irritably. "I just don't get enough done." I humbly and painfully remembered that both Clayton and my interest date at the bank had arrived at the same day.

And no matter how hard I tried, after that I never seemed to get enough done. There was always something that kept success at the far end of an economic row.

In the history books, we read that in April, 1917, the United States declared war on Germany and then in December against Austria. Almost immediately following such portentous announcements there are countless unsuspecting individuals who become actors in minor tragedies and comedies. Only a voluminous social history would hint of these, for historians speak in terms of nations and masses of people.

All three of us boys were drafted. Hugh had had a long illness which disqualified him. The draft board told Chester and me that only one of us could go; the other must stay and be a soldier of the soil. It was a dramatic time for us all. I was torn between a desire to serve my country and spare my younger brother, and the urgency to abide with loved ones.

Time was pushing us for a decision. Soon we must find the answer. Would it be the right one? Friday morning the snow was piled deep in the barn lot and my fingers were stiff with cold as I struggled to harness the team.

I must haul fuel today—how would Madge manage two babies and wood hauling and snow shoveling when I was gone to war?

Just then I heard a tuneful whistle and Chester came around the corner of the barn. He called a merry salutation. "Nice morning, Guy! ... Say, I've been thinking ... got fifty cents?" Half-dollars were almost as dear as they had been in those childhood days, but I put my hand in my pocket. I pulled out a penny.

"My wealth," I grinned. "Sorry! I'd let you have the half if I had it."

"Oh, this will do just as well," he replied as he reached out and took the coin. He flipped it high in the air, quickly covered it with his foot. "Heads or tails, brother, and you better call it right," he said. I looked at him steadily for a moment. I knew that he was finished with trying to persuade me. "If you call it right, you stay," he said. "If you call it wrong you can go. I still think it's right for you to stay."

"Tails," I snapped.

I wondered if Chester looked at the penny with feelings as mixed as were mine. It was tails. My heart sank and I dreaded to look up for there were no words on my tongue. But he was equal to the occasion.

"You just as well have let me have my way in the first place," he laughed. Yet it was hard even now to let him be the one to go.

The years moved through the war and though prices flourished my crops failed. What hogs I could keep on my meager store of feed nearly all died of the dread cholera. The good land was there, but I had bungled in its husbandry.

A baby girl was born in those lean years and we named her Virginia.

Six years had now passed since that fall when Madge and I had confidently set out to conquer an infinitesimal part of a prairie country; and our sole success was our family. We loved and enjoyed our children and we were one in our good fortunes and our hurts. Yet even this success could not survive the bleak February days of 1921 when corn prices were so low that we took a cue from our neighbors and burned it for fuel because it was cheaper; then the Angel of Death walked the prairies sowing sorrow with a lavish hand.

"It's diphtheria," was the agonizing cry of the country-side as each new child victim complained with a sore throat.

Our own little flock was rushed to the doctor for in-oculations as soon as the first warning came but we hadn't reckoned on Madge's frailty. She contracted the dread disease almost before the children ceased to complain from their treatments. There was no one to help for every family had its own battle against the epidemic.

Almost alone the good old Dr. Thomas fought the dread scourge, making his weary rounds through the country. He came as often as he could to Madge's bedside and through the long hours of delirium tried to hold hope.

She became conscious one night and I thought the crisis had passed. Instead, it was her hour of farewell. She held my hand and whispered, "Guy, you must preach—God needs you.... I'm going soon. Raise our babies right—good-bye."

Then we were four.

Madge's funeral in that pestilence-ridden, wind-swept prairie was a macabre nightmare. It was like one of those terrible dreams that come upon one in the darkness of night and in the morning only the horrible bits that confuse and nauseate can be remembered.

The Ides of March passed before I realized that another spring would come; that there was work to be done. I had lost fifty pounds of weight and was poorly prepared for spring and its labors! I had so little energy and less will to force a plow into the furrows.

Every Sunday I walked alone to Madge's grave, and her dying admonition, "You must preach," pierced my heart. Yet, always as I abandoned my lonely vigil and returned to the children at home I remembered also her hope that I would "Raise our babies right." I could find no consonance between the two and I resumed tilling. I tried to lose myself in hard work but my heart was not in farming.

The bank foreclosed the mortgage on our little place. Had Madge been alive this would have seemed a terrible tragedy; now it seemed merely an anticlimax. I worked out for wages, sold insurance, taught—anything to keep my mind busy and to provide for the three small children. It finally seemed expedient to move home with Father and Mother, whose cares were already great enough without the addition of mine. Mother had been an invalid for several years but from her bedside she supervised us all as best she could. And we in turn ministered to her as best we could. One of Madge's nine sisters took Virginia to raise.

Somehow eight years of Sunday pilgrimages to the low mound in the Honeywell burying grounds seemed to blow across the prairies. Then the Gray Angel struck again.

Brother Hugh died and exactly one week later Mother left us. I turned blindly from the room, unable to speak that evening, as one of the kindly neighbors who kept vigil at the bedside saw that Mother had passed on and pulled the quilt to the head of the bed.

"One of us'll drive you in to Chariton to get the undertaker," offered a man standing near the door.

"No," I replied, "tonight I must walk alone."

"But it's twelve miles, man," he expostulated.

"Yes, I know," I said and stepped out into the new-fallen snow that shimmered in the cold moonlight.

Just as I closed the door behind me I heard someone say, "Still grievin' for Madge."

The air was chill, and the snow was drifted almost knee-deep. I plodded sorrowfully down the twelve-mile-long road toward the county seat town. Out ahead the snow lay in a great unbroken shroud over trees and fences and farm buildings. Behind lay the beauty of God's great pattern broken by my clumsy footprints. Suddenly I stumbled in the rough frozen roadway and fell into the drift ahead.

As I sank to my knees I prayed God to bring peace to my tormented soul—a peace unbroken and pure as the snow pattern. Alone there, I made my confession to the stars of heaven: "I believe with all my heart that Jesus is the son of the Living God and no matter what the cost, I shall, from this hour, serve him in any way I can."

I rose to my feet and started forward. The going seemed easier then and I headed for the home of a Dunkard minister whom I knew. It was late when I knocked at his door but he welcomed me to the warmth of his base burner and the glow of his heart. I told my story and he listened intently. The parsonage and church were connected, and as the clock in the courthouse steeple struck midnight we stepped into the baptistry and he lowered me into the coldest water in which man was ever immersed.

After Mother's death and my baptism, I meant to teach only long enough to finish the school term. However, when fall came teaching still seemed to be the most logical means for keeping the family in food and clothes and shelter. I finally became superintendent of a small school in an Iowa coal-mining town about fifty-five miles from home and we stayed there three years.

During the last year both of the boys rode a bus four miles to attend high school in Indianola, Iowa. Soon after the term began, the school nurse recommended that Clayton have a complete physical check-up. After a long and serious examination the doctor turned to me and said, "This boy has tuberculosis!" I realized then what Mother's illness had been and that during the six years we had lived in her house my son had contracted the dread disease. The doctor prescribed absolute quiet, fresh air and a rigid diet of strength-building foods. He recommended that Clayton stay in bed for at least a year.

Everyone in the little coal-mining town learned to love "Clay" as they called him. Many retired farmers lived in the village and their wives took it upon themselves to brighten the hours for the "poor motherless boy." They brought many a tasty tidbit to tempt his appetite.

I lost myself in reading. It was one of the few satisfactory escapes to which I had access and I devoted most of my spare time to it, sometimes reading aloud to Clayton. A school patron loaned me copies of two of Harold Bell Wright's books, *The Shepherd of the Hills* and *The Recreation of Brian Kent*.

These stories introduced me to a new and fascinating country. The very word Ozarks became to me a symbol of haven—a symbol of peace and quiet. I determined that some day I too would seek out this country which had become the refuge of another weary man. And I felt that in this land so far away in feature and situation I too might experience recreation.

As the school months passed, Clayton became gradually worse. Typically, he lost the will to live and the battle became a mental and physical one. A widow who came almost daily to "cheer the little fellow" added to our problems. About a week before the close of school I learned that she had been telling Clayton about her granddaughter "just Clayton's age" who was "sick with the same kind of lung eatin' ... Doctors gave her three years to live, but law! she didn't live that long!" It was useless to tell Clayton to laugh at the ignorant old soul.

At last, out of my confusion I again cried to God for help. I picked up the Bible and prayed, "Oh, Word of God, give me the answer." The Book fell open at the nineteenth chapter of Matthew and my eyes fell on verse 29. Surprised, and a little disconcerted, I read, "And every one that hath forsaken houses, or brethren, or sisters, or father, or mother, or wife, or children, or lands, for my name's sake, shall receive an hundredfold, and shall inherit everlasting life."

That settled it, and with a deep sense of peace and comfort I accepted the decision. Aloud I said, "I'm ready. I'll start for the Ozark Mountains next week and God will guide me where He wants me to go."

CHAPTER 5

Escape to the Hills

"HOP IN, PERFESSOR." IT WAS A FRIENDLY COMMAND given by the driver of a rickety-rackety old truck. He kicked open the door and leaned over to take the battered suitcase that I carried in one hand. I tossed in the bundle I had been carrying under my arm and gratefully climbed into the windowless cab.

"I'm goin' as far as Indianola, if that'll help you any," he volunteered as he leaned across me and with a big right paw grabbed the door. He slammed it with a vigor that bespoke familiarity with the contrariness of old cars. "When you git to Indianola you'll be on Federal Highway Number Sixty-five and chances for gettin' rides from there on ought to be good," he continued above the grinding of gears and I perceived at once that I was in good hands.

"Hear you're going to the Ozark Mountains," he stated. I nodded but could not reply before he continued, "Friend of yours back there at the Hawkeye told me you was goin'. We seen you walkin' past when I was drinkin' my coffee. He says you're a right nice feller, but had a lot of hard luck. I says the Ozarks ain't no place for you then— I went through there once with a load of corn." He added this bit of explanation with the air of an experienced traveler. "It's a wild place, perfessor. Lot of killin' and feudin'. Easy place to pick a fight and an outsider ain't got a chance. My advice is, you sure want to watch your step."

There was hardly time for me to tell my story to the

trucker before he brought his vehicle to a halt where the road from Newbern intersects the Jefferson Highway.

"Here she is, perfessor," the driver said. "This is Sixty-five. Runs clean from St. Paul all the way down to New Orleans. Goes through some mighty purty Ozarks, too."

I was fumbling at the handle on the door when the driver said, "Watch your shins," and gave the door a mighty kick that sent it banging against the hood. "Good luck," he said as I pulled my luggage from the truck and pushed the door back to where he could grab it with his powerful fist. Then in a moment, amid the grinding of heavy gears, my first ride was out of sight.

The sun had scarcely driven the dew from the grasses along the roadside and here I was, ten miles on the way toward my goal.

The most difficult part of entering any new field of endeavor is in decision. All that was behind me now. I had tried personal planning and failed. Now I must try to follow God's plan. Clayton and Albert were as firm as I in the belief that their "daddy was guided by God" and that He would place me where there were opportunities for service. The boys and I had talked it all over. We'd agreed that I should go into the hills and find a cabin near any kind of work that should afford a livelihood. On the tenth of June, the day school had closed, the boys and I had returned to Newbern where Charley and Etta Shafer, who were old neighbors, had assisted me in getting the boys settled. They owned a building across the street from their own home and had offered us the use of two second-story rooms.

Into these rooms we'd moved enough of our furniture to make the boys a comfortable abode. Here also we'd stored boxes of books collected during schoolteaching days and other personal property. This was to be the home of Albert and Clayton until the Ozarks offered better things.

"I'll walk every step of the way if necessary to get to the Ozarks," I had told Charley Shafer as he helped me lift a box of books into place.

My glory was now bright enough to make the three hundred miles between the prairies of Lucas County and the rolling hills of the Ozarks seem no farther than the length of a long corn row.

"There's nothing wrong with walking," I defended. "I've done it all my life. There'll be some rides but when they don't come, I'll walk."

Both Etta and Charley Shafer were probably a little dubious about my proposed plans but they were staunch friends. They'd done all they could to help me with the moving and as they left, Charley had turned in the doorway to say, "Etta and me'll run across every day to see the boys. Don't you worry about 'em none."

The problem of financing the boys and my trip had lost its frightfulness when we'd received fifty dollars from the sale of our cookstove. It was one of the few articles of value salvaged from the tragic days behind.

Albert and I had talked long and seriously the night before and made final plans for my departure. I'd allowed myself five dollars for the trip and left the rest of our small savings for the boys. If the trip proved too long and my purse needed refilling I would hunt for work along the road. When we'd finally turned the lamp low and sought our beds Albert had memorized a complete set of instructions and had a carefully marked highway map showing my proposed route. I was to stop often at towns along the way for any messages the boys cared to send me. Should Clayton have one of his hemorrhages I could be summoned to return immediately.

Clayton had seemed a little better. Perhaps he'd responded to the excitement of the adventure or was influenced by Albert's and my surge of hope. I think that getting back home helped him some, too. It made my departure less difficult to see that he was brave and that there still glowed a spark of hope. It thrilled me to hear him say, "Dad is going to find a nice cabin in the woods where I can get well and hunt and fish like other boys."

We had talked so long into the night that it seemed as if the last glow had hardly gone from the lamp wick before the brighter light of a new day had sped me on my trek.

Clayton had bid me a sleepy "good-bye."

Albert, already a man for his age, was never one to complain, but neither was he one to deny his faith, or fear to utter his feelings. "Good-bye, Dad," he'd said, trying to smooth out the quaver in his voice. "God bless us all until we can be together again." I had seen him still standing in the doorway of the building as I'd turned the corner of the street and headed out upon the open road.

When high adventure descends swiftly upon one, events move so rapidly that there is little time or thought to realize what is happening. So it had been with me the last few days. And now that I was on my way I could not help but wonder.... Would the boys be all right? Was this the right way to do it? ... Yes, I thought so.

Rides were not long but their frequency put me in Lineville by noon. By the time I had walked from one end of the village street to the other I was in another state, for the little town, true to its name, divides its taxpayers between Iowa and Missouri.

My early good fortune with drivers who picked up hitchhikers had kept me from noticing that the temperature had mounted during the morning hours. Infrequent rides during the afternoon of that mid-June day made me acutely aware of the increase in heat. My clothes were beginning to show perspiration spots and I wondered how long white duck trousers, white shirt and shoes would remain presentable. I had covered my head with a handkerchief dampened in a creek, carefully rolled my sleeves above my elbows and unbuttoned my collar. I had a tie but it lay flat in the suitcase.

Benjamin Franklin, when he made his celebrated entry into Philadelphia, may have been a more grotesque figure than I, but he certainly could not have evoked more comment. I passed farmers and their families who had taken refuge from the parched fields and sat fanning themselves in the relative cool of trees or porch. Some of them smiled or nodded at me as I trudged along in the swelter, pausing occasionally to shift the leaden suitcase or cumbersome bundle. Doubtless they were wondering at the foolish fellow who didn't know enough to come in out of the heat. Perhaps they even thought me a fugitive walking when honest men sat in the shadows and planned the work to be done after the sun had crossed over into Kansas.

The Ozarks seemed so far away.

Suddenly I realized I was whistling. Whistling that old familiar tune learned in the church at Newbern where Grandma Baker had taken Hugh and me to Sunday school. Then the words came to me and I sang, "My faith looks up to Thee, Thou Lamb of Calvary, Savior Divine."

Just outside of Trenton, Missouri, a minister offered me a ride and persuaded me to "beat the heat and the miles" by following a course through Kansas City. I felt I should follow the marked itinerary as shown on the map left with the boys, but this road was so much longer than I had expected. When the pastor said the route he suggested would take me over the much-traveled U. S. No. 71 from Kansas City to Carthage and over U. S. No. 66 to Springfield, I decided to follow his advice in hopes of finding a shorter way. I would send a message to the boys.

The theaters were spewing their crowds into Twelfth Street when we arrived in Kansas City. My host recommended an adequate but cheap lodging place, and a free meal at the Helping Hand Transient Relief Center next morning was a boon. However, my conversation with a fellow traveler didn't add much kindling to the glow of hope for a quick trip to Carthage and Springfield.

"You'll have to take it easy, outside of Kansas City, brother," the transient had said over his cup of coffee. "Traveling man got bumped off outta here the other night by a guy he picked up. Stole his money and dumped his body on the road. Better lay around town a few days 'til it clears up and they start giving out rides again." But there was no time for such a delay. I had already deviated from my appointed route and the city was no place for a man with only a few dollars in his pocket. There was nothing to do but put Highway No. 71 underfoot. I'd told Shafer I'd walk every step of the way, if necessary. . . .

There was plenty of traffic on the highway but mighty little of it stopped for hitchhikers. About thirty-five of the ninety-nine miles behind me had seen the imprint of my shoes by the time I walked into Nevada that night. Lodging and breakfast here reduced my finances to two dollars and ten cents. Had there been a few more cents in my pocket I would have indulged in the luxury of a bottle of liniment. But walking out the soreness was cheaper so I turned my face to the east soon after sun-up.

I walked steadily without benefit of a single ride until I trod upon my own shadow. No Iowa cornfield had rows as long and as hard as that ribbon of concrete.

The cuffs of my once white duck trousers were becoming smudged and splotched from the highway and the tar off a benefactor's running board. The crease had assumed irregular lines. My shirt sleeves were now too damp to fold neatly—one dropped at my elbow while the other hung limp and unbuttoned. Tepid perspiration on my brow replaced the cool water from my fresh handkerchief headpiece. With almost every step a trickle of sweat slithered down my back and spread about my waist. The stench of the black tar which oozed from between the expansion cracks in the concrete came up in heat waves to offend my nostrils. Everywhere there was the same dry odor that comes from a piece of newspaper just before it bursts into flame. Out ahead the pavement would not lie still. It shimmered in undulating waves of heat.

As I walked on, a house grew larger through the shimmering atmosphere. It was a big friendly-looking house close to the highway. Upon its porch was an old man seated in a hickory rocking chair. "If the occupants are as friendly as their house appears to be...." I thought.

The old man saw me at once and cordially waved a salutation. I stepped through the open gate and asked for a drink.

"Water? Sure," he said, rising from his chair. "You look mighty hot. Better come up and rest yourself, too."

I was luxuriating in the comfort of the rocker when he returned with a glass of water and a large crockery pitcher of buttermilk.

"Better drink slow," he said as he handed me the glass. "You must be mighty anxious to get somewhere, walking in this kind of weather."

"Just heading for the hills," I told him as I sipped the water.

He dragged a second chair from one corner of the porch and sat down, resting a foot against a porch pillar. "Help yourself to another drink when you're ready," he invited. "Plenty more in the springhouse."

That was the best buttermilk I'd ever tasted—cool and sweet, and rich with tiny lumps of golden butter in it.

We sat for some minutes exchanging questions and answers in a dilatory fashion. I was silently urging myself to start on when the screen door opened. Turning, I saw a tall, slender, dark-eyed young woman.

"Father, dinner's ready," she said in a comfortable voice. And then she turned toward me. "We'd be mighty glad if you'd stay and eat with us. Everyone is gone today except father, Aunt Sallie Kate and I."

The old man nodded his approval and I acknowledged mine with "I'll need to wash up a little." It was a joy to wash in the cool water—to remove the grime of the road and dry my face and hands on a clean white towel blown fresh and soft in the summer sun—all the while savoring the fragrant home-cooked food.

I walked into a large homey kitchen where a cheery, white-haired woman was setting another place on the table. She greeted me with a smile.

"Young man," she said in a musical southern voice. "Ah heard you talkin' to Brothah and wondered what youah goin' to do with that quiet voice."

I was startled and uncertain how to answer but finally I stammered, "I know I'm hoarse but my voice will be all right when I get to where I'm going and can rest some."

"Oh, no, that's not what ah mean," she replied. You have a fine voice. You should be usin' it for the Lawd."

The old man had come in from the porch and we all sat down to dinner. After a dignified grace he turned to me and said, "If she says you have a good voice, mister, I guess you have. She's a pretty good judge of folks usually—had lots of training in it I guess. Her husband was judge of circuit court—one of the smartest the state ever turned out. The Supreme Court up in Jefferson City still cites his decisions."

"Yes, Aunt Sallie Kate is usually right," offered the young woman as she passed a platter heaped with fried chicken.

"You folks are right encouraging," I said. And then I was impelled to tell them something of my story. They listened sympathetically and the enthusiasm of the older man and woman was very heartening. The young woman said, a little wistfully, "I've always thought I'd like to go into the hills and teach school. I hope you have a very successful venture."

The Seth Thomas clock in the kitchen banged out two loud strokes before we left the table. I thanked my hosts for their hospitality and set off down the highway, refreshed in body and soul.

I had walked many miles pondering God's kindness and direction when I suddenly realized that I couldn't name my human benefactors.

A storm blew up from the southwest but a lucky ride into Springfield saved me from the shower. I stood under an awning at one of the busy street corners on the big square and looked about me. The tide of night had almost crept in and it was pouring rain on the deserted streets. A bronze plate on the building near me proclaimed that I was standing upon the market site of slave-trading days. Humbly, yet joyfully, I bowed my head and prayed to God, thanking Him for freedom, for guidance and love, and asking his blessing on my venture into this new world of the Ozarks.

Thus fortified I walked north on a street marked "Boonville" and entered the first restaurant I saw. I asked the proprietor if he could use a cook. He questioned me and, as Apostle Paul before King Agrippa, I answered freely. He gave me a job at fifteen dollars a week and meals and lodging. I sent an encouraging note to the boys and pitched into work.

Country folk were our principal customers at this little restaurant and during the next two weeks I made many inquiries about schools that needed teachers and communities without preachers. A truck farmer said he needed a hand and agreed to hire Albert if I would send for him.

"Things are working out," I rejoiced. But my joy was short-lived. Etta Shafer telephoned and said that Clayton was worse! I must return to Newbern at once!

I had worked two weeks and had drawn only two of the thirty dollars. I was grateful that the balance due would afford quick transportation home. However, I'd not reasoned the way my boss did. He had been plagued by transients and "It's just an excuse for leaving," he said. "You're just like all the others and you'll stay a month or no pay." There was no reasoning with the man.

The milkman had not yet rattled his way through the restaurant next morning when I left and headed north. I literally walked away from my resentment, and the sting of defeat was almost as deep as the hurt and fear that I felt.

The goal had seemed so near.

And the thoughts of returning afoot over those long, hot, despairing miles when I should have been speeding to Clayton by bus were almost too much to bear. There should have been money for his medical care, too.

The sun was shining brightly but I was plodding through darkest night.

"You look purty low, mister. Had some bad luck?" A kind, well modulated voice pierced my consciousness. Gears were grinding, the landscape was rapidly moving past. I was riding! It's a fool who becomes so dazed by his own calamities that he is unaware of the kindness left in the world. Surely I wasn't ready to teach or preach when I had so much to learn myself.

"Bad luck?" I managed an answering smile. "Well, I guess some people call it that. Maybe it's just the Lord giving me some postgraduate work." He looked at me a bit questioningly and I told him a little about myself and why I was walking back to Iowa.

"Sorry I can't help you some, stranger," he declared. "I've had sick young'uns myself. But I'll ride you as far as I'm goin' and maybe you'll have better luck there."

"Where's that?" I asked.

"I'm headed for Hermitage," he answered. "That's

the county seat of Hickory County. 'Tain't right on the main highway goin' north, but it's right close to Number Sixty-five. What kind of work you lookin' for, son?"

I felt encouraged every time the fellow spoke. He was big and husky-looking, with broad shoulders and heavily bearded face; when he spoke his smooth voice and kind manner was as balm to my troubled mind.

"Interested in teachin' er preachin', eh? Well, they's a school over in east part of Hickory County—Mulberry School—hain't got no teacher yet and ain't likely to get one soon. 'Course you might not be interested: it's a God-forsaken place."

"I'm not too particular," I told him.

"You couldn't be and go to the place I'm thinkin' about," he grinned. "Sure could use some Christianity down there, too. Don't know what they need more'n a teacher and a preacher, lest it was some first-class funerals."

It was a straw but I groped for it and began questioning him.

"That's all I know about it," he answered. "But I'll ride you into Hermitage and you go to Elzie Miller—he's the county superintendent—and if Mulberry School is still minus a teacher you can tell 'im Nig Williams sent you. It might help a little."

So, I reached the office of Elzie Miller.

"No, Mulberry district hasn't a teacher," he said. "The district voted down its levy, little as it was, and up to yesterday it looked as if there wouldn't be any money to pay a teacher." He picked up some index cards that lay on his desk. "Let's see," he remarked as he examined the cards, "there are twenty-four pupils and the community is so isolated there's no chance of the children attending school in another district."

Here, I thought, might be an opportunity for service.

"I recommended that the state pay the district the regular allotment from state funds," Mr. Miller resumed. "It's a little unusual. When a Missouri district won't do anything for itself the state doesn't like to help out. But yesterday I received word from Jefferson City that they were allotting four hundred dollars for Mulberry School."

I thought of Clayton. "Do the school directors know about this allotment?" I asked.

"No, I haven't had a chance to tell them," he went on. "If you're interested and think you can qualify I'll hold things up while you go out there. Then if you can hire yourself to the directors I'll issue you a permit to teach as soon as you get me a copy of your Iowa certificate and a letter of recommendation."

He gave me a copy of the Missouri school law and the names of three directors. "Be sure and let me know how you come out," he called after me.

Next morning a genial native directed me to the Mulberry School District and obtained for me a ride to Cross Timbers, which was within fourteen miles of my destination. It was a cool, wooded roadway that led from the little town to Mulberry and I reached the home of one of the directors by noon.

I disturbed Alonza Harmon at his noon meal; when he came to the doorway he was still mouthing a portion of his meat.

"Don't reckon hit'll be worth your while to see nobody else," he chomped dissuadingly. "We'uns don't pay only five dollars a month. Don't need school nohow."

I didn't tell him of the county superintendent's success in behalf of the district but bade him good-day and sought out the other directors. Both happened to be working at the same place. We sat on a wagon tongue on the shady side of the barn and talked for some time. I told them of my interest in both the school and the community. They were right neighborly fellows and when I perceived they favored a school I told them of the special allotment. We made a contract for the term that was to start in the middle of August.

Now the road to Iowa seemed a little less long. Moreover, I would return with a home-coming gift for Clayton: jobs for both Albert and me. I hurried down the wooded trail to Cross Timbers lest evening find me stranded where there was little or no chance for a ride. I stopped on the way to report to Harmon. He grunted and then recommended: "Reckon you better stay at Andrews'—last teacher stayed there. Hit's clost to school. Be good place fer ye."

In Cross Timbers I paid for a meal by splitting wood for two hours, and then set off for Iowa. Soon after I reached U. S. No. 65, a trucker with a load of cedar fence posts took pity on me and I rode into Sedalia, a third of my journey done.

Through intermittent stages of walking and riding I finally reached Indianola, ten miles from Newbern. I telephoned to the Shafers and inquired about Clayton. He was better! They'd tried to reach me in Springfield and save me the trip home, but I had gone. Perhaps I should have experienced regret, but somehow I didn't.

I swung off down the road to Newbern. I'd been gone just twenty days! Everything I'd hoped and prayed for was unfolding before us now. . . . God had heard my cry. . . . Though I'd walked through the valley of the shadow of despair, His rod and His staff had comforted me. . . . He had prepared a table before me. . . . Surely goodness and mercy would follow me all the days of my life.

It was pleasant to anticipate the boys' surprise when I should tell them my news—jobs for Albert and me— prospects of a home in the hills for Clayton. I chuckled, envisioning their surprised admiration when I should show them one of the original five dollars I had taken with me. ... I'd tell them all about the trip ... all about the school district ... they would excitedly ask me questions. ... And then I started: the boys would certainly ask about Mulberry School and what it looked like. How would I make them understand that I hadn't even seen it?

CHAPTER 6

The Holy Terror

"DON'T BLAME YOU FOR LIKING THESE HILLS, GUY," said Cousin Halleck Baker. Now Cousin Halleck was a prairie man, a practical farmer who did not often rhapsodize about nature, which had given him many a hard battle as well as much co-operation. We were near Warsaw, Missouri, at the western end of the 125-mile-long Lake of the Ozarks. We stood on an escarpment high above the lake watching the sunset. Its reflection traced the darkening waters with a stylus of shimmering light that disappeared into the violet hills where the lake formed a great oxbow. This was only the Ozark border country but it was a generous sample of the beauty in the highlands farther south.

We drank deeply of the spiritual nectar brewed in the out-of-doors. This was the first lap of a Colorado vacation trip for Cousin Halleck and his family and they were blessing their decision to route their journey via Missouri's man-made wonder. The evening air held a chill such as so often descends on these hills in early August. We had built a campfire in a clearing among the woodlands and Halleck's wife and daughter were preparing the evening meal. Halleck finally turned back to the fire with the air of one remembering a pleasant duty and said loyally, "'Course 'taint like Iowa." Cousin Halleck was like most other loyal sons of Iowa (had he been going to California instead of to Colorado the first thing he would have done on arriving would have been to hunt up an Iowa picnic), and I shared some of his homesickness, though for a different reason: Iowa still held, on one of her farms and resting in the good earth, some of my little family. Albert was with me on this second trip into the Ozarks but we had left Clayton with his sister Virginia, at their grandmother's in Lacona. There he was to stay until we could establish ourselves in the hills.

Clayton cared for, Albert and I had gone to Des Moines and made arrangements for my teaching credentials to be sent to Hickory County. We'd made a final pilgrimage to Madge's grave and then a round of brief farewell visits to several kinsmen. That was how we fortunately chanced upon Cousin Halleck as he prepared to set out for the Colorado vacation.

"We're taking a trip west," he said when he learned of our plans, "and thought we might come back through some Ozark country; but I reckon we can do it the other way around just as well and give you and Albert a lift. We've been wanting to see that big Lake of the Ozarks." Both Albert and I were grateful for a consideration not always shown by relatives. And so we had enjoyed our trip together; but tonight Cousin Halleck would turn westward and Albert and I would go on to Cross Timbers, which was now only twenty miles distant.

The moon was high when we reached Cross Timbers. Ten o'clock in a nine-o'clock town—no lights to be seen anywhere. We walked to the school grounds and sought out the open shed where high-school pupils stabled their horses. We raked up a scattering of hay and straw and made our bunk in a clean stall.

At the village restaurant next morning we spread our money on the counter. "If we had another nickel we'd have a dollar," grinned Albert. He ordered an egg sandwich and coffee while I compromised with coffee. Then we walked every step of the fourteen miles into Hermitage. Superintendent Miller had already received my credentials from Des Moines and had my teaching permit ready.

"This certificate will allow you to carry on until next regular teacher's examination," Mr. Miller explained. "That'll be next March. Then you'll be issued another certificate according to the grades you make."

At noon we had dinner with the superintendent. Away from the office, we discussed Mulberry School and he warned me of some difficulties I might encounter.

Forewarned and refreshed, Albert and I set out for Springfield to locate the truck farmer who had promised Albert a job. Good luck with rides and a minimum of walking put us in the Queen City of the Ozarks before dark. We went at once to the restaurant where I had worked to see if the proprietor had relented enough to pay me the twenty-eight dollars back wages. But the place had been sold and the man who had succeeded me as cook was now in charge. He invited us to stay with him that night and I helped cook while Albert earned a dollar by washing dishes. Next day when the truck gardener came Albert left with him.

This was Saturday! And school to start on the following Monday. No time to lose.

I hastened back to Cross Timbers and struck out on a trail that the restaurant man said would take me most quickly to the Andrews place. I took the dim road through the timber and it was like walking through a great corridor—the trees towered overhead like Gothic arches of the great cathedrals of Europe pictured in school histories. Yet those pictures had never shown singing birds, scampering squirrels and woodchucks or fragrant purple blossoms. This temple was alive! And so was I.

Where the trail crossed Stark's Creek at Still Hollow Spring I paused and sat down to rest on a rock ledge. Downstream a few hundred yards there was a wagon ford

where the road crossed. Upstream there stood an abandoned mill. A sun perch darted from the watercress at
the stream's edge and became leader in a kind of tag when
two other small fish followed in its wake. I watched them
until they disappeared under an overhanging rock just
ahead of the shadow of a little green heron that winged
its noisy flight upstream. Overhead the wind rustled in
the trees and the cicadas tuned up for their evening
serenade. Shadows grew long across the creek and the
sparkle left the rocky water swirls. As I leaned over to
remove my shoes and socks the pungent odor of pennyroyal that had been crushed underfoot rose to my nostrils.

I put my shoes and socks under my arms, picked up my
luggage and stepped into the stream. Its chill waters sent
sharp pains through my legs, and I stepped gingerly as bits
of gravel dug sharply into my tender feet. I nearly lost
my balance and tottered to a soaking when I stepped on
a soft patch of level green moss. The simple beauty of
this green pad beneath the waters belied its treachery and
I thereafter bore the hurt of safer footing as I waded on
across. I brushed the gravel from my soles, put on my
shoes and socks and set off across the lands of Mulberry
School District. According to the description Harmon had
given me I must be close to the Andrews place.

I trudged across the narrow, rocky field which bordered
the creek, climbed over a rail fence and was on the road
which I had seen cross at the ford below the mill. The
road was hedged in by wild blackberry brambles and
scrub oak; it was narrow as a single wagon track and
deeply rutted; large rocks protruded here and there. An
irregular tattered ribbon of grass and weeds meandered
between the ruts. This trail wound steeply among the
shadows of the heavily wooded hillside and for all the
walking of the past few weeks I found myself stumbling
and panting long before I reached the top of the ridge.

There were no telephone lines along this road but I felt certain the Andrews' would be expecting me. Several persons had seen Albert and me in Cross Timbers on the previous day and doubtless the word was out that the new schoolteacher was in the country. I had heard of the efficiency of the Ozark grapevine communication system, and as my entry into the community had taken place twenty-four hours before, it was likely that many patrons in the Mulberry district were already anticipating my arrival.

The road was no less rough as I started down the other side of the hill—and I don't know why I thought it should be. About halfway down the steep descent I saw a clearing. According to the directions given me in Cross Timbers, this place—the first past the wagon ford—must be my destination.

The clearing was enclosed by a rail fence and was settled by a group of wooden structures. Like so many chicks, several small, unpainted, dressed-lumber buildings seemed to huddle in the protecting shadow of a larger hewn-log shelter that was surely the barn and implement shed. Within a stone's throw of these utility buildings and nearest the road was a barny, ramshackle sort of house shaped roughly like a short-stemmed T. The dwelling's proximity to the outbuildings was all a part of the economy of labor as practiced by the hillman. The house resembled the barn for it, too, was made largely of rough-hewn logs. Originally it must have been two log houses with the traditional turkey trot between them, but now the center section or trot was closed with dressed-lumber boards. The front of the house looked to be about a story and a half high but the stem of the T was only a low-roofed lean-to.

This, then, was the Andrews' abode. As I walked nearer I noticed someone sitting in a rocking chair in the shadows near the front entrance. A dog barked. The occupant of the chair saw me and started toward the gap in the fence at the road, reaching it before I was directly in front of the house. I nodded and started to speak, but . . .

"Reckon yo're the new schoolteacher," she said. "I figgered hit war 'bout time ye showed up. Teachers allers boards here so I knowed ye would, too. I'm Mis' Andrews. Most folks calls me Missoury. Never knowed why Maw called me Missoury lessen it was me bein' borned on tenth of August—that's the day the almenack says Missoury 'come a state. 'Course that war long before my bornin' day," she chuckled. "Come in; Paw'll be here d'reckly." She raised her voice as we walked toward the cabin. "Paw! Oh, Paw. . . . Never knowed him to be 'round when a body wants him."

Mrs. Andrews didn't give me a chance to get a word edgewise into the conversation but I did have an opportunity to study her. She was a big woman and I felt that doubtless the primness of her dress and its ruffled collar belied her customary habits; for 160-pound women don't develop such sinewy hands and arms in work that allows them to wear starched print dresses. Her hair had been rolled into a knot on top of her head. As she preceded me up the path I noticed her shoes: broad, masculine work shoes worn by those accustomed to field labor.

"Paw!" she yelled again and a small figure stepped out of the barn east of the house. "Hurry and git done with what yer doin'. New schoolteacher's come to stay with us."

"Maw, was you acallin' me?" asked a woman who suddenly popped up at the doorway of the house. She saw me and giggled.

"Thet's my girl, Arabellie," Mrs. Andrews nodded by way of introduction. "She lives with us—ain't never married. We got a boy, Otis, too. Otis," she called.

There was another shadow at the door and Arabella's figure was eclipsed by a larger form—a form clad in overalls, though not boy's size, for this Otis was a hulk of a man.

I stepped forward to offer my palm man to man, but suddenly felt it grasped firmly in a woman's two hands that clung tenaciously. I tried to withdraw my hand but she tightened her hold and in my confused embarrassment I found myself literally tugging to be free. She giggled again and finally released me. I shook hands with Otis.

Mrs. Andrews raised her voice again. "Hurry up, Dave; yo're keepin' the schoolteacher waitin'."

Dave came up the path. He was a slight man, much older than his wife. He stooped with the weight of two five-gallon milk pails brimming with white foam. He set the pails down, swiped his hand on the bib of his overalls and smiling feebly, shook hands with me.

"Howdy," he said. "Reckon Missoury and the childern'll take keer of ye. I got to git the milk crocked." He turned and carried the milk into the house.

Light from the kerosene lamp on the table inside the house brightened as Arabella turned the wick key.

"Hain't no need fer turnin' thet up so high, Arabellie," Mrs. Andrews said as we stepped into the house. "Hit just burns up coal oil and blacks up the chimbley. Ain't ary-body goin' to be readin' none tonight."

In the yellow glimmer I could better see the Andrews' progeny. Otis was about thirty and dull-witted and Arabella couldn't have been much older than that; some folks might have thought her younger. It is difficult to judge the age of hill women after they are eighteen. Arabella had the kind of figure that a good dressmaker could have made stylish, but the clumsily cut dress which she was wearing fitted her too well in some places, illy in others. She kept looking my way, boldly, and I felt uncomfortable under her gaze.

Mrs. Andrews pointed to a chair near the door.

"Set your stuff down and take a cheer whilst me and Arabellie puts supper on the table," she commanded.

As the two women, busying themselves with supper, shuffled between table and kitchen stove, great grotesque shadows broke from the lamplight. Arabella lifted a checkered tent from the center of the table. She moved much crockery, a well-filled spoon holder, salt and pepper shakers, a sugar bowl and a honey jar, in order to locate the lamp. These beginnings were soon augmented by rattling plates and cups as the women worked.

We were in the middle section of the house, which, like Topsy, had apparently "jist growed." The chinked, hewn logs of the two original houses still showed: the ceiling and floor were wood and the two relatively new walls that enclosed the former "trot" had been covered with roll building paper of the kind that bears huge two-color flowers. The lean-to which I had noticed as I came up the road was the kitchen.

I looked about and speculated on which of the rooms would be mine. Considering the limited space for the three Andrews' and myself, I wondered if I would have to share a room with Otis.

A pole ladder against one wall extended from the floor to the board ceiling. Doubtless it led into a garret storeroom. Mrs. Andrews saw me looking at this ladder-like contraption and turned from the table. She wrapped her hands in her apron and stepped between me and the lamp. I heard my fate come from the shadow that towered above me.

"Hit's right comfortable place we'uns got fer ye, Mr. Howard." She nodded toward the ladder. "Ye'll lak it up thar. More to yerself than being down on the ground—and we'uns air agivin' ye Gran'pa's bed." She turned to her daughter. "Arabellie, git them folks up and let's eat."

Arabella whisked out and called loudly from the

kitchen door. The two men soon came in and amid much shuffling we all sat down. I was last.

Mrs. Andrews nodded to us and said, "Paw'll say thanks nights and Brother Howard'll say 'em mornings." All I ever heard of the ensuing grace was "Oh, God. . . ." Thereafter the old man's voice trailed off into an unintelligible mumble. The merry-go-round of dishes began and I quit looking for the napkin that I should have known wasn't there.

The food was filling and there was a good variety of vegetables more flavorful, certainly, I thought, than the conversation. The latter consisted, mainly, of monologue with some questions and answers when Missoury asked me about schools and Iowa. As we loitered about the table at the close of the meal she brought up the subject of religion.

"Reckon yore bein' a preacher didn't hurt none yore gittin' hired fer Mulberry School," she said. "Hillcrofts and the Charleses lean on religion purty heavy. Can't say the Harmon tribe's got ary to spare."

This statement surprised me in light of the fact that Harmon was the one who had suggested that I put up with the Andrews'.

"Ole Mandy Hillcroft ain't let no grass grow under her feet," Mrs. Andrews went on. "She's narrated it around yo're goin' to be a preacher 'sides a teacher. They're kind'ly 'spectin you to take charge tomorry."

"Well, I asked for an opportunity to be of service," I said, "and I'll be glad to help out all I can." I arose from the table. "If you don't mind, I believe I'd like to get to bed now. It's been a hard day."

"Ott, you help yore paw heft Brother Howard's plunder up to his room," instructed the elder woman. She and her daughter arose from the table and began to stack the dishes. "They's a lamp up thar."

Otis climbed up the ladder with the agility of a squirrel and relayed the suitcase through the opening.

"They's matches on the table beside the lamp if you ain't got ary," he said as he stepped down and stood aside for me to climb up. He didn't add where, in that dark place, I might find the table.

The rungs of the ladder were so close to the wall that I had to turn my feet sideways as I climbed and the Andrews family stood watching my embarrassed ascension. I need not have feared about fumbling in the dark for stray rays of lamplight came through the opening and filtered through the cracks in the floor. There was also faint moon-glow from one small window in the attic so my entry into the private suite was not entirely unilluminated.

"At least," I thought as I groped for the lamp, "I need not worry about being crowded up here. A whole attic to myself." I found the lamp which I lit and looked about me. My spacious suite occupied about one-third of the small loft. The rest was filled with the dusty accumulations of years! The furniture consisted of a small table with the lamp on it; there was a split-bottom chair—and a bed.

Grandpa's bed was hand-made, with no evidence of particular skill or design. It was solid walnut with thick corner posts and straight, high head and foot. The quilt upon it was bright colored but of noncommittal pattern and mediocre workmanship. Yet with all, I fancied that bed. It was piled high and a nostalgia swept over me as I remembered the deep, luxurious feather beds of my mother's: how we boys used to lose ourselves in them on a cold winter night. I was seized with a childish desire to back off, make a run and dive into its depths. Of course, though, there was no room for backing off and I was too tired to run anyway. I sat down on the chair and bent over to unpack my nightclothes. I blew out the lamp and sat a few minutes in the gloom, contemplating my initiation into Mulberry School District and my new home. The clink and rattle of glass and crockery downstairs subsided, the light pattern on the rafters changed as someone lifted the lamp from the table in the room below and carried it into another part of the house.

Dressed for bed, I knelt beside my chair and looked heavenward in prayer. It was as if the pale night sky were overhead: stars began to appear. The whole area above me twinkled like a Milky Way. But how, I wondered with a start, could stars twinkle here in this loft? I looked more closely and realized that what I saw was not stars. It was the moonlight drifting through the oak shingles of the roof.

I thanked God that come what might there was still the bed! The feather bed and I would defy any winter winds that tried to give us too much ventilation. I prayed long and with great earnestness that night—aware that it was probably I, not God, who needed convincing. I arose and stood at the side of the great inviting mound that I could make out in the cobweb-filtered moonlight, considering how best to enter this sanctuary of comfort. How better, indeed, then to fall full length—to indulge in the luxury of one grand plop! I pulled back the coverlet and let go—but my bed didn't sink or plop. It crackled!

Crackled? But feathers aren't crackly. What ... how ... why? This was a cornshuck mattress!

CHAPTER 7

Mulberry School

SUNDAY MORNING I AROSE AT THE FIRST COCK'S CROW and dressed with special care. At Sunday school I was to meet many of my pupils and patrons.

I recognized Jake Hillcroft, one of the school board members, standing in the group outside the church-house door when we arrived. We greeted one another and he helped me to meet several other patrons of the district as we waited for the crowd to gather. The church bell rang, calling all inside. Hillcroft turned to me and said, "We'd like for you to come home to dinner with us today, Brother Howard. I figgered you'd want to be seein' yore school and this evening we'll git Clark and Harmon and walk across and look 'er over."

As we entered the church I reflected that I could have embraced the man for offering me such welcome relief from a Sunday afternoon under Arabella's gaze.

Nearly sixty men, women and children were gathered there. They were sitting on crude plank benches and staring at me inquisitively. Jake Hillcroft led me down front where he stopped and introduced me to his mother, Mandy Hillcroft. She was a kindly person who must have been the type of good hill womanhood used as a pattern by Harold Bell Wright.

When the initial curiosity about the new schoolteacher had been satisfied, the congregation picked up hymn-books and began thumbing the pages. Mrs. Hillcroft conferred with the woman at the old Estey organ and announced a hymn by name. I wondered why she called the selection instead of the page number, but the mystery cleared when a paper-covered hymnal was handed to me and I saw that it was different from the books held by my neighbors. Nor were theirs all alike. The organist played by ear and improvised where the reeds were mute. She pumped and the congregation sang. Many in the group only casually referred to their books for they knew the words and music in their hearts. There was harmony in their voices climaxing in the amen at the end of the hymn.

Mandy Hillcroft prayed a short, fervent prayer and then suggested that the new schoolteacher read a chapter from the life of Christ and divide the audience into age groups for discussion of the lesson. I was amazed at the wide knowledge of the Scriptures evinced by the older men and women.

Just before the closing prayer, Mrs. Hillcroft announced that Sunday school would continue from week to week. "We want you'uns to come back," she said, "and fetch others along."

Mandy Hillcroft's cooking was as good as her praying. The meal she set in front of us in the kitchen of her neat four-room cabin that noon would have graced any table. The advice she gave was as acceptable as the meal, too.

A body hadn't ortter meddle in other folks' affairs," she said, "but they're some folks ye jist gotter feed with a long-handled spoon. I ain't asayin' what ye ortter do, Brother Howard, but iffen I war ye I'd be mighty careful what I done and said where yo're stayin'."

"Maw, the Andrews' bark is worser'n their bite," soothed her son.

"Ye ain't fergettin' thet turkey deal of hern, air ye, Jake?" Mandy asked.

"Ain't likely," he chuckled.

"Something I ought to know about?" I asked.

"Might as well, jist to show you what breed of cats yo're foolin' with when you have anything to do with Missoury," Jake advised. "Cousin Lily Horton bought a settin' of turkey eggs from her—come to two dollars and eighty cents. She thought Missoury war gettin' mighty generous when she tole her, 'Now honey . . .'"

"She allers uses honey when she's aimin' to stir up a stink," his mother interpolated.

Jake continued, "Missoury goes on with, 'these turkey eggs'll hatch a heap better with a turkey hen settin' on 'em. Hain't right fer a chicken hen to set 'em. Turkey'll raise more of 'em fer she knows what they needs better'n a settin' hen. Honey, I'll shore be proud to loan you two settin' turkeys—I allers tries to be naborly.'"

Mandy chuckled until she set her chair to rocking. "Lily didn't know what that old witch had in back of her head when she wanted to be naborly."

"The deal war made," Jake continued, "and nacherally when the turkey hens hatched off their broods they took them little turks right back home to Missoury lak turkeys allers do. Well, Lily started lookin' fer the critters and finally wound up at Andrews' place."

"Could she identify her poults?" I asked.

"'Course not and old Missoury knowed that, so she says, 'I'm shore sorry, Lily, but I hain't seen nothin' of them two hens I loaned you'uns.'"

"Lily tried to bluff her out but it didn't work with Missoury," Mandy broke in.

"No sir, bluffin' don't work with that woman," Jake continued. "Lily told her she recollected one of them birds and Missoury riled up madder'n a wet hen. She lit all over Lily: 'Reckon I know my own stuff,' she says. 'Here I try to be naborly loanin' you'uns turkey hens. By God!' she says, 'I bet you sold my hens and yo're shore goin' ter pay me fer 'em. They's fetchin' five

dollars apiece and you kin just fork over ten dollars.'
Well, sir, Brother Howard, that old she-devil cussed and
damned Lily a sight 'til the pore girl said she'd pay to
get shet of the whole deal."

"A body'd athought that'd keep Missoury quiet,"
Mandy offered, "but hit didn't. Cousin Lily paid her thet
ten dollars and said she didn't want any more to do with
her. Missoury ups and swears a swear and says, 'Suits me
fine—don't 'low to have no truck with such trash nohow.'"

Jake pushed his chair away from the table. "Well, we
better be hikin' out, Brother Howard, and get Clark and
Harmon and go look things over," he drawled.

Clark joined us willingly but Harmon said he figured
we could look at the place just as well without him, yet
upon our insistence he consented to go along.

Mulberry School sat high on a wooded knoll but was so
screened by scrub oak and cedar growth that I didn't see
it until we entered a clearing in front of the school
ground. Then the place loomed drearily.

It was indeed a ragged beggar sunning. In fact, it gave
every appearance of having sat in the sun much too long.
It was an unshapely thing made of large, hand-hewn oak
logs. A few of the cracks between the heavy outer covering were covered by four-inch strips, but these rough
unplaned boards bore no paint and gave to the place a
boarded-up effect adding to the air of desolation.

"Looks like the shingles were hand-made," I said by
way of comment.

"Them's oak shingles—been on twenty years," said
Clark on the defense. "Folks in the neighborhood made
'em at a workin'."

"Bet you never heard of that, did you?" Hillcroft
asked. I shook my head in the negative. "They used to
have workin's ever'time a new house war put up," he
continued. "I recollect this'n—Paw was alive then and I

come over with Maw and Paw. 'Course the house is older but the roof was put on new at the workin'. Ever'body turned out."

I noticed that many of the shingles had curled out of shape or had blown from the roof. "Looks like we may have to have another working some day soon," I remarked.

Harmon spoke quickly. "Them's good oak shingles. They jist turned up thet way 'cause they's put on in the wrong sign of the moon."

I looked about for the toilets. "What about sanitary conditions—where are the privies?" I asked.

One of the men laughed. "Don't need none. Girls go down the north holler; boys down the south'un. If you all ketches any big boys agoin' down the north holler, whop the devil outen 'em."

The well on the school yard was the only part of the entire school plant that showed care. It was ninety-six feet deep and drilled through solid limestone. Typical of the Ozark well, water was drawn by means of a galvanized-metal valved bucket four feet long and four inches in diameter. Frequently the windlass used to draw the long bucket is nothing more than a tripod of poles, but Mulberry School had a neat, substantially built well house.

The elation I felt over the satisfactory well lasted no longer than the time it required for us to step into the school building, which Harmon sullenly opened after unfastening the heavy padlock on the door.

Leaves and trash littered the planking floor. Spiders had held summer-long spinning sessions in all the corners. Many windows were without panes and oak shingles had been nailed to the mullion strips—poor substitutes for glass. Abandoned mud swallows' or phoebes' nests clung to the side of the exposed stone chimney. Wasp nests gave evidence of continued occupancy.

The seats were little more than crude benches; the

desks, deeply incised with initials and dates and crude characters, would be a penman's horror. (These had probably been purchased many years before from a more prosperous school district.) Some well-meaning backhills man had been responsible for the teacher's desk. It had been sawed out of rough oak and hammered into something with four legs and a top. The chair was a backless stool.

Across the entire space behind the desk was a kind of blackboard. It was warped. Its tongue and groove pine boards had once been painted black. Now it was gray with washing, chalk dust and time. I looked about the room and saw that there was not a single picture, curtain or window shade. The walls had been faced with wide oak board but the cracks had not been battened.

The few books which I found piled in one corner were dog-eared obsolete texts. Many were without covers, only a few by the same author. These old books, plus two erasers and five pieces of chalk, comprised our school supplies.

An ungainly cast-iron stove much in need of blacking rested in the center of the room. I knew it wasn't necessary to look inside but I did. Sure enough, it was filled with last year's ashes.

"I wish I had a month in which to get this school ready," I said to myself for I had always taken pride in maintaining an inviting schoolroom. Well, it was too late now, but I would come early the next morning and many mornings after. I'd use many out of school hours and by constant effort much of the present ugliness would disappear. There was so much to think about; so I excused myself early from the directors and struck off walking over the hills.

CHAPTER 8

Arabella

I KNOW OF NO WAY TO MAKE ANYTHING BUT A RATHER dull chronicle of what was really for me an exciting event: my first day of school in the Ozarks—the beginning of a dream come true.

The school board, all my pupils and their parents with a number of interested spectators were on hand for the school opening Monday morning. Many came late and it was nearly ten o'clock before I could open the session.

Harmon, who was the school board secretary, brought the register for keeping daily records.

"Reckon we best fix you some kind of contract seein' the other two hired you," he said, whining through his nose. If he expected a retort or a bit of explanation from me he was disappointed for I merely said, "All right, I'm ready." I indicated my desk and chair. "Sit here."

After the contract was duly negotiated the directors sat down with the pupils and patrons. Apparently I was expected immediately and without introduction to take charge. It was the first time in my teaching career that I had opened a school with pupils, parents, school directors and visitors all present. I must have been a little embarrassed.

"First," I said as I stood before them, "I would like to meet all of you people. I want to know your names and the names of the children each of you will have in school. I'll start right here with this lady."

They began to thaw out a little, answering in monosyllables the questions I asked each of them, but not a single person volunteered any information beyond the direct answer to my query.

Two young women past eighteen years of age asked if I could teach high-school work. "Yes, I'll be happy to have a high-school class," I said. "We have no books covering high-school work but I will send for some that I have stored in Iowa. You may enroll today and we'll begin without text."

Twenty-four pupils enrolled, including the two high school students. They seemed bright children, eager to learn, quite attentive and obedient. The adults remained until about eleven o'clock, when I called a short recess. When the older folk were gone, the children began to talk and freely offer information.

"They'll be lots more in school this winter when work's all done," one little fellow confided in the midst of a game of wood tag. "Lots of big boys and girls, too. That's when school gets bad. Don't see no gads this morning. Don't you do no whoppin'?"

"You stayin' down to Andrews', hain't ya?" The boy had changed bases with scarcely a pause in his chatter. "Ole Misery shore's a holy terror. Nobody don't have no truck with 'er. Jist pass and repass when they meet 'er, that's all."

After recess all the arithmetic classes were assigned work and the two high-school pupils were taught the meaning of plus and minus in algebra. The last ten minutes before noon were devoted to rapid calculation. The children were not permitted to write the two numbers to be added. They could only write the answer. I rapidly read twenty-five problems and many pupils wrote the correct answer to every one.

At lunch, pails were opened at desks or carried to the playground. The plain, wholesome food was eaten with a relish. One youngster had brought frog legs. "Done ketched me a couple big frogs. Maw, she fried 'em fer me

—shore good. Ever eat any, teacher?" he queried. Another small boy sat down beside me and opened his syrup-pail lunch container. He peered intently at its contents. "Durn," he said disgustedly. "Corn bread! Jist as fer as I kin see, not a durn thing but corn bread!" A number of the children had fried chicken. Others had young squirrel but without exception the lunch pails contained cornbread.

Several had brought jars of sweet milk, many of which had soured in the August heat. After lunch one of the older boys took charge of a project which was new to me and which I thought a neat trick. Under his supervision we dug a square hole in the ground, lined it with rocks and packed it with leaves which were wet with water from the well. "We can put our milk in here while the weather is warm," he said proudly, "and it will keep just as sweet as it would in a springhouse."

As we were going back into the schoolhouse for the afternoon session, one of the older girls said to me, "Arabella Andrews is jist an old maid. Been one four years, too. She's same age as my brother and he's twenty-nine. Better watch out, teacher, she'll shore marry you whether you wants her or not; she shore is lookin' fer a man."

When the first day of school ended, I walked along down the mountain trail to the Andrews cabin near the Hoffman Ford on Stark's Creek. I felt less frustrated and could begin to muster a grin, if not a laugh, at some of the strange things that had been coming at me so rapidly within the last forty-eight hours. When I neared the cabin I saw Mrs. Andrews—"Ole Misery—the holy terror," the schoolboy had called her—out in the field helping her husband and son shock kaffir corn. Arabella was not with them.

I walked into the cabin and was greeted by a beaming Arabella.

"Let me fix you a cup of fresh coffee and a san'wich,"

she said. Hers was the benign expression of a cat that was about to spring upon a nestling. "I was always awful hungry when I got home from school and we allers fixes a bite fer the teachers." She chattered on and on like a contented Leghorn hen scratching in a shock of wheat.

The rest of the family did not come in from their field work until dark. By that time Arabella had finally left off chattering at me and cooked supper.

At supper I answered many questions about the first day of school and listened with interest to the comments about the children, most of which evolved into gossip about the parents. I volunteered no opinions other than that I liked the school, the patrons and the children.

"We'uns air heaviest taxpayers in the district," Missoury informed me. "We got more'n a thousand acres of land and don't owe a cent on it. We'uns agoin' ter give Arabellie a half-section up clost to the schoolhouse. Hit's got a nice cabin and's mostly fenced; all new rails. They's a lot of good farmin' land on it."

Arabella made no comment but she was generous in the number of times she passed the ham and hot biscuits; and whenever I looked up from my plate she would catch my eye and giggle.

As the conversation continued, I could detect that they were very curious to know why I had come to the hill country. I told them only the barest account of my life and of Clayton and his illness, of my decision to come to the Ozarks in Christian work and my hope to eventually establish a home for us all. It was late when we went to bed that night and the Andrews' were still full of questions.

We rose before sun-up and ate breakfast by lamplight. As soon as we finished the meal, they all, except Arabella, went to the fields. Immediately I made preparations to go to school.

"Why go so early?" Arabella questioned petulantly. " 'Course I'll put up yore lunch if you've got ter go now."

It probably didn't sound any too convincing to her when I explained that I wanted to clean the building and cut the sprouts and brush from the school ground. Yet I would have used almost any excuse to get away. And as I walked to the school that second morning, I began to wonder if I shouldn't find another boarding place.

CHAPTER 9

The Pie Supper

BY FRIDAY I MORE THAN DREADED THE THOUGHTS OF a week end under the Andrews roof. I felt that such an ordeal wasn't to be endured if I had to resort to the extreme of spending Friday night in the schoolhouse. With no definite idea in mind—except that of escape—I told Mrs. Andrews Friday morning that I had a little business which needed attending and that I might not be back that night.

Throughout the day I pondered my situation and by Friday evening after school I was more determined on the subject. The idea of spending the night at school didn't seem too impractical as the weather was warm and I'd slept on floors as hard as this one. I cleaned the room thoroughly and pasted up two colorful pictures I found in an old magazine gleaned from the book pile. By five o'clock I was through with the odd jobs and for some reason was exceedingly restless. It suddenly occurred to me that I had no plans for Saturday and certainly no food for the day! I decided to walk over to the Hillcrofts' and see if Jake needed any help with his Saturday work, and perhaps I could buy a quart of milk to bring back with me.

It must have been another evidence of the guiding of a kind Providence. Jake Hillcroft had sprained a foot rather badly and was behind in nearly all of his chores. It wasn't necessary for me to ask for work for the morrow or explain my errand of the evening. They seemed very

glad to see me and were sincerely grateful that I offered
to spend the week end taking over for Jake.

I picked tomatoes and beans Friday evening but left
the hoeing of the fall garden for morning.

Mandy and Jake were sitting on the cabin porch Saturday morning when I finished the hoeing. I sat down on
the porch step to rest a spell.

"This is great country for doing a lot of thinking," I
remarked. "A man can be to himself a lot—especially if
he has a place of his own. I think I'm going to like it
here, Mrs. Hillcroft."

She paused in her bean hulling and looked at me.
"Brother Howard, iffen we'uns air going to be friends ye
jist best call me Mandy."

"All right, Mandy," I said. "It's been a long time since
I had any women folks to call by their first name."

"Us hillbillies 'druther use the given name of folks we
lak," Jake added.

"Thank you," I replied. Then I made what I thought
was a cautious inquiry. "I think I'd like to feel more settled here. You don't know of a cabin I could rent, do you?"

Mandy ducked her head and peered out over the top of
her small gold-rimmed glasses. "Ye hankerin' to get shet
of the Andrews already?"

"Well," I hedged, "I just figured that if I could get
settled in a cabin the boys could come live with me. We
could buy supplies with the ten dollars a month I'm paying for board and room."

"Iffen ye up and leave Missoury's thar's shore to be
trouble," Mandy said. She wanted to be helpful, I felt,
but her inbred, hillfolk seventh sense kept her as cautious
as her fabulous kinsman who had been sheriff as many
times as the law would allow and hadn't been shot once.
She looked at me again and said, "Missoury's the kind
that laks to run the hull country and she's bin at it a
long time."

"But I've got to get away from there before something happens," I blurted out.

Mandy nodded knowingly but hesitated before replying. "Hit might work out somehow but I'd shore go slow 'bout leadin' up to hit." She reached down to the basket on the porch floor and picked up a handful of bulging bean pods and dumped them into her apron. "Don't reckon ye mind me hullin' beans whilst we talk?" With dexterous fingers she opened the pods, gathering the plump purple beans in one hand. Suddenly she looked up from her work and asked, "Brother Howard, how in the world did ye ever start boardin' at Andrews' noway?"

"Well, I'm not right sure," I admitted. "The day I came to apply for the school, I guess it was settled. As I passed Harmon's house on my way back to town I stopped and told him I'd been hired to teach Mulberry. He recommended that I stay at Andrews'."

I saw Mandy catch Jake's eye. "Harmon said the Andrews lived close to school and that the other teachers had stayed there. I guess I just took his word for it.

"Then Saturday evening when I walked in," I went on, "Missoury seemed to be expecting me."

There was a sudden rattling of beans tossed vigorously into a kettle and Mandy picked up another handful of pods.

"She'd be expectin' ye all righty; expects all the school-teachers to stay at her place. Hit seems quare, though," she went on, "that Harmon woulda tole ye Andrews' war a good place to stay when they hates each other like pizen. Brother Howard, cain't ye see nothin' funny in it?"

Funny wasn't my word for it. "Do you suppose Harmon was getting back at me because I went to the other directors?" I asked.

The kindly old woman smiled. "What els'n is thar to figger, Brother Howard?"

"Harmon'd do that, all right," said Jake.

"Well, we'uns'll see what kin be done to holp ye fer I reckon ye'll shore be needin' it," said Mandy. "I knowed ye war a stranger here jist lak a lamb amongst wolves. And boardin' to Andrews' won't do ye any good. But I'd shore go slow about jumpin' away from thet place."

Taking my cue from Mandy Hillcroft I became doubly cautious in my actions and conversation both at the Andrews place and at school. The latter became my refuge. Each morning I'd leave for school as soon as breakfast was finished and remain there or walk in the woods each evening until the supper hour.

This unsatisfactory situation became a boon to the school, however, for I buried myself in the work. Before and after school I was more than usually industrious about the schoolroom and in the yard outside. By the second week at Mulberry the place had lost much of its desolation and untidiness. A Friday afternoon program ended the week. Now there was another week end facing me and nothing to do but prepare my guard for the two-day vacation period, for I couldn't go to Jake's again. Oh well, the Sabbath would end and I could return to the relative peace and security of the schoolhouse on Monday morning, so I struck off up the trail. I approached the cabin as wary as a stalked deer. Old Missoury was standing in the doorway, decked out in her Sunday-go-to-meeting best.

"We'uns air goin' to the pie sociable over at Hardscrabble School," she said. "Figger ye'll want ter go." She stepped aside that I might enter the cabin.

"Grab yerself that snack on the table and git yerself ready," she commanded.

Arabella was in her best mail-order dress. Her hair was frizzed to a frayed-rope likeness and she beamed with the complacence of one who has just been clever and is willing to rest.

On the table lay a green-and-white crepe-paper creation. This, of course, was Arabella's box in which she would take her pie to the sociable. She had deliberately left it there, I was sure, openly resorting to the sly trick of every country girl who wants to tip off the man she expects to buy her pie.

With anything but a girlish giggle she grabbed her work of art and began to camouflage it with the pages of an old weekly Kansas City *Star*.

"Gee, reckon I hadn't ort ter let you seen this, Brother Howard," she simpered, "but I didn't want to booger up the butterfly." She referred to an ornate thing with red clothespin body and purple wings that adorned the box.

Ordinarily I would have pleasantly anticipated a pie supper. Tonight I resented being kidnaped by the Andrews' but there seemed no way to back out. I wolfed the snack and joined the family in the barn lot.

Missoury and "Paw" were seated on a wide board laid across the front of the wagon from whence they urged the mules on their journey. Arabella, Ott and I made ourselves as comfortable as possible in the hay that padded the bottom of the wagon box. We stopped frequently to permit young folks who had set out on foot to climb into the wagon with us. The road was full of chuck holes and rocks and the gay young blades and their gals made the most of each jostle. Arabella liked it, too, and took advantage of each jolt to permit her body to bump against mine. It was so crowded in the wagon box that there was no likely escape for me from this undesirable game.

The snakelike road climbed steeply. We topped the crest of an unusually high ridge and Dave Andrews stopped to wind his mules. Across the hollows echoed the rumbles of other wagons, the bantering and laughter and singing of other wagonloads of young people. Now and then a young man would gallop past on horse or mule with his best girl up behind him, her arms clasped tightly around her hero's waist. It seemed as if the entire hill population was pie-supper bent.

A huge bonfire on a knob above the valley signaled the location of Hardscrabble school. In silhouette against the blaze were many wagons, mules and hillfolk. A round golden moon paused on the eastern horizon.

The older men were congregated in groups on one side of the schoolhouse. In the shadows on the other side of the yard a crowd of young people played "Swing Josie." Two hill fiddlers sat upon a fallen oak and their music set the pace for the dancers. The young folk sang gayly as they promenaded, dosi-doed and swung around in a great circle.

Andrews, Ott and I tethered the mules, then gravitated toward the group of older men. Missoury and her daughter bustled into the schoolhouse. The young folks who had come with us took their pie-filled boxes inside and ran to join the fiddlers' fun.

A school patron was telling me about sending his boy to school after fodder cutting when the clangor of the bell signaled the start of the program. Patrons and guests squeezed oversized bodies into undersized desks. Everyone crowded into the schoolroom until all the seats and the aisles along the walls were filled. Every window ledge was filled to capacity. Young men and their girls standing against the walls whispered and tittered.

The pupils who were to be in the program occupied the front seats. Unseen little folk took their places on the platform behind the improvised muslin sheet which waved and bulged and became patterned with grotesque shadows. Soon the curtain parted surreptitiously and the pretty young woman teacher stepped out. Holding the curtain behind her, she welcomed the patrons and announced her program.

The program was fun and everyone enjoyed it no matter how simple the verse or nonsensical the short

farce which was given by the older pupils. Its climax
came with all the earthy gusto of rural humor when a
school patron read her literary effort, "The Hardscrabble
News." The building was already rocking with laughter
at the puns and jokes about local folks when I heard:

"Our teacher's fixin' up a little extra since the new man
teacher come to Mulberry. If they ever git serious, him
being a preacher, they can save the weddin' fee to buy a
cradle."

I smiled good-naturedly but the item apparently held
no humor for the Andrews' for they alone didn't join
in the laughter.

The curtain closed on the program and the really important business of the evening began. The auctioneer
readied himself for the sale of pie-filled boxes. The handsome hillman acknowledged his vanity by frequently re-
moving a long comb from his vest pocket and running it
through his greased hair. When the curtain behind the
auctioneer opened it revealed a table filled with boxes of
many shapes and colors and was a signal for renewed
whispering and tittering, especially among the girls.

The auctioneer selected a box brave with ribbons and
bows. He held it dramatically aloft, crying, "What am I
bid fer the pleasure of eating outta this purty box with
a purty girl?"

"Two bits," came a prompt answer.

"Ah got twenty-five, do ah hear thirty?"

A boy standing along the wall nodded and the girl at
his side giggled.

"Ah got thirty, do ah hear thirty-five?" The auctioneer droned on. At last the box was sold for forty cents
and the boy against the wall stepped forward to pay for
his purchase. The auctioneer referred to a slip of paper in
his hand and called out a name. The girl who had giggled
went forward to be claimed with the box.

Most of the boxes had been sold when the auctioneer

picked up the one over which fluttered a crumpled purple butterfly. I had no choice but to make a bid.

"Start at a quarter," I said. A lad near by looked at me for a moment. Apparently thinking it was the Hardscrabble teacher's box, he upped the bid to thirty-five cents. "Forty," I said by way of compliment. Just then the boy saw Arabella. She was much too interested and the young native knew instinctively that he'd been ill advised. He refused to bid again. I marched up and paid for the box while the clerk called out, "Arabella Andrews."

Another wave of laughter rippled over the crowd. "He ought to a knowed which one to bid on. He brung her, didn't he?"

When the last box had been sold, the teacher handed a Plymouth Rock rooster to the auctioneer.

"We're agoin' to give this to the most henpecked man in the house," he shouted. "A penny a vote and we'uns adeciding it in jist five minutes."

Young Ezra Holland was the winner. Ezra and pretty Mary Gilbert had been married only six weeks and the way they walked about with their arms around each other was a neighborhood joke. "Shame on ye, Mary—henpeckin' Ezra a'ready," someone shouted.

"I'm comin' over fer dinner!" was heard from another corner.

"Pshaw," Andrews yelled. "No fair! Thet chicken shore ort ter be mine. Missoury's done quit me achoppin' wood." A spirit of good-natured rivalry prevailed, even to Missoury, who only mildly chided her husband for his outburst.

A cake was offered for the prettiest girl, and in another five minutes several additional dollars were collected on that score. Pie eating followed, and whatever else could be said about Arabella, I had to admit to myself that her mother could make good pies.

When we left the schoolhouse the moon was high over

head. As I walked around the side of the wagon I over-heard two men talking.

"Mulberry's teacher's a preacher, too, they says," came a voice from beyond the team of horses which separated me from the speaker. "Reckon he could be a revenooer. Best watch out, boys."

So that was why I had not broken the shell of com-munity reserve! Here was another hurdle in the obstacle race before me. That night as we bumped along under the moon I realized that the native folk would never accept me as one of them until I could prove that my intentions were simply to help them in every way I could.

Next morning after the breakfast table had been crumbed Dave Andrews drove the wagon to the yard gate. It was market day. Into the wagon we loaded three ten-quart buckets of eggs, a can of cream, a box of beeswax taken from a bee tree which Ott had discovered and cut the day before, and a small sack of dried golden-seal roots which Ott said were being quoted at about three dollars a pound. Town was only fourteen miles away but the journey took nearly four hours.

After our produce was unloaded at the general store Dave drove the team to a vacant lot near by where there were other teams. We soon had our team unhitched and a mule tied to each side of the wagon. Dave took several ears of corn out of a sack that had been stacked under the wagon seat. We fed them to the mules and then walked back to the store.

It was a long low building with merchandise of the same staple quality found in most any country store. The merchant, his wife, son and two daughters kept busy waiting on trade. I saw very little money change hands, however, as most of the business was done by bartering. Eggs were counted, cream tested and weighed, roots and beeswax weighed and valued. This credit was exchanged for goods: soda, baking powder, spices, rice, bulk oatmeal, calico, ginghams, denim, shoes, boots, men's hats, caps, mittens, underwear, simple drugs such as sulphur, camphor, turpentine and Epsom salts. Feeds of all kinds were sold by the pound. Each customer traded out his credit. If he didn't use it all, he took a due bill; if he spent more than his credit a charge account was made by the merchant.

We became a part of the scene. Everyone seemed to know everyone else. They visited, talked of crops, politics, church services and every event of community interest. I alone was an outsider.

CHAPTER 10

Layin' Away Gran'pappy

ONE MONDAY MORNING IN EARLY FALL THE SKY WAS dark and unusually gloomy. By the time I reached school a drizzle of rain had begun to fall and the air was quite chilly, so I built a fire. It was well after nine o'clock before the last pupil straggled into the schoolroom and lessons seemed to go poorly all morning. Just as we were beginning the afternoon session a loud rap sounded on the door. I opened it and there stood a downcast young man.

"Hello," I smiled.

"Howdy," he replied, barely raising his head.

"You're one of the Frazier boys that I met at Sunday school yesterday morning, aren't you?"

"Yep, I'm Melvin."

"Come in out of the wet," I invited. "Would you like to start to school?"

"No, I shore hain't got no time to come in," he said, shifting from one foot to the other. "Ma, she sent me to see if you'd come to the cabin tomorry afternoon and hold a layin' away meetin' fer Gran'pappy. Gran'pappy, he died last night. The old man warn't no church feller but he shore never done nobody no dirt."

"I'm very sorry, Melvin," I said. "Yes, I'll do anything I can. What time is the funeral and where will it be held?"

"Maw 'lowed hit best be about two o'clock tomorry at the cabin. We's layin' him away in the Harmon buryin' ground arter that," he continued. "Maw said if ye

84

said 'yes' when I axed ya, to tell ya to have whatever singin' an all that ya wanted."

So I was to be a preacher as well as a teacher. And my first sermon must be a funeral sermon with the responsibility of all the arrangements mine.

As I closed the door and returned to the classroom I remembered all too vividly that a funeral was an ordeal for me. The grim picture of my brother's funeral, of Madge's and then Mother's following so soon rose up to harass me. "Possibly this is God's way of seeing if I'm a quitter," I thought. It was an opportunity for service that I couldn't deny.

When the afternoon session was finished and the children were all gone home, I sat at my desk a few minutes and thought to organize myself for the task ahead. There were Bob and Ethel Norman, a friendly warmhearted couple. (They were not natives to the community but had moved in four years before my coming when Bob had lost his job during a general railroad strike.) She played the organ and both of them were good singers.

When I locked the schoolhouse and headed for Normans' I noticed the sky was showing blue patches; but by the time I reached their place the sun was shining through intermittent clearings. Bob and Ethel were at home. They seemed pleased that I was to conduct the funeral and were generous in their offer of assistance.

"Don't you give the music another thought, Brother Howard," Ethel said. "Bob and I will see to that part of it."

I hurried on to the Andrews place and got my Bible, notebook and pencil. I walked up the steep rocky slope to the top of Childers Mountain and sat down on a large rock. I could see through the timbered hills to the misty blue horizon beyond. Sassafras and sumach were beginning to turn and the woods were already a riot of reds and yellows (they seemed to drip color as well as moisture) against the blue sky. Purpling shadows of the hills with alternating lanes of light from the setting sun made a scene of rare beauty.

I bowed my head in silent prayer to God for strength and an understanding heart that this, my first sermon, might be made up of words that God in His wisdom knew should be spoken.

"Cleansin' yore soul?"

I turned in startled surprise. Lige Gurney was coming up the path.

"I thought I was all alone," I stammered.

"Sorry if I scairt ye, Brother Howard," Lige apologized. "But somehow they's times when I gits so onery I hain't fit ter live with and when I'm needin' a soul-washin' I comes up hyar. Seems lak I'm closter ter God er somethin'. Didn't think about nobody else bein' up hyar too."

Lige lifted his long arm and pointed to the golden ball of setting sun that had just begun to disappear beyond the wooden horizon.

"Purty, hain't it," he mused. "Makes a body think of a purty pitcher lak they put on them big bank calendars. Reckon this's God's paintin'. He makes hit perfect." I think he almost forgot I was there. "With winter comin' on makes a body think of a baby smilin' jist as hit goes ter sleep.

"See them colors all over the woods, Brother Howard? When I gits down in my soul and feelin' ever'thing's wrong I climbs up hyar and remembers that God made ever' one of them hills and all the purtyness."

"That's a fine way to say it," I nodded.

"My livin' gits jist lak a old shirt, all worn 'n' dirty," Gurney said, "but settin' a while up hyar with God's jist lak washin', ironin' and patchin' thet old shirt. It works plumb good again then."

I hadn't thought of a reply when he turned back to

me. "See ye got yore Bible. Yo're preachin' the funeral tomorry, I hearn. Ye shore comes ter the right place ter git hit fixed up." He got up and flicked a small rock out into space. "Lots of folks wonderin' 'bout ye, Brother Howard, but when I seen ya settin' thar so still, with yore head bowed and yore eyes shet, aprayin', I jist plumb nacherly knowed ye could be counted on."

He turned as abruptly as he had come. "Gotter be gittin' on," he continued as he started down the trail. "Ah'll see ye tomorry at the funeral. Goin' now ter he'p make the coffin."

Somehow the solemn beauty, the silence, the grandeur of the timbered hills with their multi-colored leaves gave me the inspiration I sought. Selecting Job 14:14 as my text, "If a man die, shall he live again?" I began jotting down notes representing ideas that came faster than I could write. When I walked back to the Andrews cabin there was a calm assurance in my soul that I would not fail my God, myself or my fellowman.

A score of people were already at the Fraziers' cabin when I arrived. (I had turned school out at early noon.) Melvin's "gran'pappy" had been shaved and dressed in his only suit. It was a much-worn black one which had been brushed and hung outside to air, but it had hung unused such a long time that the shoulders had taken on a greenish cast and nothing could banish the prominent faded streaks. Gran'pappy's body was just being placed in the casket when I arrived.

The casket was a thing of beauty. It was hand-made of native walnut, in perfect symmetry. The dark wood had been sandpapered and polished until it shone like burnished gold. It had been padded with cotton and lined with white crepe. A small pillow with a lace cover supported the head of the dead man. The lower part of the lid had been screwed fast and the small upper section left open so we could see Gran'pappy's head and shoulders. His knotty, worn old hands lay folded across his breast.

The casket rested on two chairs directly in front of the open window of the best room. Bouquets of wild flowers, wreaths of geranium and garden flowers, colored leaves and juniper banked the corner of the room.

The clock had been stopped at five minutes after ten, which had been the hour of death. It would not be started until after the funeral. The mirror above the homemade chest of drawers had been covered with a piece of black calico. Such was the custom in all hill-country homes when a death occurred.

As I entered the home I gripped the right hand of each of the sorrowing relatives. I tried to speak a kindly but firm, "God bless you."

Neighbors had brought in pies, cakes and platters of food so that members of the household would be relieved of any meal preparation until after the funeral. The food was arranged on the dining table and all who wished to eat were called. I was asked to return thanks before we ate. Everyone spoke in hushed tones during the meal.

After the dinner, the daughter and her husband came to me and asked if I thought it would be all right to have the funeral in the Mt. Hope Church a mile distant but on the road to the cemetery.

"They don't have no services there any more," the daughter explained. "Lige Gurney 'lowed it'd be all right an' he holds to that church. Some of the neighbors have gone up and cleaned it up. Hain't no room much in the cabin."

Her eyes filled with tears. "You already knows Paw warn't no church feller, but he shore war good an' kind. He'd lak a church funeral."

"Why certainly we can go to the church if you wish

it," I answered reassuringly. "Only God has any right to judge your father, for he alone knew him as he was."

"I'm proud to hear you say it thataway," she smiled timorously.

Melvin, the oldest grandson, came up to my side. "We got Gran'pappy's 'bituary all writ out," he said. "I'll git it fer ya."

People kept coming in wagons and on horseback. Entire families walked if the distance was not too great. After a short service at the house, which consisted of the reading of the fourteenth chapter of St. John and a fervent prayer by Lige Gurney, the coffin was gently placed in the back of a log wagon. A long procession trailed it down the road to the church.

At the church, Gran'pappy's coffin was rested on two carpenter's sawhorses placed in the aisle in front of the pulpit. Bob and Ethel Norman sang "The Old Rugged Cross." I read the obituary and offered a prayer, a quartette sang "In the Sweet By and By" and the Scripture lesson followed.

Then I preached my first sermon—a funeral sermon.

At its conclusion I stepped down from the pulpit, opened the lid of the casket and walked to the center of the room. I directed the congregation to pass up one aisle, view the deceased and proceed on down the other aisle and outside the church house. The people of the hills take their funerals seriously and the matter of "viewing the remains," as they term it, is a very essential part of the service. They would have considered it little less than sacrilegious to have omitted this solemn rite and privilege.

I conducted the procession as I had seen funeral directors do, leaving the relatives to the last. Then we went to the cemetery.

"Shore plumb purty the way you had folks take their last look at old man Frazier," one of the hillmen remarked on our way back from the cemetery. "Never seen it done thataway but hit shore war nice."

I was grateful for the expression of approval and felt my first service had been a successful one. And if I could satisfactorily preach a funeral, surely I would be capable of any other public appointment I might be called upon to fill.

CHAPTER 11

Who Burned the Schoolhouse?

I WAS NO MORE PREPARED FOR WHAT HAPPENED ON the day following "Gran'pappy's" funeral than I had been for the many other sudden turns in my Ozarkian life. When, on that September afternoon, I heard a scraping of feet on the stone that was our schoolhouse doorstep, I wondered, "What's happened now?" As I rose and walked to the door the figure turned; it was Clayton.

When I recovered sufficiently from my surprise, I put an arm around him and led him into the schoolroom. "Sonny, how in the world did you get here?" I asked him.

"I got lonesome at Grandma's and thought I could hitchhike down here like you did." He beamed through his tired smile as we walked down the aisle among the bewildered pupils. I found a place for him near my desk.

I hastened to close school early that afternoon so that Clayton might get to where he could lie down and rest. His eyes were bright with a spark of determination and hope but I knew how tiring the long trip could be to a healthy man, and this was a sick boy. His cheeks were flushed and his skin was pallid. He looked so thin.

Clayton rested on the cornshuck mattress until suppertime. I stayed close to him and away from Arabella's curious glances. I heard enough snatches of the talk in the kitchen after the Andrews' came in from work to know that Clayton and I were the subject of conversation. We stayed in the loft until we heard chairs being set up to the table.

Missoury and her family did no chattering at the table

that night and I took their sullen silence to mean resentment. They hardly spoke to either Clayton or me during the meal, and that night in bed Clayton asked me if we never talked when we ate.

Next morning I learned the reason for the ominous silence.

"His lung trouble's ketchin'," Missoury bluntly told me. "He ort ter be home. He shore ain't goin' ter stay here."

My heart leaped—in anger, yet in triumph. Here was an undisputable reason to leave the Andrewses.

"We'll make some arrangements," I advised Missoury as Clayton and I set out early toward school.

We stopped at the Normans'. I was anxious to tell them that Clayton had come for I was really happy to have the boy with me. I told these friends of Missoury's reception and of my desire to find another boarding place where Clayton and I might be together until we could get some salary, rent a cabin and get my things from Iowa.

"You can both stay here," Ethel Norman said promptly. "We know what hard luck is. If you can spare me ten dollars a month it will be enough to buy all the extra things we'll need."

"I'll give you more than that," I said, "for I'm paying Missoury that much for only myself, and now there are two of us."

"No," spoke up Bob Norman, "we'd like to help out and Ethel won't be doin' this to make money."

Clayton remained with the Normans for the day and I hurried on so that I might walk over to the Hillcrofts' before school. I told them that I was leaving the Andrews place and why, and asked Jake if he thought the school-board would be willing to pay me ten dollars so that I could settle my board bill with Mrs. Andrews.

"You've taught more'n half a month," Jake said, "an' I don't think thar'll be ary trouble getting the others to pay ye fer that much, anyway. Jist leave it to me; I'll git yore warrant."

I went on to school and pitched into the work there. Shortly after noon Jake came by. He had my warrant. "Folks seem to lak yore teachin' and says the kids air shore larnin'. Clark war fer payin' you right off. Harmon figgered it war an extra bother makin' out two warrants in one month but we took care of that. It war two agin' one."

That evening I went to the Andrews' with a light heart. Only Arabella was at the house as usual when I arrived but she disappeared when she saw me packing. I didn't see her again until I started out to the field to say good-bye to the Andrews'. She had told them of my actions and, led by Missoury, the family accosted me in the barnyard.

"What fer ye aleavin'?" snorted Missoury.

"I want to be with my boy and you told me you wouldn't keep him," I answered.

"I shore won't keep that diseased brat!" Missoury shouted. She shook her grubbing hoe at me. "But yo're goin' ter pay me fer a full month."

"Yes," I said, "I'll pay you the ten dollars."

"Ten dollars?" she screamed. "Ye skinflint; ye've et fifteen dollars' wo'th if ye've et a cent. Ye owe me fifteen dollars!"

Arabella peered at me over her mother's shoulder. "More'n thet, Maw, countin' them lunches we fixed up fer him."

I tried to be patient. "Mrs. Andrews," I said quietly, "you have no reason to act like this. I offered to pay you more than I owe you. Now I won't pay you a dime over seven dollars and a half. That's the exact amount you have coming to you." I walked abruptly away while she screamed and cursed.

She was still standing at her front gate hurling unsavory epithets at me as I crossed over the ridge headed for the Normans'.

Bob and Ethel laughed when I told them of the farewell the Andrews' had given me. "Old Missoury always does that way. She'll do or say anything to get a dime," said Ethel.

"If I were you, I'd go to Climax and buy a post office money order for seven dollars and a half and mail it to her," counseled Bob. "Then you'll have proof of payment and she can't cause you any further trouble about it."

I took Bob's advice and sent a money order. Missoury later threatened me with the law but by that time she had cashed the money order.

I felt that the days following my departure from the Andrews house were much the pleasantest since my arrival in Mulberry District. It was a great relief to be out of Missoury's clutches and from under Arabella's gaze; to be with Clayton once more and under the same roof with such congenial people as the Normans.

Bob had a good squirrel dog and a .22-caliber rifle. He encouraged Clayton to go hunting on fair days; he took him to Stark's Creek and taught him how to cast for bass and sun perch. Mrs. Norman fixed a bed on the porch where Clayton could sleep in the open air. The food she prepared was plain, wholesome and well cooked.

"Brother Howard," she said one evening. "I believe Clayton is improving every day. You can't help but notice how his color has improved and how well he eats and sleeps. He lies down every afternoon and sleeps like a baby for two hours."

Ethel was right; one couldn't help noticing Clayton's change. "The most encouraging thing is Clayton's own attitude," I said. "Now he feels that he is improving. He's happy here and that's half the battle. God is certainly blessing us wonderfully." Then I added, "Do you know how much Clayton loves you and Bob?"

Ethel smiled knowingly. "We've come to love Clayton, too, as if he were our own," she said. "We've always wanted a son. Bob and I understand your mission here, Brother Howard, and we want to do everything we can to help."

"I want to serve God by serving folks in this community," I said, "and your priceless help with Clayton is making that possible."

"Religious services have been sadly neglected here for a long time," Ethel commented as she busied herself with household tasks. "Prejudice is strong and a few, like Missoury, have done much harm. But the younger generation is seeking something solid to anchor to and if you'll only bring them the love of Jesus in word and deed you can do wonders here."

Startling news came to me Friday when the pupils told me that a preacher had come to stay with the Andrews' and that he was to start a revival that very night at Hopewell Church. That evening after school as we were doing our usual Friday cleaning the subject came up again.

"Paw says Missoury's up to no good gettin' that preacher to come," one of the older high-school girls said. "Old Missoury's jist doin' that athinkin' she'll be gettin' ahead of you." She was washing the blackboard with bold, carefree swipes. "Law, forty preachers couldn't do her no good. Folks hereabouts thinks she's plumb possessed of the devil."

Doubtless as least part of what the girl said was true but I didn't want to appear to think so. "We should all go to the services, anyway," I said, walking to the stove in the center of the room to make sure that the fire had burned out. I threw a shovelful of ashes on the firebox. "Even if Missoury had evil intentions," I went on, "the preacher probably doesn't and he is only the innocent tool of an evil mind. Mrs. Andrews is a woman who can be a saint or a devil as she chooses and I expect the preacher thinks she's a saint."

That night the Normans, Clayton and I walked to Hopewell Church. We saw the Andrews family file into the church and occupy a bench on the front row.

Brother Jones was a deeply spiritual man with an education far above the average backhills preacher. His sermon on the fatherhood of God was fine and met a favorable response from those present. He owned a violin which he played quite well as we sang several old revival hymns. After the services we talked and I invited him to come to school and make a little talk to the children. "I'll be over next Monday," he promised.

We went to church again Saturday night and the crowd was almost double that of the night before. Word was out that Hopewell had a preacher and true to the backhills custom everyone, sinner or saint, came to church. At the closing I suggested that Sunday school, which we had been holding in the schoolhouse, meet at the church at ten o'clock the next morning and that Brother Jones preach immediately following. This suggestion met a hearty approval.

We were getting ready to go to Sunday services the next morning when Freddy Stark came running up the path.

"Oh, teacher," he said breathlessly," the schoolhouse is burned down. Ain't a thing left but a pile of ashes smokin'. Burned in the night and nobody seen it."

The schoolhouse! Impossible. No fire had been kindled since Friday morning. The fire was out when I left Friday evening and the building had been locked.

A few long-faced patrons were standing about the smoldering ruins when Bob and I got there. We nodded to the group which included Jake and his mother, but no one had much to say to anyone.

I walked around contemplating the ashes. Mandy Hillcroft stepped close to my side and in a hushed voice said, "Somebody set hit afire, Brother Howard. Hit couldn't a happened no other way," She paused a minute. "They's jist some folks jist bound to rule er ruin," she ruminated. "Then startin' thet meetin', too. Hit looks bad, Brother Howard, don't hit?" I smiled at her but made no comment.

Later I picked up a stick and dug into the ashes below where the door should have been. I soon found what I was looking for—the heavy padlock used on the front door. It was badly dented as if it had been pounded with a hammer and broken. "Whoever did this overlooked hiding the lock," I thought. Being careful that no one saw me, I wrapped the broken lock carefully in my handkerchief. Continuing my search I came upon another surprising thing. The galvanized gallon kerosene can had gone through the fire without exploding and both caps were screwed on tight—it was empty! I knew that the can had been two-thirds full of kerosene when I had last used it on Friday morning. "Used our own oil to burn our school," I thought as I kicked the can back into the hot ashes. I mentioned these discoveries to no one, but joined Bob and we headed for church.

When church services were over many people asked about plans for going on with school. "I'll have to see what the school wants to do," I replied as I shook hands with many well-wishers.

Melvin Frazier was the last to shake hands with me. When he released his grip he left a closely folded note in my hand. I quickly pocketed it, waiting to read it when I was alone.

It read: "Brother Howard, ye bin good to us, helpin' with Gran'pappy's funeral. I got a chance to help you. Don't say nothing. Meet me at the big oak at dusky dark tonite."

I was stunned when I finished reading the roughly

scrawled note. Should I tell Bob? I wondered. "No," I decided, "Melvin trusts me to keep silent and I'll not betray that trust."

It seemed a long time until dusky dark and throughout my conversations with Bob and Ethel I kept pondering the meaning of Melvin's note.

"Sure it burned because somebody set it afire," Bob agreed when I showed him the padlock and told him about the can. "Everybody thinks someone set it afire, I believe, but I rather doubt it was Missoury. If she done it you can bet your bottom dollar it would have happened at a time when no one would have suspicioned her. Missoury's mean but she's smart, too. She'd know that after her tantrum about your coming over here to board and her trying to break up our Sunday school she'd be the first one to be suspicioned. No, Brother Howard, that doesn't sound like old Missoury's devilment to me."

"No doubt you're right," I said.

"Did you ever wonder if it could have been somebody that wanted to shift a little blame on somebody else—maybe even onto you?" Bob asked.

I nodded.

"Better keep your own counsel for a while, Brother Howard, and maybe we'll learn some more; let's see who hangs himself."

I kept the appointment at dusky dark. And under the big oak in the woodland gloom Melvin told me the name of the person who had set fire to the school building!

Puzzled, I turned and walked slowly to my boarding place. What could be the reason back of the startling information Melvin had given me?

CHAPTER 12

Who'll Build It Back

E VEN THE GOODNESS OF ETHEL'S BISCUITS TOOK A minor place in our conversation at the breakfast table next morning. The confusion and turmoil brewed by the schoolhouse fire was all we could talk about.

"Most everyone thinks Missoury did it or had it done," offered Ethel.

"Just as many reasons to think it could have been Harmon," argued Bob. "Doesn't he hate Missoury? And didn't he send Brother Howard there to stay because he was mad about his being hired?"

"I can't believe Harmon would take it out on me that way," I remonstrated.

"Brother Howard," Bob continued, "Harmon was the one largely responsible for killing the sixty-five-cent levy usually voted for maintaining Mulberry school. Then you said he didn't help hire you and that probably didn't set well with him. I'm just thinking he might know something about the fire."

I reached for another biscuit and topped it with golden butter and wild honey. "The burning of the schoolhouse was a great shock to me just when everything seemed to be working out for us," I said as I bit into the delicacy and deliberately enjoyed its sweetness. "Bob," I continued, "I know who burned the school!" Bob gulped. "But to say who it was would be violating a confidence so I've decided not to tell anyone the name of the felon."

Bob didn't press me about the arsonist's identity so I went on talking. "Hillcroft and Clark ought to be in favor of going on with the school if we can get a building. It's a question in my mind whether the district will vote bonds for a new school. With the Andrews and Harmons as the heaviest taxpayers we can depend on them fighting any bond issue. I'm going over and talk to Hillcroft before the board meets this afternoon."

Soon after breakfast I walked over the ridge to the Hillcrofts'.

"Jake and me have jist been talkin' about what's best fer the school, Brother Howard," Mandy said. "Everybody laks the way yo're alarnin' the young'uns and hit shore would be a pity ter stop now. Specially since the state give us that four-hundred-dollar boost. Reckon ye could go on in the church or in Harmon's vacant house?" she questioned.

"I'd certainly like to go on with the school," I declared. "Especially so if the patrons are satisfied with my work. Perhaps it's not too much to hope some plan satisfactory for both children and parents can be agreed upon by the board. We ought to begin again without too much delay."

Jake and I walked on down the hollow to see Clark. The three of us seemed in perfect agreement that we should somehow go on with school.

The Clarks had five children attending and expressed themselves as being pleased with the way the school was being conducted. They further commented on the Sunday services and expressed the hope that I would remain in the district for, they said, "Every settlement needs a preacher. When people die, like Gran'pappy Frazier did last week, hit jist don't seem right ter lay 'em away without a preacher at the funeral."

Mrs. Clark told how, during the previous winter, good old lady Beeson had passed on and all the services they had for her was a prayer at the grave by Missoury Andrews and "everybody 'lowed it were plumb disgraceful for her ter pray at all, as onery as she is."

I had a copy of the school law that County Superintendent Elzie Miller had given me, and the two directors and I went over that part pertaining to school elections. No one mentioned Ray Harmon or questioned what his idea might be in regard to continuing the school or voting bonds.

Hillcroft and Clark suggested that a petition be circulated at once. Through it we would get the necessary number of signatures to call an election. At their request I drew up the petition with five hundred dollars the specified amount to be voted upon. We estimated that would be adequate if the schoolhouse was made of native lumber. Mrs. Clark suggested that if there were sufficient funds we should plan for toilets, desks and benches and a teacher's table.

After dinner the two directors and I walked over the west ridge to Harmon's where the "official" board meeting was held.

Jake Hillcroft called the meeting to order. We sat silently awaiting Harmon's views. He cleared his throat and began in a nervous, nasal twang, "Reckon it's commonly suspicioned old Missoury burnt the school," he said. "She was just asnortin' when the teacher quit boarding there and she's done all she kin to head him off, agettin' a new preacher in."

"But whoever burnt hit," he went on, "we sure hain't got no schoolhouse now. The law sez the teacher's contract is canceled whenever a school burns, so I s'pose we might as well say school's over fer this year. Don't you boys think thet's about it?"

Clark and Hillcroft quietly expressed themselves as being very anxious that school continue and they both spoke of the feeling of the entire district relative to my school work. Finally, they suggested that we continue school in the church beginning the following Monday.

Harmon was against such a plan. He maintained the

church was too far from the center of the district, the building in bad repair, hard to keep warm and that there were no books with which to continue lessons. Clark asked Harmon if he would consent to rent his vacant house near the school site for the purpose of continuing the term.

"I wouldn't consider it fer one minute!" he replied. "Old Missoury'd jist like a reason to burn hit down. She's bound she's gonna run Mr. Howard out of the country. If you boys want to hire another teacher old Missoury didn't have it in fer, I might rent it."

The three men discussed the condition of the church and over Harmon's protest voted two to one to have me continue school there, beginning the following Monday. "We'll move the school wood, rent the church, put in a bigger stove and see about books," they promised as the meeting adjourned. No mention was made to Harmon about the petition for the bond election.

"'Twouldn't do no good and if we keeps real quiet we can get 'nuff signers 'fore the Harmons and Andrews knows 'bout hit," advised Clark.

"When it comes to taxes, the Andrews and Harmons will bury the hatchet until after voting," laughed Jake. "Maybe hit'll be a good thing at that. Might even lead to finally endin' their feud."

"What started all this trouble between the two families anyway?" I asked.

"Oh, the Andrews and Harmons have hated each other since the War between the States," said Clark. "They say their kin disputed the exact location of fence line between the homesteads."

"Each new generation has carried it on ever since," Jake added. "They've been times when hit was just a smoldering hatred, but sometimes it breaks into open warfare. Their land's been divided and redivided. Here lately they been buying it back. Ray Harmon owns almost all of what his grandpa used to and so does Dave Andrews, I reckon. They finally had a county surveyor come in and find out where the line really should go."

"Well, who owns that narrow strip of ground between their fences?" I asked.

"Oh," laughed Clark, "that's jist the devil's lane."

Jake looked at me and grinned. "Reckon you never heard of such as that." I shook my head and Jake continued. "Andrews and Harmon each moved their fences back four feet from the surveyed line and that's called a devil's lane. Hit sure is named right, too."

"Sure is," Clark added. "As the feller says, they's more quarrels between nabors starts over fence lines than any other cause, 'cept maybe dogs."

Three days later Jake and Clark came to see me. They had secured enough signatures on the petition to allow them to post notices of the special election. "The board'll meet this afternoon to order the election," Jake smiled. "Then the fun'll really begin."

"Can't find nobody that has any say 'bout the church," Clark reported. "Lige Gurney's one of the old members and he was an elder when they quit havin' meetin' there. Hit belongs to the Campbellites and the elders and deacons has the say, so the county superintendent says. Surely ort ter be all right ter go ahead."

Harmon was hopping mad about the election but was helpless to do anything to stop it.

I walked the twenty-eight miles in to Hermitage that week end to see Mr. Miller. He gave me a large collection of used schoolbooks. There wasn't a blackboard in the church so I purchased a supply of paper and pencils to use as a substitute.

When school reconvened Monday all the pupils excepting Harmon's children were present; and despite the lack of equipment school was very successful that day.

Brother Jones came that afternoon as he had promised

and gave the children a fine talk. He was still staying at the Andrews place and said he planned to continue the revival another week. He very kindly offered to make the school a blackboard if the directors would buy the necessary material.

The entire community went to Hopewell Church again that evening and everyone seemed to wholeheartedly enter into the spirit of the service. Messages which Brother Jones brought the congregation were vital, interesting gospel sermons and a general air of deep religious devotion prevailed.

Missoury rose just before the benediction and declared:

"I got a 'nouncement ter make. You'uns all knows we hain't tuck up no offerin' fur Brother Jones so we'uns goin' ter do hit now. We been akeepin' him to our house but I aims ter give, nohow, an' heavy too."

Turning to her son she commanded:

"Ott, you pass the hat!"

The congregation responded with a liberal offering.

Missoury was the last contributor. She made much of opening her purse and fumbling over a roll of greenbacks and a handful of silver. When she held her tightly clutched hand toward the hat that Ott held, something happened and her offering fell on the broad brim of the hat and then rolled to the floor.

Bill Walker picked it up from under his seat and handed it to her, remarking, to everyone's merriment:

"Here's yer penny, Missoury. 'Tis kinda heavy."

People, according to the custom in most rural gatherings, remained for at least a half-hour after services, visiting with each other and once more harmony seemed to prevail.

Then into that harmony a bombshell exploded. It brought disappointment and anger. Wednesday, Missoury and Dave Andrews had driven into Hermitage. On

Thursday the sheriff arrived and served notice on the school directors and me that since no regular services had been held in the old church by the membership for fourteen years, the church property had reverted to the original tract as the deed recited. Dave Andrews owned the original tract and under the law he was the present owner of the acre of ground the church had formerly owned. Naturally, this gave Andrews ownership of the building, too. Old Missoury proudly exhibited the tax receipts to everyone who would look at them.

With no place to hold school, the board decided that we would have to stop the session.

"We hope the bonds will be voted and a new building can be erected," Hillcroft and Clark offered by way of consolation. Harmon was noncommittal but his attitude showed his pleasure at the turn of events.

I was so disgusted that I let him know I could use the law for my purpose, too. I informed the board that since I had taught one day by their official order my contract was still in effect.

CHAPTER 13

The Indentured Teacher

THE SPECIAL ELECTION HAD BEEN SET FOR THE FIRST week in November and, while on the surface there appeared to be little activity, both sides were really working vigorously. Harmon and Andrews had a decided advantage for many families had borrowed money from them and, as these loans were secured by both real estate and chattel mortgages, the creditors were bringing pressure to force the debtors to vote against the bonds.

Hillcroft and Clark came often to the Normans' and kept me informed about the state of affairs. They said, one evening, that in case the bond issue failed, they had a plan for continuing school but did not wish to suggest it until the election was over. "Might help in votin' the bonds not to have school just now," they said.

Brother Jones closed his revival ahead of schedule for the antagonism that had been created by the stopping of school destroyed the spirit of the revival.

I spent the next two weeks helping Bob cut wood for his winter's supply of fuel.

Election day dawned clear and warm. The entire district turned out, even aged and invalid voters being transported to the polls by both factions. It was nip and tuck all day, but when the last vote was counted, the proposed bond issue had failed to carry—failed by seven votes.

Late that evening Hillcroft and Clark came over and

revealed their plan. They suggested carrying on school in two rooms of Mandy Hillcroft's small cabin.

"Ma and me kin git along with jist two rooms," Jake explained. "We kin take out the wall between the other two. Then I'd like to see old Missoury close school."

"Ye kin depend on teachin' again Monday," Clark added. "Folks kin fetch enough chairs fer their own kids. Ye can teach thataway until something kin be done about another schoolhouse."

School commenced for the third time on the following Monday. The Harmon children were again noticeably absent. The new quarters were clean, of course, but not very comfortable because we had so little room. However, the children were happy to be back in school and no one seemed to mind the inconvenience.

A few days later the Andrews' brought a woman preacher into the community who began another revival at the church. She was not as well received as Brother Jones had been because hill tradition tabooed the acceptance of a woman in this capacity. Nevertheless, she was a good, earnest worker and her meetings continued until Saturday night when she announced that her husband had come for her and she would be compelled to return to her home in Arkansas.

"How many of you would like to see this revival continue?" she asked. Every person in the room put at least one hand into the air. She turned to Missoury Andrews and said, "Would you people, as owners of this building, consent to its use for a revival or for religious services every Sunday evening if you could get someone to preach regularly?"

"We shore hain't agoin' to stand in the way of the Lord's work," Mrs. Andrews answered piously. "Yessum, anybody what wants ter preach here's welcome," she continued.

"Thank you, Mrs. Andrews, that's mighty nice of you,"

the preacher said. "I haven't asked him about it, but I'm taking the liberty of announcing that your teacher, Brother Howard, will preach here tomorrow night." Either the woman was thoroughly innocent or very acute. "I know he can preach for you from what I've heard about him," she continued. "Now, how many want him to preach his first sermon here, for you folks? Let's see the hands in favor of him as your regular pastor." Every hand went up except the Andrews'. People were agreeably surprised at the boldness of the woman and not a little amazed, I think, that the Andrews' did not verbally object.

"This is your opportunity, Brother Howard," the Normans said, as we returned home. "And may God use you, as we all know He will."

The manner in which this, my first revival sermon, was thrust upon me, and the news that it was my first, contributed to the packing of the church house. To our surprise, the Andrews' came too.

My text was Psalms 90:10, "The days of our years are threescore years and ten; and if by reason of strength they be fourscore years, yet is their strength labour and sorrow; for it is soon cut off, and we fly away."

The theme of my sermon was "Life." "Life is the workshop where we build for eternity," I began. My emphasis was upon example and works rather than judgments and pious words. My nervousness and hesitation were forgotten; so, soon, was the sermon I had carefully prepared. Ideas came to my mind more rapidly than I could speak.

When the benediction was pronounced, Charley Simmons jumped to his feet. "How many of you want the teacher to preach to us ever' Sunday night?" Charley shouted. The Andrews' were the only ones who failed to respond with uplifted hands, though they seemed a little reluctant to oppose so large a gathering.

"The Lord works in curious ways to fetch about His wonders, so the Good Book says," Mandy Hillcroft exclaimed, accompanying her words with a vigorous handshake. Many people congratulated me on the evening's service and expressed the hope that I would consent to preach every Sunday evening.

Clayton continued to improve; the sparkle was back in his eyes, his appetite was good and every day he was able to take more and more exercise.

We talked with the Normans and it was decided we should continue to board there until school was out. Then we would try to find a cabin for ourselves.

"Clayton needs someone to look out for him," argued Ethel Norman. "He should get lots of rest and wholesome food or he will lose all he has gained."

"You'll be gone every day to school and there'll be no one to fix his dinner, watch the fires and see that he sleeps regularly," Bob added. "A boy just won't do those things for himself."

Albert wrote regularly and I visited him one week end. His employer was a good Christian man and I felt satisfied that he was in good company.

A plan had been forming in my mind, which I talked over with Albert. It met with his approval. "Yes, Dad," he said, "I'd do it! You can count on me for some help, too. Just let me know."

Back at church next Sunday night I announced that I thought I knew how we could build a new schoolhouse and suggested a mass meeting for Tuesday night.

Much speculation and comment followed the announcement and it was the subject of common discussion in the community for the next two days.

When I arrived at the meeting Tuesday night, the house was packed with hopeful, interested patrons. Charley Simmons presided. He called the house to order and made a short preliminary speech.

He spoke of the importance of school, of how much everyone regretted the destruction of the old building, of appreciation for my work and interest. Then he asked if anyone had anything to say before he should call for the presentation of my plan for a new school.

Missoury Andrews rose. "I got something ter say," she said defiantly. "I told ye they wouldn't no good come from such doin's—apickin' up hitchhikers and hirin' 'em to run our school and lettin' 'em hold Sunday school in the buildin' and tell us what's allers lived here how we'uns ort ter live—ye can jis' figger ye lost the school fer good. We'uns's the heaviest taxpayers and I says ye hain't agoin' to have no more school. Folks in the district done showed together votin' they don't want no school. Hit's just the works o' the devil!" She sat down.

Mr. Simmons took his red bandana handkerchief from his hip pocket, removed his glasses and cleaned them with great deliberation as if he were playing for time for me to collect my thoughts to answer Missoury.

"Anyone else got anything to say?" Mr. Simmons finally questioned, as he restored the spectacles to his nose. He waited in nervous silence for a moment. No one spoke. Then he turned to me and said, "Brother Howard, will you please step up here now and tell us about your plan?"

I arose and went to the front. I stood silently for a moment, looking at the audience. Then, "My friends," I began, "no one could regret more than I do the loss of the school. However, I'd hesitate to say it came about because you chose to worship God in the building. No doubt Mrs. Andrews is more nearly correct when she says, 'it is the work of the devil.'"

There was an awful silence as everyone looked at Missoury Andrews.

"Here is my plan," I broke in. "As you all know, my salary here is fifty dollars a month. There is at present three hundred eighty-six dollars in the teachers' fund, as I have drawn only twenty-five dollars. With this teachers' fund I propose to buy necessary lumber, doors, windows and nails for a new school, providing the twenty-eight families in the district will board me for whatever chores I can do evenings and mornings. My older son, Albert, will send me a few dollars each month to help care for Clayton. We can construct much of the new building of native lumber, with oak shingles, at little expense. The money we have, I'm sure, is adequate for the materials if you folk want to volunteer to build the school."

I called to Lige Gurney on the back seat, "Think you could build a schoolhouse, Lige?"

"Ye bet I kin," grinned Lige. "I kin jist as good as ye kin."

"If you want to adopt this plan," I explained further, "I will enter into a contract with the school board for them to pay fifty dollars each month on the material until the bill is paid in full." And I couldn't refrain from adding, "This will relieve some of you who are heavy taxpayers of any additional tax burden.

"Now, everyone who will donate time and labor, or board me a week or so for what work I can do, stand up." Everyone in the house except the Andrews' arose.

"Thank you," I said, and I turned the meeting back to Mr. Simmons. He turned to ask Bob Norman to dismiss us with a prayer.

Missoury jumped up and grabbed her daughter by the hand. "Come on, Arabellie," she said. "Such carryin's on hain't fer them what has the love of the Lord in their hearts! Ott, Dave, git up. We air agoin' home."

Charley stood with an amused smile on his face until

Missoury and her family had disappeared through the door. Then he yelled, "Come on folks—three cheers for the parson—to hell with Missoury Andrews. I believe she's met her match at last."

CHAPTER 14

Finally, One of the Folks

I WAS NO LONGER A STRANGER; FINALLY I HAD BEEN accepted as one of the community. And when Ozark people extend their hand for a firm clasp and solid handshake and "thank you," their thanks are genuine. When the school meeting closed, all the school's patrons and many others thanked me for my offer.

Mandy Hillcroft shook my hand and said, "We'uns air shore athankin' the Lord fer ye acomin' to Mulberry."

I answered by saying, "I'm happy to be one of a community of such wonderful people as I've found here."

"Now let me tell ye 'bout these here folks," Mandy continued. "They either is or they hain't. Ones what's good er shore powerful good. Ones what hain't er like old Missoury, just ornrier than the very devil."

During my years of labor among these backhills folk, I have come to know that the native Ozarker is either black or white. A hillman is seldom tinged with gray, for false pretense or hypocrisy is no part of his make-up.

That night, back at the Normans', after thanking God that the community's wall of reserve had been broken down, I dropped to sleep almost instantly and did not awaken until next morning when Bob called, "Breakfast."

What a different world it is when you have the knowledge that the people with whom you live trust and believe in you! The sun seemed brighter and the world seemed a better place as I walked to Hillcrofts' for a board meeting. On the high ridge where the school had stood, I paused to look at the midwinter beauty of the Ozark landscape—the woods of green cedar and red-brown oaks whose leaves would stay until a new spring's buds appeared to push them off.

Mist rising from Stark's Creek looked like a silver veil winding its way up the valley. Gaunt sycamores stood as guardian sentinels to watch over the beauty of another Ozark day. I could see for miles through clearings in the mist, for the spot where I stood was one of the highest in Hickory County.

Here and there in clearings stood sturdy cabins— weathered brown without, homely warmth within. Their spirals of whitish-gray wood smoke ascended heavenward in the calm, frosty air like incense offered to a loving God for the bounty stored within those hill cabins.

Clark was already at Hillcrofts' when I arrived. Harmon came later. We discussed the amount of material needed for the new building, its probable cost, how we would arrange to have the doors, windows, brick, nails and cement brought to the school site from Warsaw, the nearest point where such material could be purchased.

"It will be necessary to figure out just how much material we need," I said. "My plan for the new school would be to make it two feet wider and four feet longer than the old one. The old building had only three windows on each side. I'd recommend the new one follow the approved plan of seven or more windows and that they be larger and all on one side of the building. But naturally, I'd like the school board to be unanimously agreed on the plan before we go any further."

Harmon kept silent during the long discussion that followed. A plan was drawn on a large native oak board. The board feet and dimensions of the lumber were computed for the entire structure. It was agreed to use native stone for the foundation.

Mandy Hillcroft, while not a member of the board,

was listening and suggested that if the roof were to be of hand-make oak shingles, she would donate two oak trees for the purpose.

I then suggested that as Ray Harmon was the only experienced carpenter in the district, he should act as foreman.

"No, boys, don't 'low to he'p much myse'f," Harmon demurred. "Lak to, but hain't got the time to spare, so I can't do hit. Seems quare to me nohow—schoolhouse aburnin' down." He looked at me. "Everybody knows who burnt hit, then you aspendin' yore wages to rebuild."

This statement made me angry for, to say the least, it was a nasty implication. I tried not to betray my feelings when I replied, quietly and very emphatically, "Yes, Mr. Harmon, that may seem strange to you. But regardless of what people may think, I know who is responsible for the schoolhouse fire." I looked directly at him as I spoke. "I also know who was hired to burn it and how much he received from the one responsible for the crime. So far, I haven't told anyone what I know, nor do I plan to do so if this new building goes up on schedule. As far as you are concerned, Mr. Harmon, I should think you would be interested in this project for the sake of your own children. And I believe you will be," I added emphatically.

His face paled and he breathed heavily as he answered in his usual harsh voice. "Yeah, reckon maybe I do owe hit to the boys. I really can't spare the time but I do owe it to them to he'p a little."

"Thank you," I said. "That will relieve me of a lot of worry, for I know you can do a fine job of it."

Four copies of the lumber bill were made for the near-by mill operators to study and bid for the contract.

"Us directors kin haul the rock and get the foundation started this week," Clark stated.

"I'll go to town fer the cement. They's got a couple dozen sacks left over at Davis' store," said Jake.

The meeting might have lasted longer but Harmon said it was about chore time and rapidly started off toward home.

"Stay here fer supper," Mandy Hillcroft said to me and I accepted her invitation.

After Harmon left, Clark turned to me, "Well, preacher, you shore surprised us atellin' Harmon you could put yore thumb on the polecat that set hit afire. By the way he backed water reckon ye musta knowed more than's healthy fer him. Harmon hain't one to back up so quick an' easy. All I got to say—yo're smarter than ye look, and I reckon me and Hillcroft hain't sayin' a word about what's happened."

"S'pose we kin figger out now who done hit," Hillcroft added, "but let's all keep our mouths plumb shet, fer we'uns want to put up that school and I shore know we'uns air goin' ter git hit done now."

Two days later we awarded the lumber contract to Sid Darnell at fifteen dollars per thousand board feet, delivered to the school ground. A contract was drawn and signed, allowing twenty days for the sawing.

A predated school warrant was drawn for the entire cost of the lumber. This warrant was payable to me; I endorsed it and gave it to Hillcroft as president of the board, with instructions to pay Darnell as soon as I had taught enough in the new school to cover the amount. This arrangement was satisfactory to Darnell—"Reckon the only way I'd lose would be fer you to lay down an die," he laughed. "You look plumb healthy to me, so I'll take the chance."

The school directors and I went to Warsaw and purchased the doors, windows, nails and other necessary hardware. We explained our situation to the dealer, who readily agreed to carry a charge account against me. The school board was to mail a warrant to him as soon as the wages due me would cover the amount of the bill.

Mr. Howard welcomes folks to the meetin'.

Mr. Howard preaching in the Sycamore Log Church in the Shepherd of the Hills Country of the Missouri Ozarks.

We hauled fifteen sacks of cement from Cross Timbers to the school site and stored them in the well house. The three directors and I, and a half-dozen other men who had children in school, dug and laid the foundation.

Everyone co-operated and the work moved fast. The first of the next week was set for the house "workin'." Mulberry district would have a new school for a Christmas present.

CHAPTER 15

The Workin'

Monday was an ideal day for the "workin'"—midwinter weather in the Ozarks is often more like Indian summer—and forty-two men and work-brittle boys reported early at the school ground.

Harmon finally came and reluctantly agreed to act as foreman, though I really think he was not a little pleased with the job. He selected five men who had had some carpentering experience to mark the lumber, and ten men with saws to cut it. Ten men and two teams went to the Hillcroft woods to cut and block the shingle trees. Five experienced board makers cut forked trees and set the forks of each over a flat block of wood preparatory to splitting the shingles. Boys were set to work to remove heart and sap wood from the shingle blocks. These blocks were worked up into shingles by board makers using mallets and froes. Two small boys who feared being left out found themselves jobs as water carriers. Everybody worked!

A great bonfire was built and kept burning throughout the day. For cooking the dinner, the men and boys quickly and expertly built a stone furnace. It was two feet wide, two feet high and about twenty feet long.

The fire was Luke Ayers' job and he scooped shovelful after shovelful of live coals into the stone furnace. The women put pots of beans, potatoes, dried apples, whole hams, coffee and cabbage on the embers to cook in perfect campfire fashion.

A group of women went to Mandy Hillcroft's and

baked corn bread in her big Dutch ovens, covering them with coals in the fireplace. "A body can do hit better in the fireplace," they insisted. "Hain't only a jump and a holler down to Mandy's."

About noon, stakes were driven into the ground, strips nailed across from stake to stake and a loose-board dinner table constructed. It was twenty feet long and three feet wide. Dishes and kettles of every size and description filled with hot, appetizing food were placed upon the table. The corn bread was brought from Mandy's fireplace when it had baked to that shade of brown known to the Ozark housewife as "plumb perfect." This bread was cut into four-inch squares which filled three great platters placed conveniently one at each end and one in the middle of the table. The boiled hams were cut in thick, juicy slices and these filled a number of kettles. Folded white cloths covered the kettles to keep the meat hot. Home-baked pies and cakes were all placed at one end of the table.

The keen air of December, the odor of cooking food and boiling coffee, the hard work, the spirit of congenial hospitality were typical of Ozark communities and their spirit of neighborliness. Noon mealtime found the lumber marked, sawed and piled ready to begin the actual work of erecting the building.

Everyone stood with bared, bowed heads as Mandy Hillcroft returned thanks. Hers was a fervent prayer for health, strength, thankfulness for food, and a petition for God's guidance in the erection of the schoolhouse.

Each worker had his own plate, fork, spoon and cup and passed along the side of the table cafeteria fashion, selecting whatever food he desired. The appetites, banter and laughter displayed about the table can be understood only by those who have been partakers of such an Ozark "spread."

"Hey, Lige,' Ye've et 'nuf now to fatten a shoat," someone yelled.

"Have to call the horse doctor fer ye," countered Lige. "You're afounderin' yo'rse'f."

"Den, if ya eats any more, ya'll shore bust," someone called.

"Gimme 'nother fried pie an git outen the way," was the answer.

Hill-fashion, the men squatted on the ground or upon logs after dinner and filled their corncob pipes with long green tobacco. They smoked and visited the customary hour before returning to their work.

By mid-afternoon the schoolhouse frame was up, the boxing all on and the sub-floor laid. An hour later the rafters were in place, the sheeting on and the gables boxed. Some of the men who had sawed and piled lumber in the morning now peeled and split shingles. Others put up a trestle on each side of the house and began laying the first row of shakes.

Ray Harmon kept his helpers busy making and fitting door frames. Windows were fitted into the frames, the facings planed and set.

The door was hung and the men began laying the tongue-and-groove pine floor. Sundown saw the building virtually completed except for the pine lining on the inside of the building and a brick flue.

A dozen men agreed to return the following day, ceil the building, build the flue and make desks, benches and a table for the teacher.

They did return and finish the job. Four smooth, soft pine boards were used to make a long blackboard. Construction of the desks and benches was slow work for they all were planed smooth and required careful fitting.

Lige Gurney donated a hickory chair with woven bark bottom for the teacher's use and school reconvened Wednesday in the new building.

CHAPTER 16

We Gather at the River

THE MULBERRY SCHOOLHOUSE WAS NOW THE BEST public building in the community, so in addition to its being used five days a week as the wellspring for the three "R's," it became the local church and Sunday school each Sabbath day. The building was much better than anything to which the pupils had been accustomed and attendance was almost stabilized. They all liked to come to the new school. Its central location made it readily accessible from all parts of the district and the decrepit building owned by the Andrews' was finally abandoned for community use.

In a letter to a friend—the Rev. Charles Harris—I explained the need for Sunday school literature and songbooks. Within a few days these came to Cross Timbers by parcel post, the gift of a wealthy parishioner of the Martensdale, Iowa, church.

Attendance at Mulberry services grew steadily. Sunday evening devotionals drew the largest crowds for the young people of the entire countryside came. Some young hillmen and their girl friends would walk as far as seven miles to attend the services. They were a bright and orderly group.

One Sunday evening several young folk came from the Owsley school district, nine miles to the northwest, across Stark's Creek. After services they invited me to preach for them one Sunday morning and evening each month. No services of any kind were being held regularly in their community, they explained. They hoped, also, that we might form a young people's Bible study society. Their sincerity and eagerness to study God's word struck a responsive chord in my heart. So on the following Sunday I asked my own congregation what they thought of my accepting the invitation of the Owsley group.

"Fine folks over thar an' they shore air needin' the Word," Lige Gurney said. Bob Norman offered to supervise a young people's Bible class at Mulberry on the Sunday night I would go to Owsley. Everyone seemed happy to share services with this neighboring community.

"Shore cain't be selfish and git nowhar aservin' the Lord," was the way Mandy Hillcroft summed it up.

I walked the nine miles to Owsley on the following Sunday morning. It was not a difficult place to find for I needed only to walk up the level bottom along Stark's Creek until I came to Uncle Zeke Cox's. The school was near by.

The Owsley schoolhouse was open and folk had gathered early to await my arrival. John Owen, the young man who taught the Owsley school, and his wife, Lela, led the singing and proved generally to be excellent helpers. After preaching we organized a Sunday school, elected officers and took a collection for supplies. John Owen named a committee of five to draft a set of rules to govern the Young People's Society for the Wednesday night meetings. Uncle Zeke's daughter-in-law was named chairman.

I went home with the Cox's for dinner and had a fine day with them and the Owens, who boarded there.

That night the church house was packed with young and old. The girls were in fresh print dresses—many of them made from feed sacks (two feed sacks will make a dress). The boys wore blue denim pants belted at the waist; a few wore dress shirts but most of them had on blue chambray shirts unbuttoned at the collar. A tie was a rarity and shoes were of the sturdy kind made for service rather than looks. A few of the men wore cotton-flannel-lined blue denim jackets which they called "wampuses." This service was one of the best I had held, inspired singing and excellent order betokening sincere interest.

That night I stayed with a family who lived three miles down Stark's Creek so I would not have so far to walk back to school. It rained during the warm night and next morning I walked out into a world dripping with the forerunner of spring showers. There was a promise of lazy weather in the air and I knew the sulphur and molasses days were near.

I veered from the creek and kitty-cornered the Andrews farm to follow the shortest route to Mulberry School. This took me across a lespedeza field toward a haystack which had been fenced with rails to protect the feed from the stock. The stack appeared so inviting one couldn't blame the domestic creatures for using it as a place of refuge. I was walking toward the stack and contemplating whether it would be more sport for one to slide down the side or over the end of the great mound of hay when suddenly I heard a loud, angry voice. I stopped stock-still and listened. It was Missoury's voice coming from the opposite side of the haystack! Then I heard the awful crack of a cattle whip as it struck something. Then the crack, crack of the whip again followed by such profanity as I had never heard before.

"Damn ye, take thet—wish to God I'd kill ye! Yo're the by-Goddest man I ever be damned! Don't know how come me ter marry sech a mangy ole houn' as ye. Damned iffen I know. Hain't I done tole ye I'd whop hell outten ye if I ever ketched ye chawin' terbaccy agin—give Gurney a nickel fer hit? Well, by God, ye'll shore run through with all we'uns got yit."

I turned from the field and headed for the woods that skirted the lespedeza. "Poor old Dave," I thought.

"Twenty years older than Missoury and being treated worse than a cross bull." I hurried into the woods and out of sight for I certainly didn't want to be any part of an Andrews family fight.

"Sure she whips him and cusses him; and there isn't anything she won't do," Bob Norman said when I told him about my experience. "Poor old Dave is a man among men—never complains; just goes on working from daylight 'til dark and the only thanks he gets is what you heard this morning."

A week or so later Willie Pennell, a young Baptist preacher, came to see me and asked if I would fill his appointment at Fairview seventeen miles away and permit him to take my place at Mulberry some Sunday. This trading of pulpits (and a general spirit of co-operation) is a common thing among ministers in the hills and a means of fostering good will. I was a member of the Friend's Society. He was a southern Baptist and proved to be one of the finest men I have ever known. We exchanged pulpits and both of us, as well as our congregations, enjoyed the change.

One day Mandy Hillcroft suggested that the Bryans, a family of seven who lived in a little two-room log cabin four miles over on Miller Ridge, be invited to come to church. "He's a moonshiner, but they's got five boys and the mother's a good woman in her way," Mandy said. "They don't go much—reckon she feels backward seein' her man's runnin' a still. Wish ye'd walk over and invite 'em to church."

"I'll go tomorrow evening after school," I promised.

One of the Bryan boys was chopping wood in the lot back of the cabin when I got to their place. A barking dog announced my coming. The boy quickly dropped his axe and looked at me with the keen alertness of a hunted animal. He saw the cabin was my destination and raced for the back door.

I knocked on the front door and someone called, "Cum in!" I pulled the latchstring and pushed the door open. I had to push hard as the bottom of the door scraped on the warped floor.

Mrs. Bryan, seated in a creaky, hand-made hickory chair in front of the fireplace, turned and nodded a "Howdy" as I entered. Her shoes were on the floor beside her chair and her stockinged feet rested on a chunk of wood that stood on end between her and the fire. Her big toe protruded through a hole in the stocking.

"I'm the teacher and preacher at Mulberry," I said by way of introduction. "Mandy Hillcroft asked me to come up and see if you and your husband and the boys wouldn't like to come and join us at services. We're having Sunday school and church every Sunday."

"Shore 'nuff—we'uns heered about ye—have a cheer." The woman jerked her thumb toward a vacant stool near the fireplace. As I seated myself I glimpsed the boy who had been at the woodpile, peeping through a crack in the partition between the two rooms.

Mrs. Bryan was not an old woman, I noticed, but her face was leathery and deeply wrinkled. Her dress was of some ancient black material, plainly and crudely made. The skirt came to her ankles. Her stringy, graying hair was braided in one long plait that hung down her back.

"Bin thinkin' as how I ort ter fotch the young'uns," she said as she spat a mouthful of amber directly over the bare toe and into the fire. "Ya kotched me achawin' my terbaccy, preacher—uster try ter hidden hit, but I 'low iffen a body's goin' ter chaw 'er a body might as well jes' chaw 'er." She ejected another mouthful of amber into the fire with an aim so accurate that I wondered if she was using the exposed toe for a front sight. " 'Low we'uns'll be a comin' next Sunday," she said.

I inquired if they had a Bible and she said they didn't

have. I explained that I made it a practice to give every family a Bible if they did not already possess one and asked her if she would like a copy.

"Be right proud ter git hit—Cedric kin read hit fer us, he's our oldest—a body shore ort ter study out the Lord's biddin', " she said.

As I walked back to Hillcroft's I felt that perhaps the hill folk were coming to trust me. Even the isolated Mrs. Bryan had heard of the meetings.

Mandy Hillcroft was pleased with the results of my visit.

"Do you suppose they'll come?" I asked.

"Shore, they'll come—whenever folks hyarabouts says they'll do somethin' they ginerally does hit even iffen they takes thar time about hit," Mandy said. "'Course, thar's a few lak old Missoury what don't, but they's few."

Sure enough, the Bryans were at Sunday school on the following Sunday. They were timid and self-conscious but the boys seemed to enjoy their class work. Ethel Norman, who was their teacher, had obtained a supply of picture cards depicting religious scenes pertaining to the lesson. The Bryan boys gave their cards to their mother with proud smiles.

That night when the invitation hymn was sung three young men and a man and his wife arose and accepted the invitation to accept Christ. These five were the first whose confessions I had ever taken.

Lige Gurney rose and said, "I know hit's cold, but why don't we'uns go down to Stark's Crick right now fer the baptizin'? Hit's the way the Apostle Paul done—agoin' the same hour of the night—shorely we'uns hain't no better'n him."

Lige's suggestion met the wholehearted approval of the five candidates for baptism so the entire congregation walked the mile to Stark's Creek. There by the light of the full moon, in the clear cold waters of that spring-fed stream, I baptized my first converts.

The six of us stood waist-deep in the cold water, hands clasped in a circle, while the congregation sang two verses of "Shall We Gather at the River?" I proceeded with the baptismal ritual, immersed each candidate and then we climbed up the bank and put jackets and coats over our wet clothing. Someone had been kind enough to borrow extra garments from the crowd so that each of us could have added covering as we walked home. The beauty of the night, the serious solemnity of the service, the inspiration that had come with the tears during the singing at the river's edge made me realize that I had found true happiness in this my niche in life. "To be truly happy is to make others happy," I thought as I walked rapidly back to Hillcrofts'.

"Never knowed a body bein' hurt adoin' the Lord's biddin'," Mandy Hillcroft said after I had changed my clothes and sat by the fire drinking the hot coffee and eating the pie which she had fixed for me.

A few days later an invitation came for me to preach at the Climax Spring Church. I arranged for Bob Norman to again take charge at Mulberry and accepted the offer from Climax Spring.

A large crowd came to the meeting where I preached on the words which God commanded Moses to tell the pursued people at the shore of the Red Sea: "Tell the people to go forward." When I had finished reading the text a man rose and politely said, "May I ask a question?" Naturally, I granted his request and then followed one of the oddest of my preaching experiences.

My interrogator peered out from under his bushy brows and asked, "Whar did them people go?"

"There is no record either in the Bible or in history answering that question," I replied.

"Thet's right, Brother," the man said as he thrust his

hands into the hip pockets of his overalls and rose to his full height before continuing. "I believes us folks here in these here hills air part of the ten lost tribes." Then he proceeded to go into a lengthy discussion on his theory. I stood patiently waiting until he had finished and then devoted only about ten minutes to the services before dismissing the meeting. The impromptu speaker had talked for more than an hour.

"Why didn't ye tell him to sot down and shet up lak most preachers does?" one of the church elders asked me. "He's plumb crazy about thet subject, an' we shore gits tarred listen' to him."

There had been some sentiment favoring a revival meeting at Owsley, so one Saturday I called upon several active church workers in that neighborhood. Among the homes I visited was that of Ray and Sara Jarvis, whom I knew to be fine Christian people and who had already manifested considerable interest in the religious training of their son, John Wesley. The boy had frequently attended the young people's midweek meetings.

"John Wesley's just fourteen and has never been converted," Mrs. Jarvis said. "He's a mighty good boy and we aim to raise him right. We'd be proud if you could have the revival and maybe John Wesley'd go forward. There's several other young folks just like him, Brother Howard, that have never made the confession."

I told Mrs. Jarvis I'd think about conducting a revival and come to some decision soon. Meanwhile, I explained, I needed to spend the rest of the day making sick calls.

"If you got time, Brother Howard, you might go visit Granny Harper," Mrs. Jarvis said. "She's old and blind and lives on the Harper place with her youngest boy and his wife. Granny's got eleven children; they're all gone but Art. I seen her last week and she asked me to say she hankered to talk to you—said for you to come some

Saturday when Art and his wife are gone—they go to town ever' Saturday."

"I've heard of the Harpers but I don't believe they've been coming to church, have they?" I asked.

"Likely not. The Harpers always kept purty much to themselves, worked hard, tended to their own business," Mrs. Jarvis said. "They never had much dealings with the rest of us."

"I'll go by there this afternoon," I said.

It was about two o'clock when I arrived at Granny Harper's and was greeted by the usual barking dog. The huge mongrel barked savagely as though ready for attack. Granny appeared at the cabin door and quieted the animal.

"I'm the minister at Owsley," I said, introducing myself.

"I'm so glad ye come," she replied. "Come in. Hit's bin a long, long time since I ever talked to a preacher." She spoke again to the dog and with her quiet voice checked the animal while I stepped into the cabin.

"Set down and he'p yo'rself ter some of them apples— reckon Art left some there on the table," she said as we found chairs. "Eat all ye like fer I got a long story I got ter tell ye." There was a considerable pause before she continued. "From what I heerd about ye, preacher, I reckon I kin trust ye ter keep a secret. Hit's always been a deep sorrer in my life, I kin tell ye. My own children don't know and nobody else here knows. But, preacher, I feel I ain't much longer fer this world and I jist gotta confess hit ter somebody."

"Mrs. Harper, you may tell me anything you wish," I said. "My purpose in coming here was with the hope I could help you."

"Well, preacher, reckon I best begin at the beginnin'," the old woman said. "My father and mother was raised up in Oklahomy. They married when Paw was eighteen and

Maw sixteen. Folks married young then. I was borned a year later. Maw was puny arter I was borned and I was the only child. We'uns lived on a farm and had a good living. They put me in a mission school and I finished there when I was fifteen. That summer Maw died and Paw took to drink. Said hit he'ped him fergit.

"One night he come home awful drunk. He looked at me and said, "Ye look jist like yore Maw and I'm agoin' to sleep with you from now on." The woman clutched the edge of the chair as she continued. "Preacher, I cried and cried and begged but he pulled out a big pistol he allers carried on his hip. He said he'd kill me if I didn't do what he said.

"When he sobered up he acted sorry. He didn't bother me no more for several weeks. He drunk worse and worse though. Then one day when he warn't too bad I tole him I was goin' to have a baby. He didn't say anything but he soon sold the ranch and we come up here in these hills.

"'Yo're goin' to live like my woman from now on,' he said when we settled here. 'And if ye ever tell folks yo're my daughter I'll kill ye.' Him and me had eleven children, preacher. He quit drinkin' and was allers good ter me in his way. Ever'body here thinks we was married an' no kin by blood at all. I was allers afraid our young'-uns would be tetched, him bein' my paw, but they was all strong, smart children. He died fourteen years ago and I can't say I cared a lot.

"Children's been abeggin' me ter ask fer a blind pension, but if I does they'll find out. Art got one of them blanks and read all the questions ter me. I got ter swear my whole life ter git that blind pension and I shore can't do it. I shore didn't live with my own paw as his woman 'cause I wanted ter." There was a pause before she continued. "Do you believe I'll git to heaven after alivin' thataway?"

"Have you ever confessed Christ?" I asked.

"Ain't never had no chance," she replied.

"Would you like to confess Him now?"

"Yep, I shore would," she said.

I took my Bible from my pocket and read several chapters of Scripture. Then I asked if she wished to be baptized, too.

"Yes, but does it have ter be did in front a crowd?" she asked.

"No, that's not necessary," I said. "If you wish, I'll take your confession and baptize you this very afternoon."

"Thank God!" she exclaimed. "I felt in my old bones ye would, brother. " 'Scuse me 'til I steps in the other room and changes my duds. We'uns can go down the hill to Turkey Crick, if ye'll holp me. Then I can be ready ter meet my Lord when I dies."

It was a quarter of a mile to the clear Ozark stream and I helped the blind woman down the path. Yet for all of her age and affliction she seemed to need little help. She walked as one guided by a divine glory. Never once did she falter—even crossing a rocky ledge at the stream's edge with the agility of a younger woman.

The water was cold but she never complained as we stepped into the spring-fed stream. Her print dress began to float as we waded waist-deep into the clear creek but presently the current struck us and pressed our clothes tight against us.

"Folks allers says nobody gits sick from being baptized and I believes hit; but 'tain't cold today, nohow," Mrs. Harper said.

I clung to the frail woman lest she be carried away as a leaf upon the current. When we were far enough into the stream for the baptizing I took a clean handkerchief from my pocket.

"Mrs. Harper, do you believe Jesus is the Christ, the Son of the Living God?" I asked.

"Yes, I do!"

"Will you always trust and love Him and to the best of your ability serve Him?"

"Yes, I believes; and if He'll only fergive me my sins I'll serve Him allers, God helpin' me."

I placed the handkerchief over her mouth and nose lest the shock of the cold water make her gasp and become strangled by the water.

"Mrs. Harper, I baptize thee in the name of the Father, and of the Son, and of the Holy Ghost."

I held her gently and immersed her in nature's baptismal. Quickly I helped her back into a standing position.

"Hallelujah!" she shouted as she emerged. "I'm blind now but some day I'll see the Lord in all His glory."

We shivered our way out of the creek and up the hillside.

CHAPTER 17

Morals, Moonshine, and a Promise

"HULL COUNTRY'S PLANNIN' ON HAVIN' A PIE SUPPER fer ye if hit's all right," Lige Gurney informed me one morning at Sunday school.

"A pie supper for me! Why?" I questioned.

"You give yore cash money fer the new schoolhouse and been givin' yore time here and other places without askin' pay or takin' up collections," Lige explained. "Some of us figgered a pie supper'd be all right. Hit'll fetch in a few dollars to he'p ye along."

"That's mighty thoughtful of everyone," I replied. "The fact that you want to help me, though, means far more than the money. There was a long time, Lige, when I felt like an outcast here. It seemed everybody was afraid of me and didn't want to have anything to do with me. This helps prove that I was wrong."

"No, Brother Howard, ye warn't wrong," Lige said. "When ye first come, folks war 'fraid ye might be a revenuer or here fer some other devilment. Folks's fer ye now, though—'cept maybe a few like old Missoury and they's mostly not even fer anybody but themselves."

The pie supper was held the next Friday night with the aid of several local fiddlers, guitar and banjo players who had been engaged to furnish the usual hill music for the occasion. Few of the fiddlers read music (playing only by ear); but the perfect time and harmony of fiddles, guitars and banjos playing together blend beautifully to the hearing of the hill bred.

More than forty pies were sold. A jar of sour pickles

was offered as a prize to the most lovesick couple. My name was instantly suggested and coupled with that of a pleasant old maid who lived in the community. Several other couples were nominated.

"A penny a vote!" the auctioneer shouted and keen rivalry began as each group tried to force the jar of pickles on the couple of its choice.

After five minutes of hilarious fun, Miss Ruth and I were declared the winners.

"You'uns got to come up front to eat 'em," someone yelled.

For once in my life I was deeply embarrassed, as I opened the quart jar of pickles and proceeded to give one to Miss Ruth and eat one myself as we sat together on one chair.

The proceeds of the pie supper amounted to forty-one dollars and all of it was given to me. This was the largest amount of cash I had possessed in many months.

Sermon preparations and companionship with Clayton generally occupied my Saturdays. I liked an occasional hunt, too. To roam the woods alone amidst the grandeur and solemn silence of the timber land seemed to add something very special to my life. It mattered little whether or not I shot a squirrel. The hunt was always a success.

But on one Saturday morning my plans were abruptly upset by the appearance of a deputy sheriff with a subpoena for me to appear as a state's witness in a trial set for the following Monday. It was the case of the State of Missouri *vs.* Zeb Fletcher. Fletcher was charged with owning and operating a still.

In my boarding around with Mulberry patrons I had stayed a few nights at Fletchers'. Hence I was subpoenaed as a state's witness.

"What am I to do?" I thought as I acknowledged the

summons. "I'll not perjure myself, yet I dare not violate the code of the hills." All day I thought the matter over and over, and at last a possible solution came to my mind. I remembered a few bits of legal information I had picked up from old W. W. Bulmann back in Iowa. That was while I was going to school and occasionally helping in the lawyer's office.

I announced at church next morning that there would be no school Monday but I made no explanation as to the reason for my not being able to teach. I made no mention of my being called as a witness against Zeb.

Court was already in session when I arrived at the county seat but I heard the first witness called. He had worked at the sawmill near Mulberry and his testimony brought out the fact that he was a government agent disguised as a floating laborer. His statements were very damaging to Zeb for he had bought corn liquor from him and had given him marked money in payment. This same marked money was found on Zeb when he was arrested, searched and lodged in jail.

A jug of corn liquor was also introduced as evidence, along with its analysis by the state chemist. The liquor showed a high volume of alcohol.

Then I was called to the witness stand.

"Be sworn!" the judge directed as he held up his hand and intoned the usual oath.

"I cannot subscribe to that oath," I stated. "However, I'll gladly affirm," and I repeated the required affirmation. The judge looked seriously at me over the rim of his spectacles. The prosecuting attorney turned to me with a self-satisfied smile.

"What is your name?" he asked.

"Guy Howard."

"Are you a minister?"

"Yes, sir, I am a minister doing mission work."

"Do you know whether or not Zeb Fletcher has ever operated a still or made or sold alcoholic beverages in violation of state law?" he asked.

I turned to the judge and spoke very deliberately, so both judge and jury could hear me well. "Your honor," I said, "as a minister doing missionary work among these people any information I may have concerning the merits of this case came to me solely because I am a spiritual advisor. And under the law, it is privileged conversation. Therefore, I ask to stand on my constitutional rights as a spiritual advisor and refuse, as provided in the constitution of the state of Missouri, to testify."

"Don't know 'bout that," the judge said. Then he spat a quid of tobacco into the cuspidor at his feet and turned to the prosecutor.

The prosecutor was leering at me. "Are you a lawyer?" he roared.

"Just a minute!" Zeb's lawyer interjected. "This witness is entirely within his constitutional rights." He picked up a revised statutes from the counsel table and handed it to the judge. "Here is the code. If Your Honor will turn to the section on privileged conversations you will see that this minister is entirely within his rights."

A few minutes of searching in the statutes convinced the judge of the point and I was excused.

I walked back among the spectators and sat down beside a man I recognized as one of Zeb's neighbors. He leaned over and whispered, "Plumb clever how ye kept from stickin' Zeb." The tone of his voice and the self-satisfied chuckle he emitted told me more than his words. The trial continued with a parade of half-frightened witnesses from the Hickory County backhills. It was mid-afternoon when the case was given to the jury. Nearly an hour later the verdict was returned. It read, "We, the jury, find the defendant guilty as charged in the information."

I arose, walked to the counsel table and addressed the judge. "Your Honor, if the court please, before sentence is pronounced I would like to make a request."

"Your request will be heard," the judge stated.

Then I proceeded to tell of Zeb's children who were pupils of mine and explained the need for Zeb to make a living for his family. This was his first law violation and I asked that he be paroled to me. "If the conditions of his parole are violated I personally will bring him to jail," I promised.

The judge called me, the prosecutor and Zeb's lawyer into another room for a conference. Everyone agreed that a parole was preferable to a lengthy jail term at state expense after the defense attorney pointed out that Zeb's family would be subjects for county relief if the father were confined in jail.

"Let me talk to Zeb," I requested. He was brought in by the sheriff.

"Mr. Fletcher," I said, addressing the meek mountaineer. "The judge has kindly offered to place you on parole in my charge; but before I accept that responsibility I want you to promise me that you'll work every weekday, obey the law, go to church every Sunday and read the Bible every day. If you choose to do this I'll assume the responsibility for you making no further trouble. If you break that pledge I'll be just as honest with the court as I have been with you and I'll see that you are taken to jail to serve all of your sentence."

"I'll shore do hit, Brother Howard," said Fletcher, "and I'll shore be obliged to ye."

Thus it was that I assumed responsibility for my first parolee.

I took this action in Zeb's case, not to defend or condone lawbreaking, but as a step toward helping a fellow man. The means justified the end because Zeb kept his promise faithfully.

A few days after Zeb's trial, I was called upon to conduct the funeral of an old man named Saxon who had lived about ten miles from Owsley. I was not acquainted with all members of the Saxon family but knew their son, Roll, a young man of about twenty-five, who had been an occasional attendant at the Owsley Church services. The reputation of the rest of the family was far from good but the funeral service, I felt, might be an opportunity to take Christ to all of the Saxons. The man who had brought me the death message said the Saxons had asked that I come that evening.

"If you'll wait until school is dismissed," I told him, "I'll walk back with you for I'm not sure just where the Saxons live."

As we hurried along to Gurneys', where I was staying that week, that I might change clothes and get my Bible, I asked the young man accompanying me if Mr. Saxon had been a Christian.

"Afraid not," he replied. "Never heard of him goin' to church none and, preacher, ya might as well know hit, they's a bad lot. Moonshinin', drinkin', fightin', ever'- thing in the book. Old Mamie's worst. She's Jake Saxon's woman. How come, preacher, all bad wimmin's called old? Old Mamie! She hain't so awful old, must be she's so cussed ornery."

After leaving Gurneys' we walked rapidly over rough wild hills along the most direct route to the Saxon cabin.

"Shore feel sorry fer ye, Preacher," my guide said as we hiked along. "Don't know what yo're agoin' to say. Even if hits so, shorely ya can't tell folks Old Man Saxon's plumb gone to hell."

We arrived at the Saxon cabin about dusky dark. The lamp was already lighted. The family was seated at the supper table and after I had been introduced to everyone present, my guide and I were invited to share in the meal.

Tillie Saxon, a daughter of the deceased man, set two plates on the table for us and brought two stools from an adjoining room. The food was abundant and good. The neighbors had brought in a great deal of it already prepared. In the hour of sorrow there was no deviating from this Ozark custom of bringing food offerings irrespective of the community standing of the bereaved family. We ate heartily for the long walk had whetted our appetites.

"Old Mamie," as my guide had called her, sat at the head of the table and watched us with shifting eyes that portrayed the nervous cunning and hatred of a coyote. When we had finished our meal, she turned to her daughter. "Tillie, go fetch me the writin' tablet an' a pencil. Preacher," she said, "ye kin write what I tells ye fer I want Jake's 'bituary writ right." Then when Tillie had brought the school tablet and pencil and set them down on the table in front of me, Mamie dictated in a deep, commanding voice. She told when and where her husband had been born, the names of his father and mother, the number of his brothers and sisters, the date he came to the Owsley community and the date he had married Mamie Dixon.

"Mamie Dixon war my maiden name," she said as her eyes flashed fire, "and by God! Preacher, I shore as hell don't mean Ole Mayme! God damn ever'body what calls me thet." Then in a calmer voice she listed the names of their children and ended her dictation with the date and hour of her husband's death. "Come in and see him, Preacher," she said as she rose from her chair and, aided by a knotty hickory cane, waddled toward the front room.

The coffin had been made by a hill craftsman and was covered with beautiful plushlike gray crepe.

"Hit looks jist lak him," the widow said. "Had to buy him a new suit of clothes and a shirt but nobody's agoin' to say Mamie didn't do right handsome by layin' Jake away."

The funeral next day was a sore trial for me, but I said, "Nothing I may say today can do Jake Saxon any harm and nothing I may say can do him any good for his record is written in the Lamb's Book of Life and sealed to wait the Judgment Day. His immortal soul is in the keeping of a merciful God. So it is my purpose today to speak to the living rather than of the dead." Then I took for a text Hebrews 13:8—"Jesus Christ the same yesterday, and today, and for ever"—and did my best to say a few words on life and death, on man's relationship to man and his relationship to God. I avoided any reference to the life Jake had lived.

After the interment, which was in a hilltop cemetery near by, Roll Saxon called me aside and said, "Preacher Howard, that war a good service. Now what does we'uns owe ye?"

I indicated a rough bench under a large cedar tree at the edge of the cemetery.

"Let's go and sit on that bench for I want to talk to you a few minutes, Roll." The bench was far enough from the crowd that there was no danger of our conversation being overheard.

"Roll," I said as we sat on the bench, "I never charge for any service that I can render people in the name of Jesus but I believe I'll break that rule today and charge you. I'm not sure you can pay, because the price'll be high."

"Hit may be high but we'uns allers pays our debts," Roll said in a stern voice.

"All right," I replied as I arose and held out my hand to him. "Promise me with God as our judge that you'll never make, drink or sell any more corn liquor. That is the price!"

He rose and stood silently with head bowed as tears

trickled down his cheeks. Then he looked me straight in the eye, thrust his hand into mine and said in a voice choked low with emotion, "I'll do hit, preacher, fer I reckon Pappy would want it thataway now."

I walked the miles back to Gurneys' and the woods seemed more beautiful than common. The fading redbud along the stream appeared in dull contrast against the blue sky and here and there upon the ground sweet william, puccoon and Jacob's-ladder were in bloom. The dogwoods with their beautiful green-white four-petaled blossoms were beginning to dominate the entire woodlands.

I took a branch of choice dogwood blossoms to the Gurney cabin.

"Oh! How purty," Mrs. Gurney said. "Let me git a fruit jar and put 'em in water. They'll keep purty fer 'most a week."

"Ever hear the story of the dogwood?" Lige Gurney asked when I laid the blossoms on the table. "See, they's four leaves on this flower—pure white. Two of 'em is longer'n th'other two—makes a cross." He pointed with the reed stem of his cob pipe to the small seemingly blighted place at the end of each petal. "See them little places? They's stained red around thar. They allers been thetaway since Christ war crucified—them blooms makes a white cross—nail holes with a spot of red means He bled when He war nailed thar sufferin' fer sinners. Story a man tole us young'uns says the cross war made of dogwood. They growed big then, but ever since the crucifixion dogwood trees bin so ashamed they allers grow sorry and scrubby-like and they allers begin ter bloom jist around Easter."

"They's usually their purtiest about Easter time, Brother Howard," said Mrs. Gurney as she returned with a fruit jar half-full of water.

"That's a beautiful legend," I exclaimed. "Do all the people here know that story you just told me?"

"Shore they do," replied Lige. "Fur back as I kin recollect, folks allers talkin' about hit ever' spring and folks here in the hills all believes hit. Shorely stands to reason as plain a marked cross as ever' one of them blooms is. The good Lord fixed 'em Himself so we'uns won't fergit His sufferin' fer sinners."

CHAPTER 18

The Victim

I HEARD NO MORE ABOUT THE SAXON FAMILY UNTIL several weeks after the funeral when, one Wednesday night, Bill Priestly joined me as I walked to the Owsley services.

"Shorely's fine meetin's ye got started," Bill said, "but I reckon the devil's gettin' in a few licks too. That low-down Roll Saxon's cookin' likker again down Smelter Holler an' he 'lows to take a batch to meetin' tonight. Don't ask me how I know, Brother Howard, but thought I'd happen along and tell ye 'bout hit."

"Bill, you must be mistaken," I said in surprise, remembering the pledge Roll Saxon had given me in the grave-yard.

"No, I hain't," Bill insisted. "'Course we'uns all knows ya don't narrate what we'uns tells ye so thought I'd let ye know what's comin'." He left me at the forks and headed into the brush.

Sure enough, when the crowd gathered at the meeting I could detect the odious stench of alcohol. The boisterous laughter of several young men plainly showed that they had freely imbibed.

John Wesley Jarvis caused a disturbance during the worship period that couldn't be overlooked, for hill folk, no matter how wicked they may be, generally have a deep respect for worship services. I was hurt and surprised the more because I knew John Wesley's father never used alcohol in any form. Both Ray Jarvis and his wife were fine Christian folks and had reared their son to shun evil.

But the boy was young and no doubt easily influenced.

I stopped the service during the disturbance and said quietly but very firmly, "This is the house of God when we gather together to worship. Please may we all respect it as such." The disorder ended.

John Wesley came to me after services and tried to apologize for his conduct. "Please, Brother Howard, don't tell Pappy and Mom. They'd feel awful knowin' I been drinkin'. Roll said I warn't man enough to take half a dozen swallers so I jist showed him. Please don't tell my folks, will you, Brother Howard? I promise you I won't never drink no more—I'm shore sick, Brother Howard."

"You get yourself home," I said to him, "and I'll talk to you later."

"Corn whisky and the evil it breeds is the curse of an otherwise Utopian land," I thought as I plodded home that night. What was I going to do about it? My goal was to help these people with whom I had chosen to cast my lot, yet because of the code of the hills how could I go about fighting moonshining? I felt more discouraged and tired than I had for some time. The path I climbed to Gurney's where I was to find a bed that night seemed so endless and steep as to tax every ounce of my energy. As I toiled wearily upward the thoughts kept nagging me: Had I made a mistake in defending Zeb Fletcher? Had I given the hill folk the impression that I condoned their traffic in this terrible evil?

When I told Lige what had happened at the Owsley Church meeting he sadly shook his head. "Brother Howard, moonshinin's been the curse of these hills fur back as I kin recollect, and my pap tole me hit war the same fur back as he could recollect. I reckon hit's never goin' to stop."

"There must be some way . . ." I protested.

"Only thing thet'll make a man quit drinkin', cussin'

and all his other orneriness is ter give him a big dose of God," Lige offered, "an' I reckon yo're gettin' a purty good start fixin' up the medicine. If we'uns keeps aworkin' and aprayin' we'uns jest naterally bound ter git some of 'em cured showin' 'em the grace of a lovin', fergivin' Lord.''

I hadn't spoken to anyone but Gurney of the shameful affair at Owsley; but as news travels rapidly in the hills the whole countryside was soon talking about the incident.

Poor attendance at Mulberry the next Sunday revealed what inroads the revival of moonshining had made in the community, and the spirituality of the entire day's services was at a low ebb.

"Shorely hoped and been prayin' moonshinin' hereabouts died with old man Saxon," Mandy Hillcroft said that afternoon. "Generally seein' folks we'uns loves adyin' makes us see the error of our ways lak the Good Book says, but reckon them Saxon's jist too fer gone fer arything ter do them ary good.''

Monday afternoon a messenger came to the schoolhouse door and brought some sorrowful news.

"Ray Jarvis asked me to come by and tell you John Wesley's bad sick," the man said. "Don't nobody seem to know what's ailin' him—eyes all swelled up and bustin' right outen his head. Doctor from Warsaw come and said John Wesley's in mighty bad shape. They'd like it if you'd come.''

I went at once down the trail to the Gurney cabin. The Bible Scripture, "The wages of sin is death," kept running through my thoughts. I probably knew more than anyone else about the whole tragedy. I knew that Roll Saxon was the real culprit. Here was a fine boy of fourteen paying with horrible suffering and perhaps even death because he had been taunted with "Only a real man can take more than half a dozen swallers."

"My God!" Lige Gurney spoke with deep reverence when I told him of the message Ray Jarvis had sent. "I'm goin' with you, Brother Howard. There's likely to be bloodshed in these hills if thet little feller goes back to his Maker."

We walked rapidly up Stark's Creek in the twilight of evening through moist air which held the tang of spring and the incense of flowers and growing things.

The entire situation seemed too much of a nightmare. But deeply as I had sensed the tragedy of the situation I was not prepared for the horror and terror I was soon to experience.

Several wagons stood in the yard about the three-room Jarvis cabin. The teams had been unhitched and tied to either side of the wagon boxes and were contentedly munching hay. A number of saddled horses were tied to trees about the premises. A single automobile was parked on the road near the front gate.

Men stood together in the dusk and talked in low tones—or stood and silently waited.

I lifted the latchstring on the cabin door and Lige and I walked into the room.

The place was filled with silent women standing with bowed heads. The only sounds came from the room where John Wesley lay in a big iron bed.

Ray Jarvis and his wife stood at the end of the bed with their arms around each other, their faces drawn and pale from the long hours of watching. A neighbor whispered that they had stood there so for most of two days.

John Wesley lay in the center of the bed, writhing in delirium and agony. Two strong men sat on each side of the sufferer and tried to hold him. Improperly distilled corn whisky was doing its lethal work and the beautiful life of John Wesley Jarvis was slowly but surely being snuffed out.

The boy's eyeballs had actually burst in bloody matter.

His face was horribly swollen, his lips thick and black, and he was wildly delirious from the fever raging within his body.

"Git that damned jug away!" he screamed in a wild rasping voice. "Shore I'm a man. Didn't I take six swallers? Oh, God! but hit burns. . . . I'm sick and goin' to puke—hits aburnin' my guts out—head's busted plumb open—git my eyes, Pappy; they's rollin' off the bed," he cried out in the voice of a maniac.

How long I stood petrified by the horrible drama I don't know, but I was finally brought to my senses when someone laid a hand on my shoulder. Turning, I saw the face of a stranger. "May I speak with you a moment, sir?" he whispered.

I followed the man out of the house and to the automobile parked by the side of the road.

"I'm Dr. Brownlee from Warsaw," he said as we sat down in the car seat. "You, I understand, are Rev. Howard."

"Yes sir," I replied.

"I'm just wondering what you may know about this boy; does he drink much?" he asked.

"I think not," I answered. "Of course, doctor, I haven't known him very long and then only as a pupil who came to a Bible study class every Wednesday evening with a lot of other young folks."

"Yes, I know that," he nodded impatiently. "But last Wednesday night he was there and there's a rumor that one of the older boys of this district talked him into drinking a little. This evening makes five full days and that's the proper time for fusel oil poisoning to be at its worst. Do you know whether or not he was drinking that evening?"

"Yes, doctor, he had been," I admitted. "I haven't told anyone what I know and I realize that for each of us this is privileged conversation. I have no desire to protect criminals, yet for me to betray a confidence when it couldn't help the boy is unthinkable. You know the code of the hills. The tenseness in that home yonder is terrible. I fear that justice in the raw may take its own course and I'm not sure we can do anything to stop it."

"That's right," the doctor said. "There may be bloodshed when that boy dies and he can't live until morning."

"Do you think there is anything I can do to help keep peace?" I asked.

"You're a preacher, Brother Howard," the doctor said. That's your job. Best watch that big fellow who has been staying at the bed of the boy—he's an uncle I think. There isn't a thing I can do but give the boy opiates to ease his suffering and even that doesn't do a great deal of good," the doctor continued, "for fusel oil in the bloodstream neutralizes morphine." He climbed out of the car and I followed him.

He returned to the bedside and I walked to the group of men still standing outside the kitchen door.

"Can you tell me where I can get a drink of water?" I asked.

Here," someone said as he pointed into the woods, "follow that path down the hill—hit's only a short piece—they's a spring by the big oak tree. Gourd's ahangin' on the tree and ya shore can't miss hit."

I followed the trail about a hundred yards down the hill to the big tree. A yellow gourd, hollowed out to form a dipper, was plainly visible in the gloom. I drank of the cold water and replaced the gourd.

Just as I turned to retrace my way to the cabin I stopped suddenly as someone stepped from the shadows and said in a low voice, "Brother Howard, kin I talk with ya?"

I recognized the voice. "Roll Saxon," I burst out, "what are you doing here?"

The Walkin' Preacher fording a creek in the back hills.

In an Ozark school room.

"Let's walk over in the woods a ways," he suggested.

When we were fifty yards deeper in the shadows he stopped.

"Brother Howard, do they think John Wesley drunk some bad whisky?" he asked in a frightened voice.

"Roll," I countered, "no one should know the answer to that question better than you do. You promised me before God to quit that liquor business. You have deeply disappointed me. I hate to have to tell you this, but in the sight of God you are just as guilty of murdering that boy as if you had put a bullet in his heart." I paused for a moment. "Roll, John Wesley won't be here in the morning," I continued, "and if you are, that will only be reason for more tragedy and sorrow. My advice to you is to get out of here while you can and never come back. There's trouble coming when that boy dies."

"Much obliged," he said and turned and walked rapidly through the woods. I could soon hear him running.

John Wesley was dying by the time I returned to the sickroom. He suffered his last in the middle of the night. "Thank God," Mrs. Jarvis said. "He's gone now where they ain't no pain or suffering."

Ray Jarvis's brother, Lew, arose from the side of the bed where he had sat almost continuously for three days. He passed his hand over his eyes, shook his head, walked out into the kitchen. He reached above the door and took down a .25-20-caliber Winchester rifle, then walked to the cupboard and got a box of cartridges. He selected three, and dropping them into his shirt pocket slipped quietly out of the door.

I quickly followed him outside. "Lew," I said softly, "may I go with you?"

"No, Brother Howard," he said as he opened the gun and satisfied himself that it was already loaded. "I got some business tonight that I jes' naterally got to do alone." He snapped the breech.

"Let me walk with you to the foot of the hill and I promise I'll not go one step farther," I said.

"All right," he replied and we walked silently ahead.

"Lew," I said, as we neared the lower end of the path, "I can't blame you for wanting to kill every last one of the Saxons tonight, but why send your own immortal soul to hell just to satisfy your vengeance?" I pleaded and prayed with him for nearly two hours, and at last he consented to return with me to the cabin.

Just outside the door he handed his rifle to me. "Here," he said, "take this gun lest I change my mind—killin's too good fer them Saxons."

I unbolted and unloaded the rifle. Then Lew turned again to me, half-defiantly, "Brother Howard," he said bitterly, "the Bible says 'an eye for an eye and a tooth for a tooth,' and by God, they shore got John Wesley's eyes."

"Yes, Lew," I replied, "but a later law says, 'Vengeance is mine, saith the Lord.'"

Together we re-entered the cabin.

CHAPTER 19

The Challenge

WHEN LEW AND I RE-ENTERED THE KITCHEN, A neighbor touched me on the arm. "Ray and Sara want to talk to you," he said. "They're in there." He nodded to indicate the bedroom.

I set the rifle against the cupboard and rapped gently. Ray Jarvis opened the door. "Come in, Brother Howard," he said wearily. "We'uns decided to hold the funeral day after tomorrow and seein's how hits warm-like hit'll be outdoors in the graveyard. Cousin John says some of the folks reckoned they warn't room enough in the school-house. Me and Sara want you to take charge."

I nodded assent.

"We shore do thank you fer quietin' Lew down," he continued. "Got enough trouble a'ready."

Mrs. Jarvis turned and spoke in a calm, resigned tone. "Brother Howard, Jesus died for us all an' I shorely believe John Wesley's been crucified, too. If hit only saves some other mother's boy from drink I'll know John didn't die fer nothin'."

I was deeply touched by her application of Christ's philosophy. "Mrs. Jarvis," I told her, "that is one of the noblest statements I have ever heard and it could come only from the heart of a devout Christian and then from the bleeding heart of a mother. The mother of Jesus, when she knelt beneath her Son's cross, must have felt much as you do."

I asked if there were any service I might render but they both suggested I go home and rest until time to return to the funeral. Lige remained to sit up with the body.

It was early dawn when I walked slowly through the woods toward the Normans'. There was a radiance of silver light from the late moon. Far down the valley one could hear the melancholy gerrum! um! um! of the bull-frogs. From here and there came the plaintive coo of the Mourning-Dove. Far over the ridge I heard a crow cry out his rasping caw! caw! caw! as his slumber was disturbed by some night prowler that had ventured too near his rookery. It was peace and quiet following violent storm.

I climbed the winding path up Childer's Mountain and stopped on the bald summit to catch my breath. The beauty of the hour with its swelling sounds contrasting the events of the earlier hours filled me with conflicting emotions. There was the terror and agony of the death hour; Lew's burning passion for blood vengeance; the calm steady voice of the mother in her Garden of Geth-semane; and now this peace as of another world.

With a stump as my prayer rail, I knelt and poured out my soul to God, asking for an understanding heart; for faith and love and courage to be equal to the task before me. I prayed God to somehow use me at the funeral to prevent bloodshed and to impress upon the hill people that drink was the one great blot upon this Utopian land.

Thirty minutes more walking brought me to Normans.' I tapped lightly on the kitchen door. Bob, I knew, was a light sleeper and during times of trouble the hillman seems to possess a sense of knowing when anyone is near his cabin in the night.

"Who's there?" Bob called, instantly awake.

"It's Guy."

"Be there in just a minute," he answered. The doors of most Ozark homes are never locked (except on occa-sion when evil is in the air.)

Bob unbolted the door.

"Just a minute and I'll light a lamp," he said quietly as I entered the cabin. "Ever'body else's asleep."

We sat down at the kitchen table and Bob began to fill his pipe. He was full of questions. "Did the boy die?" he asked. I nodded.

"Fusel oil poisoning, they say," he prodded. "Be a wonder if these hills don't echo with shooting like they did when the country was new and night riders were meeting.

"Tell me about it, Brother Howard. Did the boy make any statement before he died? Was the sheriff or prosecuting attorney there?"

"No, Bob," I began. "Neither the sheriff nor the prosecuting attorney was there. And I'm not sure any statements John Wesley made during his wild delirium would stand in court, anyway. Bob, laws and courts will never settle the corn liquor curse of these hills. There's only one way the scourge can be stamped out and that is for the hills to do their own stamping. It seems to me that now is the time to strike but where or how I don't know. Perhaps the opportunity will be the funeral sermon. I pray God someway I may sow seed that will yield a hundredfold."

"Yes, I think you're right," Bob said. "We'll have to do our own stamping. Another tragedy like John Wesley's death, getting the stuff at church 'n' all, too. . . ." He shook his head. "Much more of such as that and these hills will be as bad as they used to tell about. I think you're right," he continued, "that now is the time for some action and the funeral may be the place. Too many preachers nowadays are preaching to please folks and letting the devil win the battles."

He paused and we sat silent for a moment. "It looks like the Lord might be giving you a chance to show what you can do, now," Bob continued grimly. "There's one thing sure, every mother's son of us, except the bootlegging crowd, will be back of you, including a lot of them that drinks a little on the sly, too."

"How big is this bootlegging crowd?" I asked.

"There aren't over a dozen really mean bootleggers," Bob answered. "They run together like a pack of sheep-killing dogs. There's a few decent folks who make a little liquor now and then because their fathers made it. They make it mostly for their own use, though. Oh, they'll sell a grown man a jug now and then," he admitted, reluctantly, "but you couldn't get one of them to sell or give a boy a drink. In fact, if a boy come hunting it, they would tell him plain out no boy ought to drink. Yes, I reckon now is the time to go to work."

"I suppose if the moonshiners were crowded, they'd put up a mean fight," I said.

"Only ones that'll fight you will be the real white-trash, bootlegging bunch," answered Bob. "The others that have been running stills are sure to quit and you can depend on nearly everyone of them helping you stamp out bootlegging. They're all scared. They haven't any more use for the likes of the Saxons than the best folks in the hills have." (So there are gentleman moonshiners, are there? I thought to myself.) "Brother Howard," Bob continued, "I hope God puts it into your heart to speak plain and straight from the shoulder at the funeral." He arose and knocked the ashes from his pipe. "You better go to bed, now," he ordered. "I'll have the folks let you sleep as late as you want. You look tired."

I awoke a little later than the usual hour. When I went into the kitchen the family had finished breakfast and were sitting around the table discussing the one topic everyone else in the hills was probably discussing—John Wesley's death and funeral.

"Why, you're dressed like you were going out logging," Mrs. Norman said, noticing my old clothes and high laced boots.

"No, not logging today," I said. "To the river fishing. I want to think and prepare a sermon for the funeral and someway fishing always helps me think."

"Not a bad idea," said Bob. "Living's a lot like fishing, I guess. Our lives go bobbing up an' down from good to bad just like a cork on a fish line riding the riffles when a perch nibbles at the bait. Put Brother Howard up a good lunch," Bob instructed his wife. "A few slices of that smoked ham ought to help his thinking, too, Ma. He's got a man's-sized job ahead of him."

When I set out, Bob walked a piece with me.

"We'll be praying the good Lord helps you find the right stone to slay Goliath," he said. "Corn liquor is the giant enemy of these hills."

"Thanks, Bob," I replied. "Goliath had a weak spot and our giant is sure to have one, too."

I dug a large supply of earthworms from the soft mucky soil below the spring and then walked slowly down the spring creek watching for crayfish and schools of minnows.

An early morning shower had left the low ground muddy and the river was sure to be tinged from the streams flowing into it. The sun was warm and there wasn't a cloud in the sky. "What a grand day to fish," I thought as I garnered a dozen crawdaddies.

I walked away from the spring creek and headed up the well-marked path leading across the ridge toward Stark's Creek.

Halfway up the ridge I saw George Saxon, Roll's half-brother, coming along the trail toward me, his rifle cradled in the bend of his left arm.

"Good morning, George," I said, pleasantly.

He walked to within six feet of me, then stopped. It was obvious that he had been drinking. His eyes were glassy and staring.

"Preacher, ya best git outen this country whilst yo're all in one piece," he snarled.

"You aren't very friendly this morning, George," I said.

"Damned if we'uns need furriners comin' in stirrin' folks up an' raisin' hell lak ye been doin'," he barked. His voice was vibrant with hatred. "Hit's time fer ye to git out and damned quick." He turned abruptly and walked on down the trail.

I was dumbfounded. What had so soon aroused George Saxon to such bitterness? Roll must have told George that I was the one who'd advised him to get out.

Should I return to the Normans and tell them of my encounter with George Saxon? Should I really take it seriously and guard myself? No, I reasoned, that won't do for the only real safety would be to have all the Saxons imprisoned, and I scarce had complaint or proof sufficient for that.

"Well," I said to myself, "the fish are waiting. I hope they're hungry."

I walked on to Stark's Creek and found a likely-looking pool. The fish were striking well and within a couple of hours I had the legal limit of beauties. I moved up the bank and laid my lunch out on a large flat rock. George's warning kept recurring to my mind. Perhaps I should follow the outlaw's advice and get out. Sometimes it seemed as if everything had been against me since my arrival in the hills, anyway. Maybe I was really butting in where I wasn't wanted. Then I thought back over the last nine months, and how God had guided me. I was grateful for much happiness, for Clayton's improved health and Albert's good situation. I thought back, too, on how in Iowa I'd felt that God showed me the answer to my problem when the Book fell open to St. Matthew 19:29.

"Why not let the same method answer the problem now?" I thought. "Yes, I'll do it." I took my Bible and notebook out of my pocket. Closing my eyes in prayer I asked divine guidance for the answer. Then, as in Iowa, I held my Bible firmly in both hands. I removed my hands and the book fell open. I read.

"He shall cover thee with his feathers, and under his wings shalt thou trust; his truth shall be thy shield and buckler. Thou shalt not be afraid for the terror by night; nor for the arrow that flieth by day. Nor for the pestilence that walketh in darkness; nor for the destruction that wasteth at noonday. A thousand shall fall at thy side and ten thousand at thy right hand but it shall not come nigh thee."

I sat motionless and pondering these words. The die was cast, and doubt banished. I opened my notebook and began jotting down an outline for the funeral sermon. When this was finished I arose, gathered up my fish and tackle and walked whistling back to Normans'.

Next morning, after a hearty breakfast of fried fish, Bob suggested that we ride to the funeral in the wagon. "It'll take us about two hours and a half to drive it clean around the road so we better start about eleven o'clock," he said.

The funeral had been announced for two o'clock and when we arrived more than a hundred people were already there. A look of uneasiness and smoldering indignation showed in the faces of many of them. I knew that theirs was a feeling that could become highly contagious as the services began at the open grave. Ozark people are deeply emotional and a collective emotional build-up was sure to follow. Only a small spark would be needed to change that crowd of peace-loving hill folk into a revengeful mob.

I tried to show a steady calm that I did not feel. We held no rites at the house—only a short prayer service. The casket was tenderly carried to the log wagon by six of John Wesley's companions. At the cemetery it was placed on two carpenter's sawhorses at the side of the open grave.

Friends and neighbors had banked the newly turned earth with spring flowers. Seats had been arranged by laying heavy oak planks across large logs spaced about six feet apart, and every seat except the front row reserved for the relatives was soon filled. In addition to those seated, scores of people stood about in the little cemetery careful lest they tread on the grave mounds. A low platform about ten feet square had been erected near the side of the tomb but far enough away to permit the casket to be placed between the platform and the place of interment. There was a four-foot aisle to be used by the crowd when it passed by for the last look at the corpse. A young man with a fine tenor voice took his pitch from a tuning fork, and the services began with singing by the congregation.

The singing helped relieve the tension. The calm, quiet sorrow of Ray Jarvis and his wife had a good influence for they sat on the front row, heads bowed in silent grief. Ray's arm was about his wife's shoulder. Under similar circumstances many a hill father and mother would have cried and wailed like the hired mourners of Bible times, but the Jarvises bore their grief with a quiet dignity that would have become the most highly cultured people. Their emotional stability was a great contribution to the peace of the community.

Another hymn and the reading of the obituary by a visiting minister brought the services to my turn. I read a single sentence from the Bible: "Behold! I stand at the door and knock." I spoke slowly and deliberately. "My friends, it is not my purpose this afternoon to speak of this young man who died so tragically for nothing I can say will do him any good or any harm. His record is written in the Lamb's Book of Life and his immortal soul awaits the Judgment Day in the keeping of a merciful God." (These were much the same words I had used at the Saxon funeral, I reflected as I paused.)

"Therefore, I plan to speak to the living rather than of the dead." Then I spoke of the opportunity which God gave everyone to accept Him; to live, to serve, and if need be, to stand alone against popular opinion, as Joshua and Caleb of old did when they reported enemies, walled cities and giants in the promised land but nevertheless declared, "God is with us so let us go and possess our inheritance."

"We have a promised land," I reminded them, "but there are enemies, walled cities of sin, and giants of evil abroad within it. These we must overcome to have a land of peace and love where everyone is neighbor and servant of God. Jesus died in awful agony to make possible a perfect condition for peace in the world. John Wesley died, too, in awful agony. As responsible men and women with a duty to almighty God and to our neighbors I bring the challenge that we rise up as an army of Christian soldiers and stamp out the curse that has crucified this boy. Then he, too, will be victorious in death.

"But," I cautioned, "this curse is not a person; it is not a thing. It is an evil idea. It is what we think that counts in our lives. We must stamp evil from our minds and hearts and in that way we will fight the curse that took this loved one from our midst."

From all over the vast crowd of hill folk came dozens of firm, convincing "amens" and I knew then that the battle cry had been sounded and heard.

"Let us pray," I said.

The remainder of the services passed in orderly quiet. The committal ended, men and women began to congregate in groups talking in low, serious tones. Some came and asked me to recommend a course of action that would break up the curse of the Ozark still.

"That is your problem, now," I answered, "and may God guide us in solving it."

Bill Priestly came to my side and extended his hand. "Howdy, Brother Howard, ye 'bout ready to start home? If ye air I'd lak to walk along with ye."

"Why yes, Mr. Priestly, I'm ready to go and I'd enjoy your company. I came with Bob Norman," I added, "so wait here while I tell him that I'd rather walk home. This is one hike I really need."

"I want ye to leave off that Mister Priestly stuff, Brother Howard," he said to me when I returned from talking with Bob. "This here's jist plain old Bill."

I thanked him and we started briskly down the trail.

"Brother Howard, that there war an awful good funeral sermon fur the occasion," Priestly commented. "I heard lots of others say the same an' they all 'lowed ye hit the nail plumb on the head. Ever'body war lookin' fur trouble to start fer Lew shore set a heap of store by John Wesley and he's awful hotheaded." We climbed over Carl Garner's rail fence and short-cut across his tomato field.

"Ye handled hit right smart," Bill continued. "The bootleggin' bunch is shore to quit fer a while. When they start agin they'll find the whole country's workin' agin' 'em. Stills'll be busted up and they's likely to be a few of the bad ones lak the Saxons tarred and feathered or worse.

"I've made a little liquor all along fur my own use, Brother Howard, but I'm shore goin' home and bust up my still even if it war Pap's. I don't never 'low to make ary use of hit. They's others agoin' to do the same fer we'uns jist figgered hit wouldn't be much use fightin' somethin' we'uns doin' ourselves."

CHAPTER 20

Closing Day and Dinner Spread

BILL AND I TALKED SPASMODICALLY AS WE WALKED along through the woods and across fields, but my mind was filled with so many conflicting thoughts that for the life of me I couldn't have repeated much of that conversation to the Normans if they had been at the gate to greet us. Their circuitous route over the hill road was so much farther than the trail Bill and I had taken I knew it would be some time before they arrived home. Bill angled across the back forty toward his cabin as we parted company.

The weight clock on the cabin wall was bonging out five musical repetitions as I entered my own place of abode and went immediately to bed. I slept the sleep of the dead until the Normans returned and Bob sent Clayton to waken me for supper.

Conversation about the table that evening was, of course, of the funeral and what the Normans had heard or observed following the services. The concensus of opinion, Bob believed, was that the funeral sermon was just what the community needed. He said that constructive action by the hill folk was almost certain to follow. I hoped it would be the right kind of action. George Saxon's threat was still on my mind but I had kept it secret.

"How do you think the Saxons and the bootlegging gang will behave now?" I asked.

Bob laid his knife across his plate and folded his arms, resting them on the edge of the table.

"I believe they'll lay low for a few weeks, anyway," he said. "If the law should come out looking into John Wesley's death, some of them might see the handwriting on the wall and quit making altogether. But I tell you, Brother Howard, it's as hard to part a Saxon and corn likker as a duck and water; so unless folks right here make it mighty hot for them they're sure to start makin' again some time."

"Maybe they'll just take a pot shot at me so I can't make it hot for them," I laughed.

Bob looked up in surprise and then chuckled a bit reassuringly. "No, they'd not bother you. They're too cowardly for that. They might kill most anyone else they hate but they're smart enough to know that the minute you were found shot in the back, the whole country would rise up and hang every one of the varmints. Why, it'd be only a matter of hours until they'd swing on a rope halter and every Saxon knows it. Say, you're not going soft on us now are you, Brother Howard? And after the way you showed your colors, too." Bob was kidding but he didn't know that I wasn't.

"No," I replied. "I just thought they probably would hate me for what I've said and done."

Mrs. Norman tactfully changed the subject.

"Some of the women of the school district asked me today if you planned on having a program and spreading a dinner the last day of school," she said.

I was startled to realize how time had flown. "School's out in two weeks, isn't it!" I exclaimed. "And I've been so busy with other things I haven't even given the last day a thought." The youngsters at school had spoken about it a time or two but I had procrastinated. "Whatever is the custom here we'll gladly follow," I assured Ethel.

We discussed plans for the program and entertainment

for the school closing while Mrs. Norman cleared the table, washed and dried the dishes.

School the next morning was a quiet relief following the tenseness of the day before in the Jarvis cabin. It was a welcome escape despite the usual restlessness that increases in ratio to the nearness of school's ending. I began at once to prepare for the closing-day program. I assigned parts in a playlet, arranged readings and songs to be ready for the final entertainment.

It was a pleasant surprise to learn that nearly all of the children knew their parts in full two days after the rehearsals started. Ozark children have almost no chance for self-expression in general public appearances excepting with the opportunity that comes once a year on the last day of school. Therefore, with the pride only a father and mother have in their children, parents often do everything possible so their progeny may make the best showing at the program. The child with the chance for self-expression, coupled with the spirit of excelling in the face of keen competition, gives everything to acting his part.

My hardest task was to teach the children in the playlet the proper voice inflection in their speeches. The smaller ones, especially, wanted to repeat their parts in a singsong monotone. Their idea of public speaking had come from the impression given by preachers, as listening to preaching furnished their only knowledge of the art. Many illiterate preachers deliver their entire sermons in a swing-along chant. A hillman summed up such a preacher once by saying, "Hain't much to hear but shore hell on the sperrit!"

The afternoon before the program, the children decorated the schoolhouse with great bouquets of wild flowers. We erected a long table out of doors by using rough boards set across cedar posts driven into the ground. The older boys laid out and marked a baseball diamond with powdered lime from near-by limestone bluffs. Three horseshoe courts were made ready. We needed plenty of recreational facilities as we expected a big crowd for the basket dinner. As little Ray Pense said, "If you all wants to fetch folks out jes' feed 'em."

Clayton had written Albert about our last-day school picnic and he was at Normans' when I got there that night.

"Thought I'd come spend the day with you," said the grinning Albert. "Gee, Dad! Clayton's looking well," he said as we walked down the hill to the spring to get a pail of water for Mrs. Norman. "They tell me you've done some good church work here, too, Dad. Boy, I'll never forget how blue you and I were our first night in this country. Remember when we slept in the school stable? I'm sure glad now that we came here, Dad," he continued.

"Yes, son, the Lord has been very good to us. Here for the first time in my life I feel I have found my real place. I know now that doing mission work among these hill folk is my job and it is the only work I shall ever follow hereafter. There's no money in it—not even a good living—but we can always make our bread and butter at other things."

"Better come help me on the truck farm this summer," Albert suggested.

"I'd like to, son, but when school's out tomorrow I expect to work in the woods with Bob to square up Clayton's and my board bill," I answered. "Then I'm going to take my Bible and a few clothes and go out over the Ozarks preaching, organizing Sunday schools and young people's meetings and render any other Christian service that I can. Mrs. Norman will take care of Clayton, and he is doing so well here that by fall he's sure to be able to work every day."

"Well, it seems to be the only thing to do," Albert agreed. "Looks like we'll have to make the living until Clayton is completely cured; then maybe we can get a little home." He hesitated a moment and then said, excitedly, "My boss tells me I can get in the C.C.C. camp later after I'm a legal resident of Missouri."

"Now, Albert, you don't have to do that just to help Clayton and me," I said.

"Oh, I like forestry and I'll have a better chance for advancement than most of the boys. I had bookkeeping and typing in high school and that ought to help. There would be twenty-five dollars of my pay each month from the government to help you and Clayton. I'd be allowed five dollars, my board and room and clothing until I get a rating."

"Son, the C.C.C. ought to be a fine thing for you," I said. "If you applied yourself to the work and took all the extra things the C.C.C. night school offers you ought to get a rating some time."

Albert was quick to follow up his case after I had shown an interest in it.

"When I get in the camp maybe you and Clayton can rent a little place. Then you could teach and do mission work; and if we all saved our money we ought to be able to have a place of our own," he continued as we walked slowly up the hill from the spring.

"We'll wash here, Albert," I said as we stopped at the bench under a large spreading juniper tree. The basin was a tin one that rested on an enormous block of wood. We hadn't finished our toilet before Mrs. Norman called "Supper!" from the kitchen door.

Evidently the whole country had declared a holiday in deference to the school closing, even if the oak leaves were as big as squirrels' ears and it was traditional corn-planting time.

People came in log wagons, on horseback and on "shanks' mare." Each group brought a large basket woven from hickory withes, small willows or peeled honeysuckle runners. The baskets were filled with every imaginable variety of food that is pleasant to the palates of hill people. The women and men separated at the school yard, as the women took the baskets to the outdoor table and the men collected in groups to talk or gathered around the courts where several lively horseshoe-pitching games were in progress.

A group of men rolled a big log to a level spot at the edge of the school ground, peeled off the bark with their razor-sharp Barlow knives and started a game of mumblety-peg. The contestants straddled the log and played by flipping a knife in the air with the smaller of the two blades fully open and the larger blade half-opened. The position of the blades as the knife stuck in the green wood of the freshly peeled log determined the points earned. The man with the most points after an equal number of throws was declared the winner and he played the next contestant.

Boys and younger men played work-up on the ball diamond before an audience of "sparkin' "-age girls. Heroes of the moment were applauded with riotous laughter, frequent giggles and lively banter. The younger girls and small children picked wild flowers in the near-by woods.

Out at the side of the schoolhouse the great stone furnace grew hot as the chosen ones made coffee and baked corn bread.

Everyone spoke pleasantly to me. "Thank God," I thought, "I've broken down the barriers of mistrust and the boys and I are now accepted as part of the community."

When all was ready for the spread, one of the women brought the hand bell from the schoolroom and rang it.

Mr. Simmons didn't lose the opportunity to act as spokesman. He stood on a stump and told of the progressive school we had conducted and the spirit of neighborliness and good feeling that had grown up in the district. He concluded his remarks by saying, "We'uns air all shore proud of our teacher, Brother Howard, an' his boys, and we all hope they keep on livin' here amongst us, fur we know now they're shore all wool and a yard wide."

Lige Gurney's fervent prayer of thanks and a plea for divine blessing had hardly soared heavenward before everyone began to fill his plate with food.

There was baked chicken, goose and guinea hen, fried and roast ham, canned beef, mashed potatoes, hot dumplings and noodles, corn, peas, tomatoes whole and tomatoes pickled, tomatoes preserved and tomatoes in sauce, candied sweet potatoes, pinto beans with lean pork, salads, fried pies, open-face pies and closed pies, light cakes and dark cakes, cookies, yellow butter, milk and steamy black coffee and at least a dozen varieties of home-canned fruit. Everyone ate with keen appetites as they laughed and joked with each other.

"Lafe," ye old cuss, ye; bet I know whar this drumstick come from," one man said as he waved a large piece of fried turkey leg. "Bin layin' off myself to git him fur I been hearin' him gobble mornin's."

"Gobble! What ye talkin' about, man?" Lafe replied. "Don't ye know season's closed on turkeys? Thet's a leg of Ma's old Plymouth Rock rooster." He winked slyly and both men laughed boisterously.

When the last dish had been scraped bare and there was nothing but crumbs left on the cake platters, the crowd slowly gathered in the schoolhouse for the program.

When everyone was in the building, except a group of men who stayed outside at the open windows and the door, I called the house to order. I thanked them all for coming, and for their help in making the new building possible and told them how much I appreciated being one of them. Then the program began.

Shouts of laughter and the applause after each performance told how much they all enjoyed it. When the program ended I asked if anyone had anything to say. It would have been a grave error to have omitted this closing-day courtesy to the patrons. In the hill country one must be very sure he has a substitute that will meet with ready approval before he deviates in the slightest from the usual way of doing things. I wasn't taking any chances.

Lige Gurney arose and began speaking: "My young'uns air measurin' corn cribs, water trofts and sorgum pans. They kin figger out to a gnat's heel what they'll hold," Lige said. "Then, by gravy, them young'uns of mine kin tell jist how high a big barrel-stave tree is by measurin' the shadder. Learned how to cure roup in chickens a puttin' thet purple stuff in the drinkin' water and we'uns agittin' more eggs than ever. Thet's the kind of learnin' young'uns air needin'."

It was Ernestine Tucker who arose next. "I'd lak to say a few words," she began. "We'uns all want Brother Howard ter know how much we'uns appreciate this here schoolhouse he put up fer us. We'uns hain't got much ter give, but the folks want ter give him something. Us women in Mulberry has made him a quilt." She stepped to the front seat, picked up a pillow case and shook a quilt out of it. She untied the string that bound it into a roll and held it up for inspection.

"Hit's a friendship quilt," Ernestine continued. "Got over a hundred names on it. Brother Howard, we'uns all wants to give this here ter you 'cause we'uns all loves you," she said turning to me.

I was overcome with feeling for I knew Ozark hill folk do not give gifts to anyone unless they are in full accord with the acts of the recipient. There were tears in my eyes as I managed a husky, "Thank you, everyone."

"Before we go I jist wants to give hit out we'uns havin' meetin' here Sunday and Brother Howard's preachin' for us. Come to church all of you'uns," Mrs. Tucker added.

Brother Bybee from over on Stark's Creek dismissed us with a prayer. The "amen" of that prayer ended my first year's teaching and nine months of mission work in the Ozark backhills.

CHAPTER 21

Mission to the Hills

FOR FIVE WEEKS AFTER SCHOOL WAS OUT I WORKED with Bob in the woods. A newcomer had purchased a large tract of land which he expected to use for a cattle ranch and Bob and I had taken a contract to clear it for him. We cut saw timber at fifteen cents per hundred board feet, and by working diligently from sunup 'til sunset preparing the great oak trees for the sawmill, we averaged about three dollars a day, which was big wages in the Ozarks in 1933.

During the first few days my body protested painfully and my muscles were sore and tired; but we kept at it and soon the muscles hardened and I could pull the long crosscut saw hour after hour with anyone. As my muscles became hardened, my breathing easier, I ate and slept better than I had for years.

During the long days in the woods I planned sermons, mentally outlining and phrasing them to the rhythm of the saw. This habit has carried through the years of my mission work in the Ozarks and many a sermon has been born in my mind as I walked all day. The practice has, too, relieved the tedium of walking mile after mile, keeping mind busy and oblivious of body.

Of course, I continued to preach and conduct other religious services. Every Wednesday at four o'clock in the afternoon we put our double-bitted axes over our shoulders and walked home to do the chores and eat an early supper so that I could walk to Owsley School for the young people's meeting. Those who had been attending

merely because it was a place where young people congregated had dropped out after John Wesley's funeral.
Now there were about forty in regular attendance, but
they were zealously studying each chapter of the New
Testament.

I preached somewhere within walking distance of my
boarding place every Sunday. Sunday services in the hills
were generally preceded by preaching on Saturday night.
If a play party or hill dance had been planned the young
people frequently first came to church in a group and
then returned to their fun after services.

Many pioneer games were a part of a Saturday night's
fun. It was quite a sight to see the young people out of
doors when the moon was full, exuberantly going through
such figures as "Buffalo Gal," "Captain Jinks," "Skip-
come-a-Lou" and "Swing Josie" to their own singing
and clapping and music made by a hill fiddler. Sometimes
the fiddler was accompanied by one or more "git'tar"
players.

I frequently attended the play parties with some of
the parents. After the games the older folks usually retired
to a cabin and sang old-time songs, visited and had a
general good time until eleven o'clock when sandwiches,
hot coffee, thick pie and cake or gingerbread were served.
Everyone planned to be home before twelve.

"Hit'd be plumb shameful to be out partyin' so late hit
tuck part of the Lord's Day," Vernie Plummer said on
one occasion as he rounded up his brood. Vernie's children were not old enough to be "sparkin'" so they came
to the frolic with their parents and returned home in the
same company.

We neared the end of our work in the timber. Life had
settled into a pattern of peace and contentment, for I had
faith that I would be able to find work for the rest of the
summer and the school board had asked me to teach Mul=
berry School again when fall came. Committees were

working unremittingly and with considerable success on the liquor problem and the Saxons seemed to have been cowed. I received no more threats and heard that George Saxon had gone to Springfield in search of work.

Then as a river that is flowing quietly and smoothly suddenly becomes turbulent or must alter its course, so suddenly did the current of my life seem to alter once again. Bob was recalled to his railroad job.

I rejoiced for Bob, for he and Ethel were of the best and it had grieved me to see them so near poverty. But for me it was a discouraging reverse and I could not conceal the fact. I could shift for myself without a worry but what should I do with Clayton? Typically, that was Bob and Ethel's first concern, too, and Ethel didn't rest until she had made arrangements for a new and desirable home for the boy.

I was not well acquainted with the Bybee family but the recommendation of the Normans as to the character of Dewey and his wife, Anna, was sufficient. Theirs was a large and productive river-bottom farm where Stark's Creek wound its way in a great U-bend through much level, productive land. The valley floor in the bend of the creek was all good plow land with more than sixty acres in the field.

The Bybee home was a four-room frame house that stood on the brow of a long gentle slope south of Stark's Creek. A screened porch extended completely across the north side of the dwelling.

There were three Bybee children—two girls and a boy. (The boy was several years younger than Clayton but after a few months' association the two became real pals.) It was a family of industrious, quiet, honest folk.

The Bybees raised large flocks of chickens, ducks and turkeys. Their livestock consisted of two span of good mules, a dozen milk cows and several brood sows. The cattle and hogs had the range of an entire half-section excepting for the cultivated fields which were fenced in with rails.

Dewey Bybee was a great hand to fatten hogs. When the butchering hogs were almost ready for "hog killin'" he enclosed them in a rail pen from four to six weeks and fed them entirely on corn, milk and water. "Akern-fed meat, onless hit's finished off on corn, air flabby and don't have the solid fiber of corn-fed animals," he explained. "Hogs fattened up on akerns and finished with corn makes the finest eatin' meat there is."

I had not planned on accepting any of the money Bob and I had earned in the timber for I felt I owed more than I could ever pay for the wonderful way in which the Normans had taken care of Clayton and befriended me. But Bob and Ethel wouldn't have it that way. They insisted on giving me my full share. We finally compromised on twenty-five dollars, which allowed me to give Mrs. Bybee fifteen dollars to be used for buying some clothing for Clayton. Seven of the remaining ten dollars went to replenish my own badly depleted wardrobe with a new pair of shoes, white duck pants and a cheap white cotton shirt. I never wore a hat—have never worn one—so I saved on that item. It was my plan to get along each day as best I could with what old clothes I had and always save the newer garments for appearances before audiences.

I shared Clayton's first day at his new home, where Mrs. Bybee fixed him a comfortable bed on the porch overlooking tree-bordered Stark's Creek. "We'uns'll take just as good care of him as if he war one of our own," she told me and I felt convinced that this was true.

Early next morning, with a few personal necessities packed in the old suitcase, I once more took leave of Clayton. There was much less regret and a much greater sense of security in this leavetaking compared to the one in Iowa a year before. Although I may have known a little more about where I was going when I left Iowa, I was surer of my purpose now and Clayton was healthier and happier.

I walked to Cross Timbers and started down the long paved highway to Springfield, sixty miles away. Again, after almost a year in the hills, I was on the road walking, I knew not where. Not aimlessly walking, it is true, but with no more definite destination than to explore the "Shepherd of the Hills" country, my original mecca, where I expected to find many communities without regular religious services.

I had walked a considerable distance when a man driving a Packard coupé pulled up beside me. He brought the car to a quick stop, flung open the door and practically growled out his, "Want a ride?"

"Thank you," I replied. I stepped quickly into the car before he could change his mind. "It was mighty good of you to give me a lift," I added, smiling. I hoped the smile would be infectious, but it wasn't.

"Damned if I know why I picked you up," he continued to growl. "All you hitchhikers ought to be in jail."

I just grinned again but didn't say anything.

"You didn't thumb me for a ride and you weren't waiting at the edge of town," he resumed. "And you're clean. You can never tell what devilment a hitchhiker is up to these days." His voice was loud and explosive.

"Can't blame motorists in the least for passing up hikers on the highways," I agreed. "I guess there are some pedestrians on the road waiting to be picked up so that they may rob their benefactors. Maybe you're right—we all should be in jail.

"However, before you pass judgment on me, may I say that once I had a car almost as good as yours? I had a farm and a winter job, teaching school. But I gave up trying to make money to come into the hills, walking into the poorest communities to preach in abandoned churches,

organize Sunday schools, young people's societies, to serve
God by serving the 'least of these.' Often I don't make
five dollars a month, but I live with the hill people among
whom I work, so I don't need much money. You're probably right, though, a man who gives up a chance to make
money these days ought to be in jail." I spoke calmly
and ended with a shrug of the shoulders. Maybe I tem-
porarily half-believed it myself.

We drove along in silence for at least five miles. Then
the man turned to me and extended his right hand. "Put
'er there, Gunga Din," he said with a friendly smile.

"Thank you," I said grasping his extended hand, and at
that moment a lasting friendship was born. Dal Swiers
told me of himself, his family and his work and asked
many questions concerning myself and what I hoped to
accomplish in my work. And as we talked, time passed
rapidly and we were soon in Springfield.

"This is as far as I go," my benefactor said, "but how
about you doing me an honor and having a bite of lunch
with me?"

He parked his car before the Kentwood Arms, Springfield's smartest hotel.

"Thank you," I answered. "I'm sure the honor and
pleasure would be mine."

We luxuriated for two hours in the hotel's dining
room. Here's the prince and the pauper, I thought whim-
sically over my coffee as we sat there; and then I wondered, which one of us is the real pauper? I'm rich!

I did enjoy to the fullest the fine food, the attentive
service, the soft music and the association with this well-
educated man. This was a part of the world I had left
behind me and had not re-entered for more than a year.
I was grateful for this brief respite, though I felt no
hungering desire for it to be more than that.

When we left the hotel and shook hands to say good-
bye, my friend left a ten-dollar bill in my palm. "Use it,

parson, to buy Sunday school supplies for one of the many abandoned churches you'll find in the hills south of here." He laughed: "And tell them it's from an old hardware salesman who isn't as bad as he sounds."

Through the years of doing mission work with its trials, hardships and dark days, the pleasant memory and friendship of Dal has given me many a lift. Many times when I trudged wearily along the hill roads he has picked me up with his pleasant invitation. "Hop in, parson, for a lift, a visit and a dinner with old Dal."

"After all, Brother Howard," he'd say, "I'm just like the hillbillies you preach for. Iffen they's arything we'uns kin do to he'p ye, be right proud to do hit. I am proud to give aid to a man like you, parson."

That friendship has taught me that no matter how burdened a man may be with the cares and tension of the modern business world he usually has the potential spirit of the Master in his soul. It may be buried deep among other cares of his life but he longs to serve God by serving those less fortunate than himself. I often hear it called a "heart of gold," but to me it appears as the Christ Love blossoming into applied Christianity.

Ruminating upon the goodness of the food I had just had I window-shopped for an hour or so in downtown Springfield, enjoying the displays of colorful, up-to-the-minute merchandise. Then I boarded a streetcar and rode to the end of the south run and walked the remaining four miles to the truck farm where Albert worked, hoping to have a little visit with him before I went farther southward.

CHAPTER 22

Shepherd of the Hills Country

B EYOND WHERE THE BLACK OF THE HIGHWAY SWERVES sharply to the west and follows the contours of the hilltop fold the rolling hills of Taney County without so much as a guardrail to mar the vista.

So this was my promised land—the "Shepherd of the Hills" country!

I moved forward to the grassy highway shoulder, to the brink of the scene, and gazed in awe at the undulating waves of hills that spread about me. I was scarcely conscious of the steady stream of cars that whizzed back of me in a haste that denied their occupants a leisurely appraisal of the magnificent sight.

Colorations of mingling hardwoods and cedars varied from wave to wave with brown bald knobs, where the prairie grass cured in the sun, making tiny islands in the sea of hills. What the region lacked in grandeur of height it more than made up for in the three-hundred-and-sixty-degree expanse of countryside. Where the sun shone full upon the scene masses of color took on greens and browns, but where the shadows began to flow up the deep valleys the hills took the cast of faded blue overalls that have been too frequently washed in hard water and lye soap.

Albert would have liked this, too, I reflected. He'd remarked on his love for the Ozark country last night as we lay in bed talking until the roosters started their three-o'clock bragging. I had slept late, resuming my journey southward so long after sun-up that it was well past noon when I walked through Nixa and started the trek over the "thank-you-ma'ms" that make of the farm-to-market highway between Nixa and Highlandville a veritable roller-coaster—if one is riding something more than shanks' mare.

Opportunities for rides had been few on that road, and while there was much traffic on U. S. Highway No. 65 beyond Highlandville the drivers were in much too great a hurry to stop for a hiker. I walked much of the road and as I stood on that hilltop I felt myself lucky, indeed, to have walked into such a scene.

Here was where Harold Bell Wright had lived and written the books that brough him fame and brought tourists to the hills. Here it was that Brian Kent had found himself; that Young Matt and Sammy Lane had walked the trail nobody knows how old; here the Bald Knobbers had made their grisly rides; Preachin' Bill had philosophized and Uncle Ike had held forth at the Forks.

I drank deep of the scene, inhaled the sweet summer air and was refreshed for the walk toward Branson.

I crossed Roark Creek in late afternoon and paused at Branson long enough to get a light supper. Then I hiked on across the Lake Taneycomo bridge and walked through Hollister where I admired the picturesque village's Queen Anne architecture.

Outside the village I saw a great institution surrounded by a beautiful farm on which scores of sleek dairy cattle grazed in front of a background of white stone buildings and rolling hills. At a highway filling station I learned that this was the School of the Ozarks, an institution maintained for Ozark boys and girls who, without its assistance, would not be able to achieve a high-school education. Its pupils, the filling station attendant told me, were taught agriculture, home economics and basic business office practices. All were required to work in the school shops or upon its farm lands in exchange for the schooling they received.

From the station attendant I learned also that I was about twelve miles from the Arkansas line. The sun would not set for two hours or more and there would be a long twilight. I was curious about the rugged country along the border for I had heard so much about it, so I put Point Lookout behind me and headed southward.

I stopped for a drink of cold water at Kohler's Station.

"Going south?" a truck driver asked me as he tested the air pressure of his truck tires.

"Yes, I am. May I ride with you?"

"Sure, put your stuff in the back and git in the cab. I'm about ready to take off. Better always grab a ride before you git into Arkansaw. The patrol picks up hitchhikers there." I rode with this trucker as far as Harrison, Arkansas.

The electric lights on the Seville Hotel were blinking their call to tourists by the time I reached Harrison, but my meager purse would not let me consider the luxury of a Simmons mattress. I wandered about the business district until most of the townspeople had gone home. When I started to sleep on a bench in the courthouse yard I was roughly awakened by the night watch. We moved to the spot of light from a white way post and I showed him several letters of introduction which convinced him that I was not a vagrant.

"You seem to be all right," the night watch said and then we sat down and talked for some time.

"I'm just batchin'—wife's dead and my boy's in the navy. I sleep days, so you can use my bed and get a little rest tonight."

We shuffled down the street as I thanked the man for his generosity.

"Here she is," he said as we stopped at an old brick residence. We climbed the dark outside stairway. "Come in and make yourself to home," he said as he unlocked the door and turned on the light. "This here's an oil stove; there's bacon, eggs, bread, butter, coffee and cream in the cupboard. If you ain't had any supper just fix what you want! You can sleep in my bed 'til I come in tomorrow morning." He turned to leave, "Brother Howard, I got to git back on duty." He left the apartment and went back to his round of door shaking.

One's spirit is always lifted above the gloom by some new friend who lightens the darkest hour with the touch of kindness and service. My new policeman friend could never know how much his kindness in sharing his bed and food with me had cleared my sky of the dark clouds of discouragement.

"Hain't no man ever licked 'til he quits, then he's licked for good," the watchman advised me in his deep firm voice when he came in next morning. "You've got the biggest job in the world, Brother Howard, and I'm nothing but a big flatfoot but I'll be prayin' fer you."

I left his one-room abode refreshed by a night's rest, my stomach filled with his bacon and eggs and his benediction ringing in my ears. I retraced my route northward toward the Missouri-Arkansas line. I had satisfied my curiosity about northern Arkansas and decided to return to the "Shepherd of the Hills" country.

Whenever I am traveling through a part of the hills with which I am unacquainted, I make frequent stops at homes to ask for a drink. As I tarry I ask about religious services, Sunday schools and churches, explaining that I am a missionary preacher. The hill folks invariably ask, "What church do ye hold to?" but I avoid answering that question by explaining that I work in any church where no regular services are held.

I was not paid by any church or mission group, nor did I ask for any offering. My entire purpose, I always explained, was to serve God by serving His people. People were usually quite curious about my lack of church affiliation and lack of interest in the collection and I believe that because of this I was invited to preach where I would have otherwise been denied an audience. In a few communities with a reputation for being hard or tough I have been gratified with the response to God's word.

All this day long I repeatedly received the answer that "preachin' air bein' held to our church." The evening sun was beginning to glow red with the dust of Kansas when I stopped at a neat house on the old Springfield-Harrison road. It was surrounded by a new picket fence, and the clean lawn, the tidy lots adjoining the barn, the lush fields; and a well-kept nursery bespoke industry, prosperity and pride in caring for a farm home.

The owner, a Mr. James, and his wife were Yankees—New Yorkers who had come to the Ozarks by way of Kansas. Their sons were graduates of the School of the Ozarks which I had passed the day before.

"Yes," Mr. James informed me, "we maintain regular church services—after a fashion. A small group of us started Sunday school at Lone Oak about a year ago and have managed to keep going. Frequently some illiterate, roving preacher comes through and stays a few nights preaching hell-fire and brimstone.

"It's the typical emotional, noisy type of preaching usually heard here," he said. "Such a man is coming to-night. If you'd like to stay with us we'll all go to the service and hear him."

"I'd like to," I replied.

"It may be this man will stay only one night," my host continued. "He came to the church at the invitation of the Paytons, whose reputation is none too good." Mr. James busied himself with milking preparations. "Maybe you could stay and preach for us," he resumed. "We seldom hear good preaching since we don't get up to the School of the Ozarks very often."

"Thank you for your confidence," I replied, "but I might be a poorer preacher than any of them."

"Well, at least you seem to have more education than the average preacher we hear around here," Mrs. James interrupted. "We'll have to take a chance," she grinned.

I helped my host milk his twelve Jersey cows. The chores done and supper finished, we were on our way to the services.

When we arrived at Lone Oak country church, Mr. James introduced me to John Payton, who in turn introduced me to the preacher. "He's kin to us," Payton explained in a manner that I interpreted as being meant to impress me.

Services began with singing which continued until it evolved into a frenzied praying and testifying. The preacher led the emotional orgy. The believers stomped on the floor, cried, laughed, screamed, danced and jabbered in a wild jargon of "tongues."

"Got the ol' devil on the run," the preacher shouted. "He hain't no bigger hereabouts then a seed tick! Glory to God! Hallelujah!"

A lank mountaineer on the front row arose and began worming his way through the crowded aisles toward the rear of the building. Mr. James leaned close to me and whispered, "That's Gump Latson. Gump's a grown man but he's never developed mentally. Isn't all there. Good feller, but just no sense."

The preacher, angered that this poor man was causing a break in the tempo of his service, stopped and snorted, "Well, if arybody else's got kidney trouble we'uns'll have a little recess."

Gump stopped, looked around and grinned his silly way until his mouth almost severed his head from his neck. "Yo're wrong, Brother," he laughed. "Hain't my kidneys—hit's my bowels. Reckon I et too much last year's 'lasses."

When the tumult had subsided, the preacher opened his Bible and read from the second chapter of St. Luke.

His pronunciation was faulty to the point of being ridiculous. When he came to the place in the story that tells of wrapping the babe in swaddling clothes, he read it, "and wropped the babe in saddlin' clothes." Finally he closed his Bible and looked around.

"Brethren," he said, "I come here tonight expectin' ter preach but I finds a strange feller here thet says as how he air a preacher, an' brethren, I shore aims ter find out!" He turned to me with a leer. "Brother, you do the preachin'," he challenged and sat down beside John Payton.

I arose without a word of remonstrance; but if I ever silently prayed for divine guidance, it was in the few seconds it took me to walk to the front of the church.

"Let us bow our heads in prayer," I began. As I prayed it came to me that there seemed an almost sinister implication in the preacher's "Brethren, I shore aims ter find out." I remembered that I was in a country whose citizens had a reputation for being suspicious of every stranger lest they be taken off guard by a federal agent.

I took as my text the words from James 4:14, "For what is your life? It is even a vapour, that appeareth for a little time, and then vanisheth away."

I talked on Christian service and explained that to use one's life best was to serve others in works as well as in words. . . . Nothing is to be gained by fighting the sinner. . . . Love him and his soul even if we do not love his ways. I illustrated with my story about Zeb Frasier, the bootlegger against whom I had refused to testify. I related how he was found guilty and how I asked for him to be paroled to me—not because I loved his ways, I emphasized, but because I loved his soul.

This story had a magical effect on the greater number of my hearers for I could notice at once looks of pleased surprise and general relaxation. From that point on, the congregation followed the sermon with interest.

I finished, thanking the other minister for being so considerate of a stranger, and asked him to pronounce the benediction.

Church services in the hills offer social diversion as well as spiritual enlightenment to the hill folk; so, as is the usual custom after the benediction, the people gathered in little groups and visited. Folks seemed friendly but noncommittal.

Silently we walked the two and a half miles from the church to the James home. I felt uncomfortable. Had I done the wrong thing? We entered the house and Mrs. James disappeared into the kitchen to fix us a snack.

"Preacher, you'll do," James laughed as we sat down. I looked up, startled but relieved. "I felt sorry for you, the way the other fellow put you on the spot, but you did yourself proud. You certainly told the Paytons, in the nicest way I ever heard, that you aren't here to check up on their liquor making. It was funny to me, for I realized that you knew why they put you on the spot. But your sermon set things right. This community is notorious for its stills. I believe if you'll consent to come back at a future date and hold a revival meeting at Lone Oak, you could do much good. I suggest a future date instead of now because the booze element will have time to think things over. When no federal raids on their stills follow your appearance tonight, you'll be in a better position to do something."

"I sure would like to hold a meeting here," I admitted.

"Write us when you can come," he continued, "and we'll see that the meeting is widely announced and you can be sure of large crowds."

I thanked him for his advice and made my plans to be on the move again next day. We made a nightcap of the huckleberry pie and coffee which Mrs. James set before us.

The next day was one of the warmest I have ever experienced in the Ozarks. I trudged a pine-timbered trail fourteen miles through the Gobbler's Knob country to Kirbyville. Once I took a wrong fork of the road and soon came to a dead end. At its terminus was a newly built cabin that was guarded by a barking dog.

The young man and woman who appeared in the door to see what had aroused the dog were very friendly and invited me in to rest and eat lunch with them. We chatted amiably throughout the meal. After we got up from the table I opened my bag and got a Bible which I gave to them. I remarked upon the beautiful timber land around us.

"We're hired here to watch timber for some speckelators," the man said as he referred to the owners of the great tract of virgin pine thereabouts.

I was thinking that I must get on the road again when a tall, slender, weather-aged man appeared in the doorway. He was carrying a rifle in the crook of his right arm.

"Jist thought I'd mosey over and see if ye war in any notion gettin' a mess o' squirrels," he said to the younger man. He watched me in a cool, calculating way.

"Ah've got company now," the young man said.

"Oh, don't let me hinder you," I interrupted. "I must get on toward Kirbyville anyway."

"I saw you got a pitcher machine in your suitcase," the wife said. "We hain't never had ary pitchers tuck of our baby." She stroked the hair of the pretty three-year-old girl who sat on her lap.

"I'd be glad to take one for you."

In a few minutes the little girl was ready and I got a picture of her and the beaming father and mother standing in front of their new cabin.

I placed the camera back in the bag, then turned and asked the hunter if he was going in the direction of the road leading to Kirbyville. "I seemed to have lost my way," I explained.

"Yep, reckon I kin hunt thetaway well as ary. Be right proud to show ye the way," he answered.

While I was afraid of the man (for he surely wasn't hunting squirrels on such a hot day as this one) I tried not to show any fear. I closed my bag and started off with him.

Evidently he was convinced in his own mind that I was telling the truth and that I was not a federal agent for he became very friendly and quite conversational. Our talk finally got around to liquor making, however, and I repeated the account of Zeb and his parole to me. My guide showed uncommon interest in the story. Then, without warning, he told me that his family had made liquor for years. I was astonished for he was the only Ozark hillman who confided in me at our first meeting.

"Jist fer our own drinkin'," he insisted. "Hit's plumb good likker. Won't hurt a body if they uses ary horse sense 'bout drinkin'. Law, hit hain't my fault iffen folks makes a hog outen theyselves."

"But drinking makes people do things they wouldn't do if they were sober," I reminded him. "You said you had four boys. If you make the stuff they're sure to drink and make and sell it, too."

"Brother," he replied, "reckon thet's right. My oldest boy, Buck, he's in the pen at Jeff City now. They's right nice to him up thar, though. Feller writ a letter fer him to mail home a spell back. Steve said hit war a nice place. All the fellers thar wears shoes summer an' winter and Buck said they et Sunday bread ever' day. They ketched him to the still and 'course he wouldn't give hit away. Hit war mine, too."

We parted company at Highway 80.

I walked west in the heat for half an hour, finally being overtaken by two men in a pick-up truck. They invited me to ride if I could bump along in the small truck and I climbed in for an answer.

They drove as if the devil was behind them and I held to the low sides of the truck as best I could. The road was rough and winding. Finally we rounded one unusually sharp turn; the car wheels struck a rut with a terrific impact and I was thrown clear of the truck, alighting on my back and shoulders.

Everything went black.

When I came to I was lying in the truck where the men had put me and was being driven toward Branson and a doctor. The doctor told me that I had suffered three broken ribs. "You need to go to a hospital for a few weeks," he said.

"But I can't," I replied. "I haven't any money to pay for hospital care."

"There's a government work camp where they are building an airport about four miles from here on Dewey Bald," the doctor said. "Transient Camp, they call it. They've got a kind of hospital with a young doctor in charge. It won't cost you anything to stay there as it's one of the government relief agencies. I've been called there a few times to administer anesthesia and I know it is all right."

"I'd better get started, then," I said, as the pain in my side reminded me of my broken ribs.

"I'll take you out in my car," the doctor volunteered.

Dr. Davis at the transient camp was a skilled young man and he soon had my ribs set and taped in place. Then for two weeks I had fine care in the screened luxury of a tent that bore the label "Hospital."

CHAPTER 23

Government Refuge

MY STAY IN THE TRANSIENT CAMP AS A NON-PAYING guest of the United States government was a pleasant and interesting experience, notwithstanding the broken ribs. Dr. Davis gave me the best of care and the food was wholesome and well cooked, if plain. The two hundred forty men of the camp afforded an interesting study in human nature.

Most of them were from the ranks of boomer transient labor. They were men who had followed booms in industry, men who had been on the move, always looking for greener pastures. There were oil drillers from Oklahoma, lumberjacks from the far northwest, cowhands from the plains and skilled craftsmen from almost every branch of industry. One out of five had fought in World War I; a few were veterans of the Spanish-American conflict. Without exception they were men with no local citizenship, though they were citizens of the United States.

These men had never remained in any community long enough to establish legal residence; therefore they were denied all federal, state or local relief except for the transient camps and the "Sallys," as they called the Salvation Army Shelters. They were men who had known intermittent seasons of prosperity and days of hunger. Most of them were too proud to seek the bread lines and soup kitchens of the depression era.

When Dr. Davis discharged me from his care, Leon Shapell, camp superintendent, called me into his office.

"Rev. Howard," he said, "we need you in this camp. Would you be interested in staying with us and doing some social work?" Such an offer as this came as a complete surprise and there were many questions I had to ask.

I insisted that I might not be qualified for the responsibility but Mr. Shapell said that he often did things on "hunch" and that my experiences as a teacher and a preacher should have given me much preparation.

"I know of no better place for studying the human being and his social problems than in those two professions," he said.

Mr. Shapell and an assistant, Dr. Davis, had been doing the best they could with the social work in addition to their regular duties, but for some time they had realized that it was a separate job. Each man must be checked in and checked out; often clothing must be issued; case histories were taken and recorded and checked. There, it seemed to me, was the big job and the one requiring the most time and patience—to talk to these men and ferret out their real stories, their real needs, some of which they themselves were not conscious of.

The educational differences of these men were surprising: Some could neither read nor write, most of them had a very meager education, but a few were university graduates. Many had criminal records. Rehabilitation was the goal.

"If you desire to do mission work, here is a great opportunity," the superintendent concluded. "The salary is good, and camp maintenance goes with it. Your nights will be your own and you'll find plenty of places within walking distance where you can preach if you want to."

I wasn't prepared to answer the superintendent immediately for I had come to the Ozarks to do missionary work among the simple hill folk—not among worldly transients.

"Thank you, Mr. Shapell," I replied. "I'd like a few days to think this over. I will go to see my two sons and talk it over with them. I'll return on Monday and give you my answer."

"That's quite satisfactory," he countered, "for we shouldn't want you to take the position unless you're sure you'd like it and would stay with us."

"I had expected to return to my school in Hickory County by the first of September," I went on. "However, my oldest son now has a certificate to teach and I could ask the school board to let him substitute for me."

"It seems to me they owe that much to you," the superintendent said. "Didn't you tell me when I was recording your case history that you rebuilt the schoolhouse for them?"

I rode into Branson on the supply truck and started walking to Springfield. A traveling man stopped and gave me a ride all the way to the Queen City. Then I walked out to the truck farm where Albert worked.

Albert was happy at the idea of teaching school and thought he might like that even better than the C.C.C.

His employer suggested that Albert remain on the job while I went on to Hickory County and laid my plan before the school board.

"The board will be sure to accept your recommendation," he insisted, "and since Albert has been there, they'll know the type of young man he is, so nothing would be gained by his going now, and I really need him here."

I left at once and was very fortunate in getting rides, arriving at Cross Timbers just before dark. I spent the night there with my friends the Kuglers and reached Mulberry about ten o'clock the following day. I lost no time in seeing the members of the school board. They agreed to accept my resignation in favor of Albert and also to issue him a contract as soon as his certificate to teach was recorded with Elzie Miller, county superintendent, and filed with the board.

I spent the night with the Hillcrofts and went to Bybees' the next day. Clayton was in fine spirits and showed continued improvement. "He works in the field almost every day," Dewey Bybee informed me with pride, "and he's a plumb good hand, too." Clayton readily agreed to the change in my plans and joyfully anticipated having Albert's companionship the next fall and winter.

Next morning I walked to Hermitage to record Albert's certificate.

Superintendent Miller welcomed me cordially. He started to open a file on his desk as he said, "I've got a surprise for you."

"Good or bad?" I asked.

"It'd look good to me," he said as he took an envelope from his file and opened it. He removed a blue slip from the envelope and handed it to me. "Think you can use it?"

I looked at it in surprise for it was a warrant for seventy-six dollars. "How'd this happen?" I asked.

"Some folks call it a bonus but it's really just the rest of the salary due you," Superintendent Miller said. "Here in Missouri the fund remaining in the teachers' fund after a school year is ended must revert to the state or be paid to the teacher." He grinned. "I never heard of anyone turning any money back."

No one could have been more pleasantly surprised than I was. What a fortune it seemed to be! I took care of Albert's business and then hurried to the county seat bank where I bought seventy-five dollars' worth of travelers' checks. Ross Coon, the cashier, would not let me pay him the customary fee for issuing the checks. "No, Brother Howard, your service to Mulberry is worth far more to this bank than the fee for these checks, and we are only happy to show a little appreciation." He even provided a ride to Springfield.

I bought Clayton a fine .22-caliber rifle, a pair of high laced boots, a shirt and a pair of whipcord boot pants. These were delivered by a neighbor, and a fire glowed warmly within me as I reflected upon the moment when he would open the surprise package. I knew just how much his boyish heart longed to possess these things. It was reason enough for me to offer prayers of thanks to our Father for the money I had received that morning and for the wonderful sunshine that seemed flooding the lives of myself and my boys. It has been my experience in life that always, when the skies are overcast, when trials are heavy and we feel we have almost reached the end of the road, somehow, without effort or anticipation by us, something happens to relieve the situation. I know this is God's mercy and loving parenthood.

From Springfield I reported by phone to Albert, then started walking once more down the highway toward Branson. It was late at night when I quit the road for a bed in a small tourist cabin near there, for rides had been few and short. I spent a little time in town the next morning and it was dinnertime when I walked into camp. Mr. Shapell gave me a hearty welcome.

During the first four days in camp I was an interested spectator, following Dr. Davis on his rounds of social service work, studying my job. By Friday morning I was ready to go to work.

Our camp was made up of two long rows of tent-houses which faced a common street. The houses were floored, and sided with lumber up to a height of four feet; from the top of this low siding they were screened to the eaves. Each tent held two rows of bunks and each bunk had an upper and lower berth. The bunks were furnished with sheets, a pillow and sufficient blankets to keep one warm. Eight men called one of these tents "home."

Fifty yards below this tent city, near the banks of a small spring branch, the combination mess hall, kitchen and commissary wafted its odors to the treetops. This building was also used as a recreation hall. After the day's work was done and the dining hall cleared up following the evening meal, the men sat around the tables talking, reading, playing games or gambling. Many played poker—for stakes that were never large since the men received only one dollar a week unless they were foremen or assistants. Assistant foremen were regular bankers with their two dollars a week and a foreman was considered a capitalist with his three dollars weekly.

A living Ozark spring ten inches wide and a foot deep brought us water that was cold as ice. Our cooling plant for the storage of meats and perishable foods was an improvised icebox ten feet wide and twelve feet long that straddled the spring branch.

A rude bathhouse had been made a few yards below the dining room where the stream had been dammed to make a pool four feet deep. Bathtubs were the circular galvanized kind used by housewives on washday, and bathers had to carry and empty their own bath water. Many of the men took a bath every evening, and during the sultry summer months the bathhouse was a busy place throughout its forty by twenty feet. Along one wall was a bench three feet high where washpans, soap and small mirrors were conveniently placed. A barber held forth with a charge of five cents for a shave and a dime for a haircut.

Each man's medical report was attached to his case history and I learned that an average of ten per cent of the men had syphilis. A few were infected with gonorrhea and five per cent were tubercular. Those in an infectious stage were quarantined and treated. Most of the men, however, were quite healthy.

The average age of the men was fifty-two years. We divided them into two groups; laborers and skilled craftsmen. The common laborers had attained an average fifth-grade education; the average for the much smaller skilled-labor group was slightly above thirty-five semester hours of college work.

Frequently an entire transient family applied at the camp for relief. They usually were traveling in a covered wagon or jalopy, seeking a place where cheap land and fuel might be found. Food, gas and oil or a night's lodging was usually the extent of the relief they sought, but one family lived in a tent and were cared for a year until they became citizens of the county. Their case was then automatically transferred to the local agencies.

When two women applied for transient relief at the local relief agency in Branson I was called into town to interview them. Thelma had sunk into some of the pitfalls of a modern age. She had married when she was twenty a widowed husband twelve years her senior. Both she and her husband were well educated. He was a high-school superintendent with a very adequate salary. Their home was modern and the wife had too much leisure time. This, coupled with the difference in age and the husband's long daily absences, led to disaster. She met a glamour boy at a bridge club. Soon she was seeing him every day.

"I loved him," she sobbed to me. "I believed him when he said, 'I've traveled all over the world and have never loved anyone until I met you, my dream girl, and you're married. I can't believe it, for you belong to me.'

"I ran off with him. He deserted me in Kansas City, and now I've got to find a place where I can be cared for until I have his child."

She told me that she had written her husband but he bitterly replied that he would not take her back or help her under any condition. She became a ward of the government.

The other girl was a pretty twenty-year-old Ozark daughter. She had married against her father's wishes a young Ozarker with a dark background. A few weeks after their marriage her husband was convicted of a bank robbery and sentenced to forty years in the penitentiary. The girl had gone home and confessed her mistake and asked her parents if she might return home and make the best of the unfortunate affair. Despite her mother's pleading the father had been stern and unforgiving. "Ye've made yore bed, now go lay in hit, fur ye've shamed us ferever," he said as he turned her out.

"Can't git no work atall," she told me.

"How have you been living?" I asked.

"Been sellin' myself to men what wants me," she confessed wearily. "Didn't do hit 'til I got so hungry it war that or steal. They send you to the pen like they did my man for stealin', but this other seems like hit don't make no difference."

"Where have you been living?" I asked.

"Nowheres. Just agoin' up and down the main roads; ridin' with truckers, mostly. They allers buy my eats and give me a dollar fur sleepin' with 'em. Hell of a life, mister, but what's a girl goin' to do?"

She gladly consented to go to a Salvation Army Rescue Home in St. Louis, and after a few months in a Christian atmosphere joined the Army to save others from the kind of life she had been leading.

Once a quite dignified little man came to my desk seeking relief. He expressed himself in wonderfully perfect English which stamped him indelibly as an educated man. His case history, as he gave it to me, revealed parents of English nobility. He held a Master's degree in English and mathematics from Oxford University. He was a certified public accountant.

"Tell me," I asked, "why are you here?"

"Disgrace to confess it, sir," he replied, "but wine and women have ruined me as it has ruined many another good man, though I'm not to blame for liking the taste of wine. It was always served on our table at home. I was graduated at Oxford and Father sent me to Johannesburg, South Africa, as a government accountant. My job was to collect the Crown tax on diamonds mined there. I took funds that belonged to the Crown and fled to America. Father paid up my default but the disgrace has kept me from going home to England."

"Joe," as we called him, was perhaps the most talented man I have ever known. He wrote many beautiful poems and has given me many of them for use in sermons.

One Saturday afternoon he came into my office. It was obvious that he had encountered a mountain bootlegger. "Tell me what you are preaching to the sinners tomorrow and old Joe'll write you a grand finale in verse." He was unsteady of body and loud of mouth.

"I'm taking my text from Proverbs," I replied. "'Where there is no vision the people perish.'" He turned and went out.

I hardly had time to forget that the man was gone before he reappeared with a little poem that seemed to be a lament of his own blasted talents:

> "Wearily we look upon the past,
> And memory of former years
> Bring to our eyes tears.
> But may we recall, Oh God!
> Thou hast allayed our mortal fears;
> And given us hope that clears
> The mist of skies o'ercast.
> We look into the future—
> There appears a beacon light
> That ever nears:
> The pinnacle we all must reach at last."

Sixteen-year-old "Bud" boasted that he had been on the road for four years.

"I haven't done a lick of work since I was twelve years old," he crowed. "Don't 'low to work neither," he declared defiantly. "Pa and Ma separated when I was twelve. I lit out then. Pa, he's married to 'nother woman and she won't have me around. Ma, she lives in Kansas City and I can't live with her neither so me for a hobo's life. And 'tain't so bad," he added flippantly.

I should have known that Bud's boasting was a cover for the hurt in his soul, but I was shocked at his callousness and judged too quickly. "Hard as nails," I thought. "Doesn't care for anything. He needs a good lecturing to set him to thinking." So I proceeded to remonstrate. As I finished I asked him, "Why don't you go to Kansas City? Get back into school. You can work mornings and evenings and have a home with your mother. That's where you belong. She isn't remarried, you said."

He dropped his head. When he looked up, tears were plowing furrows through the grime on his cheeks.

"Oh yeah!" he said, his voice betraying the bitterness he felt. "Ma, she's a whore and I don't never want to see her ner hear of her again." Then he broke into childish sobbing.

It was my turn now to hang my head in shame. What could I say to him? There was no word of encouragement, no hope, nothing I could offer that wandering boy to bring a ray of light to his warped and disillusioned soul. His father and mother and their broken home had had the say. I arose and placed my hand on the boy's bent shoulder. "I'm sorry, son," I apologized. "But don't let it lick you. You know, a fellow is never down until he says so himself. Come with me and let's have a bath and some clean clothes."

If people would only stop and think before they throw

their lives away. I thought, just what effect may these deeds have upon how many other lives? One may think, "It is my life and I can do as I please with it and it's no one's business if I choose to go to hell," but that's a mistaken idea, for you can go neither to heaven nor to hell without casting sunshine or shadow upon fellow travelers.

Truly, you are the "master of your fate," but you are at the same time "your brother's keeper" and you have no right to blast another's hopes or to bring disillusionment to his soul. We all have influence and our daily example is but the craftsman's hands that mold the common clay at the potter's wheel of life.

CHAPTER 24

Sycamore Log Church

ON THE FIRST SUNDAY AFTER RETURNING TO CAMP I walked across the hills to the Gretna Church. The little group of forty gathered there for Sunday school welcomed me warmly. When they learned that I had preached in Hickory County they asked me to conduct worship services for them following Sunday school. "How about you preachin' for us every Sunday morning, seein's how you're living at the camp?" a spokesman invited after services. It is always refreshing in this world where a confessed believer quickly grows cold and indifferent to spiritual needs, where pursuit of pleasures and greed for material gain overshadow the thankfulness and praise, to find people who are eager for God's word. So I agreed to return the following Sunday morning.

After dinner back at the camp I walked to the neighborhood of the abandoned Table Rock School, halfway between Branson and our camp. Some of the men in camp had told me of it. I contacted the people who owned the farm adjacent to the school ground, for the school site had originally been purchased from them and the land and improvements had reverted to them according to contract.

The building was in quite good condition; there were benches, I learned, stored in the loft under the rafters to be out of the way of the young people who had been gathering there regularly for Saturday night dancing.

I offered to rent the building for two dollars a month (to be paid in advance) and to take excellent care of the building on condition no one else was to use it without my consent. They were a little reluctant to the latter agreement, for the dancers, when they used the place, paid a little higher rent than I offered. But since much drinking and subsequent brawling seemed to occur each dance night the owners didn't quibble about renting the place for religious services.

I learned later that they had been warned by the sheriff that such public brawls as had been staged in the building would not be tolerated in the future. Evidently these were the factors which caused them to decide to lease the building for religious purposes.

On Monday evening after work two of the transients went with me and we swept the floor and cleaned the building. We lowered the benches from the loft and arranged them for church services. Then I went about inviting the various hill families of the neighborhood to church on the following Sunday night. An invitation to the transient men was posted on the bulletin board in the recreation and dining hall at the camp.

I would preach twice next Sunday—at Gretna in the morning, at Table Rock that night.

The hill folk who attended services at Gretna on the previous Sunday had done well in advertising "preachin'," as they called it, for a surprisingly large crowd greeted me there. The entire Sunday school of the now famous Sycamore Log Church started an hour early so that its members could walk the four miles to Gretna before services began at eleven o'clock. The little Gretna Church was packed, and the way that group of Ozark mountain folk sang the old hymns of their forefathers was soul-stirring.

"Come up the mountain next Sunday afternoon and preach fur us," the people of the Sycamore Log Church invited after the benediction.

"I'll be happy to come and preach at three o'clock," I answered. "My time is already taken for both the regular morning and evening services." Instead of one church now I had three!

That night at Table Rock about threescore hill people came to the services and, with the two dozen men from the camp, there was standing room only. I explained the need for services, suggested that a Sunday school be organized and told them of my desire to do all I could with no pay or offerings to be accepted. They were much pleased with the idea of regular services. "Sunday school's shore a heap better'n dancin' all night Saturday," Jess Lewallen said.

Many of the small group of men from the camp said they would come to every service. I learned from their conversation as we all walked back to our camp that night that some of them had not attended a religious service for many years.

On the day when the men were paid their weekly dollar, one profane inebriate took his hat and went to every transient in camp soliciting nickels to pay the rent on the building. "I never had no raising, just growed up in New York's East Side, but the people who have always tried to help me have been Christians, so the least I can do to show my thanks to the Christians will be to see you don't have to pay that rent yourself," he said by way of explanation of his action. Thereafter he never failed to have the rent collected and ready on the first day of each month until a pie supper was held and we raised enough money to make a payment on the building.

Just when things appeared their brightest, a letter from Albert brought an eclipse to the glow of good fortune. The Mulberry School directors hadn't given him the teaching contract as they had verbally agreed. Instead they had signed with a relative of an influential patron.

Albert would have to continue his farm work because he had passed up a call for the C.C.C. and would now have to await his turn again.

One hot day there came to our camp a young man whose bearing, language and mannerisms labeled him as an educated, cultured and experienced business man. But the ash-gray pallor of his face was the brand of a long prison term. I had to ask him about his past for completion of the camp record.

He answered frankly, "I was released from the state penitentiary a week ago. I left my native state and came here to start again. I realize how handicapped an ex-convict will be seeking employment in a highly prejudiced and competitive world. I was sent up for embezzling funds from the bank where I was cashier."

"Why did you do it?" I asked. "From your case history, I gather your people were prominent and wealthy."

"That's right," he answered. Then after a moment's reflection he added, "I drank; and when one is only slightly under the influence of drink everything looks rosy.... I started playing the market, and soon was taking money that wasn't mine. It was only a matter of time until I was caught."

I advised him to go back to his home town. "Take up life anew. It's the proper place for you. Quit your drinking and be a man."

His answer taught me a lesson that I have never forgotten. "Sounds fine," he shot back at me. "But that's the one place where I can't whip drink; it is kept in our home as well as served at every social function. Did it ever occur to you, as a minister of the Master, to be slow to criticize me or any other man? Sure, we're down and outers, ex-cons, addicted to drink or drugs, profane, soured on life. But after all, we may be working a thousand times harder to be Christians than you are, for you were born in a Christian environment and we were not.

Wasn't it the same Jesus you preach who said, 'Let him that is without sin cast the first stone'?"

From that hour on I have seen men saved from the depths by Jesus' atoning blood because to the best of my poor ability I have followed this ex-convict's advice of not criticizing my fellow man.

My introduction to the Sycamore Log Church was a red-letter day in my Christian life. This little church, built at a cost of much love, labor and eighteen dollars in money proved to be a spiritual shrine for me. It was located in a little dell surrounded by cedars that bordered a meandering mountain stream. The clear blue water sang nature's doxology as it tumbled over its rocky bed a few feet from the doorstep. The building, as the name implies, was constructed of heavy sycamore logs. The belfry across the center of the roof above the door was made of small logs. As I entered the building, my eyes were immediately focused upon a plank which bore the inscription, "I will lift up mine eyes unto the hills, from whence cometh my help." It hung on the log wall above the pulpit. The floor was of smooth, washed gravel from the mountain stream. The roof of hand-split oak staves was supported by ridgepoles which extended the length of the building. The pulpit was a three-pronged fork of a large walnut tree cut to the proper length and set upside down. Benches were all of rough oak lumber. The chaste simplicity of this woodland temple, the song of water harmonizing with the soft sighing of wind through the cedars, brought tears to my eyes. It was like the singing of an angel choir, "Peace on earth, good will to men." It must have been some similar sacred spot that inspired the psalmist to declare, "Be still, and know that I am God."

Many times since that first day at the log church, when the dark hours of discouragement have led me through my own Garden of Gethsemane, I have walked miles and miles to kneel in that rustic shrine and pray alone. An hour alone with God in the Sycamore Log Church is to my soul what sunshine and warm rains of spring are to Mother Nature's sleeping children.

Mary Elizabeth Mahnkey beautifully pictures the church in her verse:

> "They have builded a church of sycamore logs
> Down in the Ozark Hills;
> Near by the rippling water,
> Near music of whip-poor-wills.
> A sacred shrine there in the mountains,
> Where old fires of holiness glow,
> And from ridges and rocky hollows
> Come people I used to know.
> Gathering at early candle-light
> Just as we used to do,
> When we bashfully sat together,
> Young lovers, ardent and true.
> With sly jokes of the marrying parson,
> Our kind old Uncle John Spear
> Who baptized and buried and married us
> For nigh onto forty year.
> O, take me back to my Ozarks,
> To the little log church on the hill,
> To find my lost faith and courage
> And old friends who love me still."

Mission activity in the hills near the transient camp and the social service work among the transients was so much to my liking that time passed quickly. Each new week brought some unusual character to my desk for admittance to camp.

Into our camp there came one day a man who had once been a famous surgeon. But drink, drugs and general dissipation had left only an empty shell of a once skilled and useful man. I sought to have a heart-to-heart talk with him.

"Brother Howard, it's no use," he said. "There was a time in my life when I might have been a Christian, but that day is gone. Morphine is now my master. The finer things of life are not for me. All I care about now is the little pleasure the drug gives me and I know I shall die that way. Brother Howard, there is one favor I want to ask of you. Tell people everywhere you preach the story of Old Doc and his ruined life. It may save someone from my fate," he added.

He was the only person I have ever met who impressed me with the fact that he had committed the unpardonable sin. Apparently he had crossed into that abyss from which there is no return. A few weeks later "Old Doc" died from a lethal dose of morphine, and as I stood by the side of his open grave in the potter's field I told the men of the camp of Doc's request to warn others against following his example in life.

Work was completed on the airfield late in October and the government ordered us to make preparations to move the men to Camp Clark, an army camp near Nevada, a hundred miles away.

While we were awaiting final orders to move, the men built a great octagon pen of poles. The walls were six feet high and the cracks between the logs were chinked with clay. Around the entire inside of the pen crude benches were made of long oak poles. A bonfire of dry logs was kept burning in the center of the pen. The men congregated around the fire every evening and listened to the camp musicians and their violins, guitars and banjos.

"Just like home," one man said. "All some of us guys have known for years is a blanket close to the fire in some railroad jungle near the switchyards."

We finally moved to Camp Clark, where the brick barracks were comfortable and roomy quarters for the members of three local camps which were combined into one camp of five hundred men. On the first Sunday at the new camp I went to church in Nevada. As I left after services, I overheard the comment, "Oh, he's just a hobo from the bums' camp."

I soon learned that the local political boss dictated every policy of the transient camp. Corruption, graft and favoritism were substituted for the honest service given at the Branson camp. I longed for the hills, the hill folk and the opportunity to preach, so on April eighth I drew my pay and set out on Highway No. 54 to walk the seventy miles back to Cross Timbers where my Ozark missionary work had started.

CHAPTER 25

The Country Preacher

ONLY THE QUIVERY OWL WAS OUT TO GREET ME AS I walked into Cross Timbers, where I went to the home of my old friend, Alva Davis, and called out his name. He answered at once and took me in and made me comfortable for the rest of the night.

"Things around here are about as they were when you left, as far as I know," he told me next morning. "Feelings about the likker making are quieted down some at Owsley. Everybody thought the Mulberry school board used you both plenty mean not letting Albert teach as they agreed," he said. "Don't believe they'd ever had any more school out there if you hadn't rebuilt the school for them. Harmon's the one that did the dirt, I guess, but I hear the teacher for the next term paid one of the directors twenty-five dollars for hiring him. Don't it make you purty mad?"

"They did make it hard on both the boys and myself," I answered, "But I'm sure everything will work out all right in the end."

"What do you plan on doing now?" Alva questioned.

"I'll work at anything I can get to do; work for my room and board if nothing better is to be found. I'll preach wherever I can and something is sure to turn up so that the boys and I can get a little place where we can be together again. I'd hoped to get a school but there are so many more teachers than schools and it's so late it may be hard to do," I said.

"You and your boys have lots of friends around here,

Brother Howard," Alva said. "There are a few like Harmon, old Missoury and the Saxons that still hate you, but everyone knows what stripe they are, and they can't hurt you any. Honesty, truth and fair dealing are things that lies don't destroy."

I bid the Davis' good-bye and walked the seven miles to Bybees' to see Clayton. He was still improving and was becoming the picture of health—cheerful and happy. He called Anna Bybee "Ma" and she was as proud of his improvement as though he were her own son.

Albert was working on a near-by farm and I learned the two boys had been together at every opportunity. They both were dating girls frequently. Whenever young people had a play-party, Albert and Clayton were accepted as a part of the group.

"You'uns air more'n welcome to stay with us until you can rent a place and have a home of yore own," Bybee said. "I'll have out a tol'able big crop this year," he went on. "Couldn't pay you much wages fer your work but you kin eat and sleep, and I'll need a hand to help me and we'uns'll do all we can to help you."

Clayton and Albert both wanted me to stay where we three could be together more often, so I arranged to work out my board and room with the Bybees.

When Sunday came the boys and I walked to the Fairview church where Willie Penell was still preaching. As he and I had previously exchanged appointments on several occasions, he insisted on my preaching that day. But I begged to be excused, explaining that I seldom had the opportunity to hear anyone else preach. Willie was so sincere, so real, so in earnest in his preaching that he made me feel good to be back in the hills worshiping with the people I knew well and loved as my very best friends.

William Sundwall, the presiding judge of the Hickory County Court, took the boys and me home with him for dinner after church. One would never know that a depression existed anywhere to see the bounteous spread the Sundwalls set. There were thick slices of country-cured ham, light fluffy mashed potatoes, home-canned corn, peas and tomatoes, golden-brown gravy made from the ham fryings, tall full-blown brown biscuits. There were pickles, jellies and preserves, a generous vessel filled with rich, thick cream, a huge mound of yellow butter and a large pitcher of sweet milk, icy cold from the spring-house, and coffee. Then to finish the meal, providing one still had any capacity for food, we were offered gooseberry pie and molasses and raisin cake with canned Elberta peaches that floated in a rich sugary syrup.

Mrs. Sundwall was a kindly, cheerful person, and aside from her love for her husband and her pride in his accomplishments, cooking was her one compelling interest in life. She measured the success of her endeavors by the heartiness with which one ate at her table. She must have felt well pleased indeed with that meal by the way the boys and I did justice to it, yet the supply seemed inexhaustible; for when we arose from the table, it appeared as if there were almost as much left as there had been when we sat down.

We could not sit comfortably, so we passed up the living room and its rocking chairs and went outside. The judge took us to the barn lots to show us his fine cows, hogs and horses. We walked beyond the barn to view the crops. His fields of corn, alfalfa and small grains, like his livestock, reflected careful tending. He had the prosperous farmer's pride in the fruits of his labors.

Other visitors were awaiting us when we returned to the house for a refreshing drink of clear cold water from the spring. Some near neighbors had "dropped over" for a Sunday afternoon's visit.

The womenfolk went into the house to visit with Mrs. Sundwall, who had finishd "reddin' up" in the kitchen,

and we men sat around smoking and talking until someone suggested pitching a game of horseshoes. One game
went into another and another until the visiting neighbors said, "We want to go back to meetin' tonight so got
ter git on home early and do the chores."

After they had gone and the boys and I reflected that
we, too, must go, we were invited with true Ozarkian
sincerity and hospitality to spend the night with the
Sundwalls. But we didn't feel like imposing upon these
kind, generous, hospitable folk. Albert needed to get
back to his job, and Clayton and I wanted to be on hand
to help Dewey Bybee early next morning, so we declined
with regrets.

"Well, good-bye then," said the judge, extending his
hand, grasping each of our hands in turn in a warm
friendly shake. "Sure proud to have you back in the community, and I pray the Lord'll bless you. Times are bad
right now, not much work except government projects
that's all controlled by politics, but I have a few days'
work now and then and I'll shore call on you when I can
use you."

"That's very kind," I replied. "We'll appreciate any
opportunity to earn an honest dollar."

We thanked Mrs. Sundwall for the delicious meal she
had prepared for us and told her how much we enjoyed it,
and then set off down the dusty trail through the cool
summer woods for Dewey Bybee's.

None of us spoke as we walked along, Albert and I
side by side, Clayton a few steps behind whistling a low,
happy tune, as was his boyish habit.

Albert went on to his working place after supper at
Bybees', and Clayton and I retired early. We both slept
on the screened porch, and Clayton was soon lulled to
sleep by the rhythmic hum of the night noises. I had
time to reflect that life was very sweet, and to breathe a
prayer of thanks to our Heavenly Father for many bless-

ings: Clayton was strong and healthy, Albert had work and we were once more united in a community of friends.

"Let's go to Owsley," Clayton proposed on Wednesday evening soon after my return. "They're still carrying on their young people's meeting. We could start a little early, and go by for Albert. It won't be more'n a mile out of our way."

"Yes, I'd like to do that," I answered, happy at this suggestion. "It's good that my boys want to go to church with their father," I added, casting a glance in his direction. I knew Albert and Clayton were good boys, and they had both accepted Christ, but I had been separated from them so many months that I harbored a secret fear regarding the spiritual safety of my offspring. Clayton made no reply to my comment, but I knew from the grin on his face that I had no reason to worry.

We learned that the attendance at Owsley had dropped slightly since I was there ten months before. John Owen and Lela, his wife, were still the leaders and they had good helpers in the Cox's, Phegleys and Jarvis'. A new family had moved into the neighborhood. They had proved experienced leaders and good workers.

I was cordially received and accepted an invitation to return and preach on the following Sunday morning. As we walked home, Albert spoke again about applying for entrance in the Civilian Conservation Corps.

"Looks like we're having a hard time getting started here," he argued. "I think I'd like forestry work. Judge Sundwall said he'd help to get me in. He's going to Hermitage in the morning and Dad, if you don't care, I'm going along and try to get in the C.C.C."

You know that I have no objection, Sonny," I replied. "You seem so sure you'll like it. Doubtless you're right when you say there are opportunities in the C.C.C. for you and we would be better off to get a place of our own. There's an eighty-acre farm a mile and a half west of here that we could rent for fifteen dollars a year. It has a comfortable two-room cabin, a few acres of plow land, some fruit and lots of good garden ground. There is a good well on the place. We could keep a few chickens and perhaps a cow to furnish us milk and butter, so we could live comfortably. Clayton and I'll work at anything, even if the wage is low. The people around here are more than willing to help anyone who helps himself. I can preach and help them in many little ways in repayment. Then when you get out of the C.C.C. we'll have a place for you too."

Albert was in high spirits when he returned from Hermitage. "The county case worker promised to send me out to the C.C.C. in the first call," he said. "It won't be more than six weeks and it may be much sooner."

Clayton and I did everything we could to aid Dewey Bybee in getting his crops planted. My Iowa-acquired knowledge of farming was a help. I planted corn, ran a binder, stacked grain and hay. We relieved Dewey of the milking and other chores. Neighbors gave us an occasional day's work. I preached at Owsley every other Sunday and attended the young people's meeting regularly.

Efforts to get a school were fruitless.

The weather was extremely hot and dry during the entire harvest period. We cut all of Dewey's grain and then began cutting for the neighbors. His binder, one of the few in the community, was good as new and often we cut grain from early morning until midnight. We took turns shocking and running the binder. As many of the farmers worked together in the harvest, they brought a number of good horse and mule teams and allowed us to change the four-horses hitch every three or four hours. Thus we had teams that could work steadily.

Our binder did not stop except for frequent oilings which took only a few minutes' time. When dinner was called we ate in shifts so that the binder need not stop.

Many times Dewey and I worked sixteen hours without rest excepting at mealtime. But with all its labor and heat the harvest was an enjoyable event.

The binder was frequently kept running on Sunday. Naturally I disapproved of this and while I did not harangue the men for their part in the work or condemn them with a sermon, I flatly refused to work on the Lord's Day. Everyone was nice about it and seemed to admire the fact that I always went to church and rested between services on the Sabbath. The example of applying the Christian principle in daily living must have had more influence with these men than any words of condemnation I might have spoken, for a neighbor told Dewey, "That preacher shore practices what he preaches and that's what a body admires to see in a feller. Hit's lak that pome he was sayin' in a sermon t'other day. 'I druther see a sermon than hear one any day.'"

We were nearing the end of the grain cutting when Albert received his call to report for duty in the C.C.C. camp at Lynchburg in Laclede County. The camp was only seventy miles from Cross Timbers.

Clayton and I accepted no cash pay from Dewey for we felt we owed him far more than the value of our work. The care, encouragement, and congenial atmosphere provided by the Bybees had aided Clayton to overcome his illness and we were grateful.

The Owsley community decided to start a two-weeks revival meeting late in July. My name was among the list of preachers who had been suggested for the task of conducting the protracted meeting. Since I was a candidate and my presence might prove embarrassing, Clayton and I left immediately after the Sunday morning worship services. But as it turned out, I was the unanimous choice.

I felt that this new task was a great responsibility and I wasn't any too sure that I could do it for it would require preaching a new sermon every night for three weeks with two sermons each Sunday. Twenty-six sermons to be prepared and preached in three weeks!

A committee of twelve was selected to prepare a list of the non-Christian people in the community. The committee spent several hours daily calling on people—invited them to attend church and prayed with them. They tried to make those called upon realize that there were others concerned about their souls' salvation. But they were over-zealous with old Horace Doubt.

Horace Doubt had recently moved into the neighborhood and of course everyone in Owsley and adjoining communities speculated upon which church his family "held to." All the denominations for miles around sent representatives to wait upon the Doubts. The newcomers attended the Baptist, Methodist and Campbellite churches and worshiped with each group. Such behavior was unheard of in the hills.

"Them folks don't stand for nothin'," was the way Aunt Sally Lawless put it, and hers was the general idea of the community from Cross Timbers to Climax Springs.

Doubt was doing his fall plowing about the time our revival started and he always worked his three big bay mares in a multiple hitch instead of the usual double hitch. He named his animals Baptist, Methodist and Campbellite and would yell at them and call them by name until he could be heard a mile down the valley.

Although members of the three faiths distrusted one another, they finally got together at the suggestion of several revival zealots and sent a delegation to ask that Doubt cease making fun of the churches.

He was plowing when the committee delivered their manifesto to him.

"Law, folks, I hain't makin' light of the Lord's work. Here's three horses and every one's a durned good 'un," Doubt said as he leaned against the plow handle and looked upon the committee with an amused smile. "I have a hell of a time ketchin' and hookin' them three mares together. They're allers bitin' and kickin' and squawlin' at each other, but folks, when I git them three hooked up together and lick the cussedness outten them I kin plow this field. Ever' one of them horses's got a little habit that makes a feller think of you'uns. Now there's old Methodist thar in the furry. She's a plumb good horse and does her full share but when night comes hit don't take no water at all to do her. Old Campbellite thar in the middle never lags a lick but hit takes a sight of water for her; old Baptist thar on the land side keeps her singletree tight all day long but when night comes durned if she'll eat lest I feed her in a stall by herself."

Old man Doubt straightened, adjusted the reins around his hips and grasped the plow handles.

"Sorry, folks, if you'uns think I war pokin' fun, fer I shore warn't aimin' to," he said as he tilted the plow point into the soil. "Giddap!"

He moved on down the field and left his committee grinning sheepishly.

CHAPTER 26

Housewarmin'

WHEN GRAIN HARVEST WAS FINISHED I HAD ABOUT fourteen dollars. With this money Clayton and I rented a small place that had a little cabin on it. Albert's first C.C.C. check came. It was twenty-five dollars and with our rent already paid this seemed a small fortune to us.

We took our windfall to a public sale and bought a table, a bed, a small cookstove, and odds and ends of small items such as stew pans, cups, saucers, knives, forks, spoons and tin cups. These helped make our two-room cabin less bare. Mrs. Bybee made us a bed tick which we filled with fresh oats straw and we had the quilt given me by the Mulberry School. We sewed up sheets out of feed sacks and sawed two large blocks of wood for chairs. Thus we set up housekeeping. The cabin was a very humble place but for the first time in many months we were in our own home.

We were eating breakfast that first morning when one of our neighbors came and asked us to help him saw wood. I had expected to remain at home and get things straightened up, but we both knew that unless one has a justifiable excuse, refusal to help a neighbor constitutes a grave breach of sociability in the Ozarks. There was no valid justification for not helping him, so we both gladly consented to go and left our breakfast clutter on the table.

We finished the wood sawing just at sundown.

"You'uns best have some supper before ya go back,

fer I'll bet yore old woman hain't cooked ya none," the neighbor jested. "I'll drive ya home after supper. Hain't no trouble. And nohow, my woman wants to go up to Wright's fer a set of quiltin' frames," he added before I could protest. We hurriedly ate a bite and then set out.

As we rounded the curve in the trail above our place we saw through the woodlands a bonfire burning in front of our cabin.

"Must be some 'possum hunters out tonight," my neighbor said laughingly to Clayton and me.

"Yes," I answered, as I realized what had happened, "and they caught the 'possum asleep this time. Of course you knew all day what was going on here."

"Shore, but 'twoulda spoilt the fun if we'un's told ye," he rejoined.

"Welcome, neighbor," the folks around the campfire cried as we climbed out of the wagon. I was so overcome with feeling as to be that rare specimen, a speechless preacher.

This, I knew, was an old-fashioned housewarming of the kind neighbors nearly always hold for a minister whenever he enters a new field in the Ozarks.

Our benefactors had papered both rooms with wallpaper. This was a signal honor bestowed upon us for when Ozark cabin walls are papered at all, either newspaper or wrapping paper is usually deemed adequate. Neat feed-sack curtains hung at the windows and pillows encased in slips with beautiful hand-worked edges were on the bed. A rug made by sewing together three twelve-foot strips of hand-woven rag carpet was spread upon the floor. Hand towels, tea towels, dishes, pans, a lamp and three hickory chairs had been donated.

Our table was loaded with food: meats, lard, butter, flour, meal, potatoes, sweet potatoes, cabbage; the prize of all was a five-gallon jar of sauerkraut—enough for a family of five! A cupboard had been built in the corner of the room which we used as a kitchen. It extended from the floor to the ceiling and the shelves were more than two feet wide in the center. Dozens of quarts of canned fruit, vegetables and meats stood in neat rows upon its shelves.

Since nearly everyone who lived in that community was present, I knew now that these hill folk had fully accepted the boys and me. I knew they loved us and appreciated my efforts to help them, and that this house-warming was their way of showing appreciation.

"Git yer partners fer Miller Boy," came a shout from the group of young folk about the bonfire outside. The hill musicians were seated on a large log which the young men had just carried in from the woods and placed near the fire. Two of them carefully unwrapped fiddles from pillowcase coverings, and the third young man took a guitar from its case and tuned up with the fiddlers. These players, like most of the hill musicians, couldn't read music nor could they count time, I'm sure, but they knew harmony and seemed possessed of an inherent sense of rhythm which enabled them to produce a type of music that pleased their fellow men and set their feet tingling.

Mountain music is expressive of the hillman's way of life. Its wild emotional strains harmonize with his being. He has learned his music from the orchestration of the many familiar sounds of nature: the calls of birds, water gurgling over rocks in sun-splashed streams, the "chug-arum" of frogs, the chirping of crickets, the rustle of leaves as a breeze outruns a sudden summer storm. These are songs in the hillman's ears as he daily roams the woods, plows the fields or fishes in the crystal-clear depths of a rock-bed mountain stream. It all bespeaks a free, happy and contented way of life.

Musicians of the hills are held in a certain esteem that sets them apart from their more ordinary fellow men. The three sitting on the log in the full glow of the brightly

burning bonfire were well aware of their importance.
They made their deliberate preparations while the audience waited impatiently. The "fiddles" and "git'tar"
finally tuned to their satisfaction, one of the musicians
yelled, "All to yer places, let'er go!" And the music began.
Everyone joined in the singing, as they moved in a circle
two by two, boy and girl, boy and girl, around the bonfire. The circle was a double one with the boys on the
outside, the girls on the inside. They circled back to back,
reaching arms backward over their shoulders to meet
those of their partners, and with hands thus joined behind
them, they moved to the right, keeping time with the
music and singing:

> "Oh, happy is the miller boy that lives by the mill,
> When the wheel turns around with a free good will,
> One hand in the hopper and the other in the sack,
> The ladies step forward and the gents fall back."

The players suited actions to the words of the song.
"Swing Josie," "Captain Jenks," "Skip-Come-a-Lou"
and "Pig in the Parlor" followed as the players chose them
one after the other.

The small children and elderly folk crowded into our
cabin. A half-dozen babies slept on the bed with two
small children. In the kitchen a ten-gallon tub of coffee
on the stove gave forth a tantalizing odor as the women
prepared refreshments. Pies, cakes and sandwiches were
piled high.

The men who had grown too old to share the excitement of a play-party sat on the floor and leaned against
the walls. They exchanged bits of news of common
interest, discussed prices, farm conditions, foxhunts,
politics and crops.

"Hogs shore hain't afetchin' nothin'," one man la-
mented. "Takes a hull hog to pants me, pants goin' up in
price like they air. But Rosyvelt hain't give no orders yet

fer a feller to go 'thout pants, so all you kin do is take
what they gives you and pay what they asks," he summed
to the merriment of the group.

"Judge, you get the young'uns to come in," Mrs. Bybee
announced at midnight. "Then everybody can pass along
the tables and help theirselves."

When the two rooms had filled, Judge Sundwall called
for everyone's attention. "We are shore glad Brother
Howard and his boys have moved into our neighborhood," he began. "We welcome them, and know they'll
be fine neighbors and do all the good they kin. Every
community needs a preacher alivin' among the folks. He's
there when young folks decide to hook up in double
harness," he continued with a merry twinkle in his eye,
then added more seriously, "and we all knows how he'll
go anywhere, any time, to help the sick or needy or for
funerals. Brother Howard's beginnin' a revival meetin'
at Owsley week from Sunday so let's all go. And now,"
he said reverently, "let's all bow our heads while Brother
Lige Gurney returns thanks."

The grace ended, eager hands reached for the food.
Possessing no false modesty, these hill folks saw no reason
to stop eating so long as there was food and one still had
an appetite for it. They ate their fill and the young ones
wished for greater capacities.

Midst much bantering and jesting, the happy band of
people was soon on the way home ere the final crumb had
been picked from the plates.

Clayton and I stood in our cabin door after the last
guest had gone and heard the echoing voices of the young
folk ringing through the woods as, homeward bound, they
gaily sang hill ballads.

CHAPTER 27

My First Revival

IT WOULD HAVE BEEN PLEASANT TO LUXURIATE IN OUR newly acquired cabin, but there were too many meeting arrangements yet undone. I had preached scores of sermons but this was my first revival and I must not fail. Subtle whisperings of error sniped at my morale as I worked. "You can't do it.... You'll fail— You'll fail.... You can't prepare a new sermon every night...." Hardly an hour passed that I did not silently pray for strength and courage and an understanding heart equal to the task ahead.

One sleepless night I stole quietly out of bed, dressed in my work clothes and walked the trail to the bald, rocky summit of Childer's Mountain. There, in the vast and solemn silence of the hills that below me were bathed in dim moonlight, I prayed and meditated. Stark's Creek wound its tortuous way down the valley past stately sycamores which stood as guardian sentinels clothed in white and mossy green-gray uniforms. This visit was so satisfying that I returned night after night to gain the moral courage needed to lead the Christian soldiers of Owsley in battle against Satan.

Workers soon had the schoolhouse ready for the revival. We scrubbed the floor and washed the windows. We built twelve wall brackets for the polished kerosene lamps which were to be used to illuminate the room. We brought an Estey organ from the home of a neighbor and set it in a conspicuous place at the front of the room. Several long benches were carpentered to augment the school seats, and on the evening of the revival opening our improvised church was ready. Billy Sunday might have had a bigger auditorium, but he couldn't have been more hopeful of it as a fortress from which to fight the devil.

"Prayer" was the subject of my first revival sermon; the text was Job 42:10, "And the Lord turned the captivity of Job, when he prayed for his friends: also the Lord gave Job twice as much as he had before."

"If we pray in faith, we must back our prayers with works," I said at the end of the sermon. "A great harvest of souls is what we are seeking. Support your prayers by working with those souls you would see saved."

It was time for closing. I admonished the congregation: "Everyone of you please do one of two things: boost this meeting or go out and knock it as hard as you can. I'd rather have you good knockers than to have you so indifferent you say nothing."

When we arrived home that night Clayton asked if we could bake a pan of biscuits and open a quart of the pear honey we got the night of the housewarming.

"All right, son," I consented. "I'm hungry, too." We built a fire in our small stove and prepared a supper of hot biscuits, butter, pear honey and coffee. Clayton went to bed as soon as he had finished eating, but I studied until two o'clock.

The revival crowd increased each night. Sometimes every seat was filled; many stood along the walls and children sat upon the platform that extended across the entire front of the building. One felt the presence of a satisfying spiritual influence in the meeting. When good old Uncle Tommy Horton prayed, it seemed as if he opened the very doors of heaven. He had been born and reared in the Owsley settlement and his daily life, his every deed and thought were that of a devout Christian. Everyone knew and loved the silver-haired old man.

One night toward the last of the first week Uncle Tommy came to me and said, "Brother Howard, if ye have the guidance of the Holy Spirit in preaching on this text, hit'd pleasure a body to hear ye preach on the question Pilate asked the Jews at Jesus' trial. He said, 'What shall I do then with Jesus which is called Christ?' Ever'one's got to answer that question. They's a lot of conviction in the hearts of sinners here night after night and if somebody starts it off, others'll shore foller."

The suggested text appealed to me and by the time I had walked the trail home I had the nucleus of a sermon in my mind. Next day the sermon outline came easily and I felt sure a good service would follow that night.

When the congregation finished the first bar of the invitation hymn five young women came and knelt at the altar, ready to accept Christ. They became wonderful personal workers during the rest of the meeting and helped with prospective converts during the next week. Not all the prospects were converted, however. Ford Barker, for instance. He was a handsome hillman and a born leader. He came to services every night, and it was obvious that the young people were influenced by him. On the night Clayton and I had supper in the Barker home, Ford walked to church with us. I spoke to him of his influence and stressed that as others were following his leadership he was obligated to God to put that influence to work in the meeting.

"Brother Howard, I expect to be a real Christian when I confess," he answered. "I aim to live as near like Christ as I kin. I allow to work at it every day like you been preachin', and I'd start now; but I'm afraid I couldn't hold out. I know them young folks that's been saved. They shorely believe they's really saved now, too," he continued, "but they're weak. Brother Howard, you'd be doin' 'em a real service if you'd cut you a ellum club

and bash 'em in the heads while they're fitten to die."
I remained silent as we walked along, so he continued,
"They won't stay with you. Too many things to lead
'em astray. I don't want to be thet kind of Christian, so
reckon I best not try it."

I was unable to persuade him from that decision.

"Better forget Ford, Rev. Howard, and go and see
Ceph Boothe," Effie Cox urged a few nights later. "Invite him to come to church. He lives with his aged mother
and their great problem is Ceph's drinking. He's not old,
and could be a very useful man. You may help him."

The Boothes' sole income was the small pension which
the mother received from some undisclosed source. Ceph's
economic stature was as low as his physical condition.
His affliction, he told me, was cancer of the stomach
which drink had caused. When I suggested that we attempt to get him into a St. Louis hospital for treatment,
he seemed grateful that someone was interested in his
condition. I invited him to church and he agreed to go if
he could sit in a cushioned chair. I promised to get one for
him, and he shaved, changed his clothes and went with me.

That night I preached on the subject "The wages of
sin is death," and ended by telling the story of two men.
I told of Dr. Charles Medbury, pastor of the great University Place Christian Church in Des Moines, Iowa, and
how he lived a life of service and died in the pulpit following a great sermon. "His hours of service were all
figured up, his pay check was ready," I concluded. "It
was drawn on the Bank of Glory and signed by the Son
of God."

The other man, whose nickname in the community
where he lived was "Old Rip," had led a vile, degrading
life. One of my high-school chums and I stood by the
side of a livery stable stall and saw him die in the throes
of delirium tremens. "Every demon of hell tormented
Old Rip in his last wild state. 'Hold me! Hold me!' Old

Rip screamed, as he died. 'I'm slippin' into hell.' His hours too, were figured. His pay check was ready. It was drawn on the Bank of Eternal Damnation and signed by Satan himself," I said, ending the sermon.

The young people's choir sang "Where He Leads Me I Will Follow" and at a signal the entire audience joined them. Ceph sat with his head bowed, and I saw that his temples were white. I walked to him, put my arm around his shoulder and said, "Ceph, let's settle it tonight." He silently shook his head and refused to talk with me. That was his last opportunity to make peace with the Creator for he died within a month.

The people at Owsley asked Clayton and me to spend all our time in their community during the revival. They wanted us to visit from day to day in the different homes, but I begged to return home each night where I felt the quiet of our cabin would afford greatest opportunity for study and rest. Besides, I had a laundry problem that could best be solved at home. The only dress clothes I possessed were a coat, a single white shirt and one pair of white duck trousers. These required daily laundering so that I could be freshly dressed for each evening's service. Each night after we returned to our cabin I put my white shirt and pants to soak in soft, sudsy water. Next morning I boiled and rinsed them and hung my wardrobe in the sun to dry. Later in the day I carefully ironed them, pressing stiff creases down the front of each trouser leg.

I took great pride in doing my laundry, and was much pleased one day when Mrs. Dyer said, "Brother Howard, I don't aim to be nosey, but some of the women asked me who does your laundry. Your clothes are always so clean and white I really think some of the women who are kinda proud of their own washin' are a little jealous of your washwoman," she laughed.

"You've certainly paid me a very pretty compliment,"

I replied. "It just so happens that the only dress clothes I possess are these which I wear every night and I launder them myself each day."

"My goodness!" Mrs. Dyer gasped. "Just wait until I tell them that! The men here in the hills think it's disgraceful to have to help with a little wash and only the timid ones ever do it."

Each new session of the revival became easier for me than the preceding one. A number of texts were suggested each night, and I generally selected one of them for the next night's sermon.

Several ministers of various denominations came to the services for I had made it plain from the first that my only purpose in conducting the revival was to see souls saved. Whenever the invitation hymn was sung, I stressed the fact that any convert was free to place his membership in the church of his choice.

"Shorely must be aworkin' fer the Lord fer ye hain't beggin' fer money nor a talkin' denomination," one man said. He organized a chicken shower for me on a Saturday night during the meeting. Every family represented at the services that night brought an offering and more than thirty hens were donated. At least a half-dozen different breeds were represented in the flock, but Clayton and I were pleased to have them.

"It's agoin' to look bad fer our preacher iffen folks sees him apackin' chickens home through the woods after dark," Lige Gurney laughed, "so reckon you'uns best fetch them chickens to my wagon and I'll drive him home to save his repytation."

Early on the morning following the chicken shower, a boy and girl walked down the trail to our cabin. They were bashfully holding hands when Clayton saw them approaching.

"Behold! The bridegroom cometh," he laughed. "It's a

wedding sure, Dad. I guess you can put them out of their misery if they have a license and ask for it," he teased. "Be sure and don't tie any slip knots."

The boy timorously approached the front door of our cabin. He was dressed in denim overalls and a blue chambray shirt which had been left unbuttoned at the collar. His shoes were freshly blacked. The girl wore a dress made from flowery feed sacks fashioned to fit her slim body.

"We'uns 'lowed ter git married," the boy explained when I met them at the door. "We got our license, but we shore hain't got no money."

"I never make any charge for Christian service, son," I said. "I'll gladly marry you. May I see your license?"

The boy took the license from his hip pocket and handed it to me.

"We'uns shore agoin' ter pay ye fer amarryin' us, even if we cain't now," the boy declared as the girl nodded her head approvingly.

"We'll have to have two witnesses," I explained.

"Won't you and him do?" the girl asked, pointing to Clayton.

"Clayton can be a witness, but since I am marrying you, we will have to have another," I said.

"I'll run over to Gates' and get Aileen," Clayton said. "Want her to see what a wedding's like anyway," he joked. Clayton and Aileen had been sparking.

Clayton returned, accompanied by Aileen, and I properly married the young couple. They took the whole affair very seriously and there was something sacred in the awkward manner in which the groom took his wife in his arms and kissed her at the completion of the ceremony.

I gave them a Bible and explained that any marriage, to be successful, must be built upon the sure foundation of love. "God's word teaches much of love. Love is the perfect demonstration of pure unselfishness and God's love for all of us is the highest example of it. He proved that unselfish love when He gave His only son for our sins," I said to them.

"We'uns'll read the Bible," the girl declared, "and we shore aims ter go to church on Sunday. It shore he'ps everything ter keep clost to the Lord."

After the newlyweds had gone and Clayton and Aileen left for the Gates' I hurriedly walked to Owsley for Sunday school and worship. I was not preaching the morning sermon that day, but I wanted to be on hand to propose that the church acquire an acre of ground and build a community edifice. It should be a union church where all denominations were welcome. I appointed a committee of six to investigate the advisability of such a movement.

The revival meeting continued all the following week, with several more converts, but near the end of the third week interest began to wane. I felt it was best to close the meeting so I announced that it would close with a basket dinner at the church and a baptizing in Stark's Creek on the following Sunday.

Sunday came with weather as tantalizing as the food that bulged from the baskets which the hill folk brought for the dinner.

The usual contingent of small children were skittering rocks across Stark's Creek when the congregation single-filed through mullein and fleabane daisy to the natural baptistry at the ford. The older folks congregated on the creek banks and the children filtered through their ranks or climbed to vantage points in near-by sycamore and sour gum trees to await the coming of the band of converts. The candidates for baptism had prepared themselves for their part in the ceremony at the church-house. Some of the men had on white cotton summer pants and shirt, others wore overalls. The women and girls who possessed white garments, and most did, wore them. My own meager wardrobe allowed me no choice. I removed my coat and put it across a bench, picked up my Bible and led the little band to the creek.

The words of "Shall We Gather at the River?" swelled through the woods as we paused at the water's edge. I opened my Bible and read the story of Phillip and the Ethiopian eunuch from the Book of Acts, then handed the Book to Clayton, who stood near by. The converts joined hands. I took the hand of one and unhesitatingly led the solemn queue into the clear cold waters of the stream. When I felt the chill swirl about my waist I stopped and turned to face the singers, who had finished their hymn and bowed their heads. I raised my hand in prayer. Then one by one I immersed the converts and guided them to a new line on my left. When the last young woman had emerged, we all grasped hands to form a complete circle. Thus we stood for another hymn and closing prayer before we dripped our way out of the creek.

The baptized women folk returned to the church where, behind blankets stretched across one corner of the room, they exchanged their wet clothes for dry ones. The men who had extra garments went into the brush. I followed them, removed my cotton shirt and trousers, wrung them as dry as possible and put them on again.

As I walked home that evening, keeping in the feeble sunlight as much as possible so that every ray of available warmth would help to dry my clothes and comfort my flesh, I recounted the work of the last month. I had preached for twenty-two consecutive nights and the result of the revival meeting, with the eighteen converts, was far better than I had dared to expect; I had performed my first wedding. My soul gave birth to a new confidence as I realized that now I was filling the niche in life that God intended for me.

CHAPTER 28

The Schoolteacher

CHILDREN ARE AS FREE WITH LOCAL GOSSIP IN A RURAL
Sunday school as they are in the district schoolhouse;
and when, one Sunday morning in early August, just
before time for the new term of school to start, I heard
Ancel Bratton and Orpha Jones discussing the new schoolteacher at Owsley, I listened with interest.

"I seen her, and boy, is she a looker!" Ancel was saying in a low voice when he should have been attentive
to the devotionals. "She was down to Pa's store with the
Dyers yesterday."

"Reckon she's going to stay at their place?" Orpha
asked.

"Reckon," the boy whispered. "Maybe you'll git to see
her if she comes to church with the Dyers."

"What's her name?"

"Gordon, or something like that. . . ."

The name meant nothing to me but I felt a natural
curiosity about the district's new schoolteacher for in an
isolated community the active, knowing workers with a
sense of leadership are so few that I anxiously wondered
how helpful the new teacher might be in our church
work. I knew the Dyers seldom missed a preaching service
and as no new schoolteacher can refuse a first invitation
to attend church I thought she could be expected that
morning.

I was watching when the Dyers drove up the road in
their topless two-seated carriage. Sure enough, they had
an extra passenger, but I didn't get a good look at her

until she stepped out of the vehicle and walked up the path to the church door. When I moved outside the open doorway to extend my hand of welcome, the newcomer smiled at me. I was so startled that I couldn't speak, for the new teacher was the same young woman who had taken me in and fed me on that hot July day I had first trudged into the Ozarks!

Mrs. Dyer started to introduce us: "Brother Howard, this is Miss Gordon, our new . . ." but Miss Gordon was already saying to me, "Brother Howard, it's nice to meet again. I've often thought about you and wondered what all might have happened to you after the day you had dinner with Aunt Sally Kate and Father and me."

"You remember that, do you?" I replied. "I didn't even think to ask your name then; but your kindness and encouragement meant a lot to me—more than you'll ever know, Miss Gordon."

"So you people know each other!" Mrs. Dyer exclaimed in surprise.

"Yes," Miss Gordon answered quickly. "We met more than two years ago."

"Then you ought to spend the day with us, Brother Howard," Mrs. Dyer invited. "You and Miss Gordon can have a long visit this afternoon."

"Thank you, Mrs. Dyer, I'll be glad to," I replied.

I met them outside after the services.

"You ought to be quite a walker by now, Brother Howard," Miss Gordon said. "I too like to walk, especially where there is so much natural beauty as you have all around you here."

"Would you care to walk back to the Dyers'?" I asked hopefully. "It's less than two miles, and if we take the short cut through the woods we can be there almost as soon as they. They'll have to drive the long way around."

"Sure, why not, Miss Gordon?" Mrs. Dyer urged. "You'll probably get there before us at that."

"Then let's do," Miss Gordon replied enthusiastically as we set off down the trail. The young lady was the first to speak.

"Doesn't it seem strange that we should meet again after only a chance meeting so far from here and such a long time ago?" she said. "You were a stranger there. Now, I'm the stranger. You spoke of my helping you, then. Now you have the opportunity to help me, for these people are so different from the people I've always known. Apparently they love and trust you, Brother Howard, and I want you to help me in working with them, for I want them to love and trust me, too."

"Yes, perhaps I can help you, Miss Gordon."

"Call me Mary Louise, please. All my friends do," she smiled. "Then I won't feel so alone."

"Thank you ... Mary Louise." I felt my face flush warm with embarrassment but I was pleased. "Yes, these people do trust me, I think, and I hope they love me, but it has been a long hard task to convince them that my motives were not selfish ones."

We walked slowly up the long slope, then paused at the summit to look out across the broad, timbered valley of Stark's Creek. The day was clear and warm and the visibility almost endless. The entire horizon seemed even higher than our vantage point and a misty blue defined every Ozark mountain rim.

"Isn't it like a painting of a beautiful scene in a deep-blue frame?" I suggested.

"Yes, it is a beautiful picture—a masterpiece painted by the Master Artist's hand." She spoke softly as we stood enthralled by the colors of the wooded hills in their first faint showing of gold, yellow and red.

"The woods will grow more beautiful every day until the leaves begin to fall," I prophesied.

"I'm looking forward to it," Mary Louise said dreamily. "I've always lived on the prairie, but I've read so much about the beauty of the hills, though this is the first time I've really seen them."

The walk to Dyers' seemed so much shorter than usual.

Dinner over, Mary Louise and I went to the rustic lawn seat beneath a great juniper tree, where we sat and visited all afternoon. We exchanged teaching experiences, talked of our hopes and visions; of how during dark hours in our lives God had always led us out into the light. For both of us, the Ozarks represented a quiet retreat. And so the afternoon passed. When we were eating supper Mrs. Dyer said that she would be unable to attend the evening church services as she must go to see her aged mother.

"Would you accompany me to church?" I asked Mary Louise.

"I'd like to go," she replied.

"Why not have Miss Gordon whistle for a special musical number?" Mrs. Dyer suggested. "She whistles grand. I heard her in her room yesterday, and she told me that she whistled for church services in her home town."

"Say, that would be fine," I replied. "The audience will surely enjoy it."

My sermon subject at church that night was "Hope" and when, following the Scripture reading and the announcement of my text, Mary Louise rose to whistle she tactfully selected "Whispering Hope" for her solo. She stood in front of the teacher's desk that I used as a pulpit. Her black hair and eyes brought out the perfection of her fair complexion; her pale-blue dress was as a chaste aura about her. She was tall and slender and her sparkling personality and stately poise made of her a striking figure. With the first bars of her solo, a solemn hush fell over the audience. The notes were as high and clear and liquid as the trill of the mocking bird. The music seemed to float away in the distance as it ended.

"You have added a great deal to the day," I told Mary Louise as we said good-night at Dyers' door.

It was almost eleven o'clock when I arrived at my cabin home. Clayton was in bed but he wasn't asleep.

"How about some bacon, eggs and coffee, Dad?" he asked.

"Suits me. I'm hungry, too," I replied.

I had always been comradely with my children; hence they had been unafraid to tell or ask me anything and I told them a great deal. The hours that Clayton and I spent together held more of the comradeship of two boys than a father and son relationship. So, this night, as we ate and drank our coffee and milk we chatted of the happenings of the eventful day.

It seemed that I had been asleep for hours when I was half-awakened by a timid rapping on the door. Then I heard a sob followed by more rapping. I sat up in bed wide awake.

"Yes?" I called.

"Please, Brother Howard, kin I talk to you?" a girl's voice said between broken sobs.

"Just a minute," I answered. I jumped up and quickly dressed. I lit the kerosene lamp and saw that Clayton had not wakened, so I went into the kitchen and shut the door between the two rooms.

"Come in," I said as I opened the door. My visitor was a twenty-year-old girl whom I recognized as the hired girl from a neighboring farm. "Sit over here," I indicated the corner near the stove, "and I'll fix up a fire. You're shivering."

Dry wood on the cookstove's live coals blazed quickly into warmth.

"Now tell me what's wrong," I said to the visitor. "What brings you here at this hour of the night?"

"I've heard lots about how you help folk when they's in trouble and I'm in awful trouble, Brother Howard." There was utter despair in her voice. "I'm going to have a baby."

Between fitful sobs, she told me her story. Her mother was dead. She knew nothing of her father. The people who had reared her were not relatives and she was afraid to tell them of her condition lest they turn her out. She had been keeping company with a hill boy for about a year; when she named him, I feared, for he was of a family whose general reputation was none too good. He worked on a small farm near by.

"We's been agoin' steady 'til two weeks ago," the girl said. "He jist quit without sayin' nothin'. Now he's agoin' with 'nother girl down the river. She's purtier'n me."

The girl admitted that she had not told the boy of her condition.

"Why didn't you tell him just as soon as you knew?" I asked.

" 'Fraid to. He might take out where nobody'd find him."

I warmed the brew that remained in the coffee pot and filled two cups.

"Here, let's drink some of this," I suggested. "Then you and I will hike over and see Darrel. If we go to-night we'll be sure and find him at home and no one will see us going."

She looked up with a faint glow of hope in her face.

I awakened Clayton and told him that a neighbor needed help and that I might not return until next day. Then we set off. The night was chilly so the girl and I walked rapidly and shortly arrived at the farm where the boy worked.

I left her in the woods pasture fifty yards from the cabin while I went nearer and called out a lusty "Hello."

"Who's thar?" the farmer asked as the door creaked open. I told him who I was and asked to see his hired hand.

"Sorry to disturb you," I said, "but I want to speak with him at once."

"Reckon the law's alookin' fer him," the farmer grumbled, "but his pap's the one that's cookin' off likker. But I reckon yo're only tryin' to he'p him," he said as he shuffled away to awaken the boy. The youth soon appeared tugging at a gallus on his overalls.

"Let's go down the trail a ways, son," I said as he stepped through the door. "I don't want anyone to hear what we say." We walked away from the cabin and headed toward the girl's hiding place.

I told him how the girl had come to my home and confessed her condition.

"Are you to blame?" I asked him point-blank.

"Reckon I am," he admitted. "Only reason I quit her was them folks she lives with's allers cussin' me out on account Pap's makin' whisky."

"Will you marry her?" I asked.

"Shore will," he answered. I quietly called the girl out of hiding. But her appearance did not startle the boy as I had expected. Neither spoke nor displayed any of the emotions that must have been suppressed within them.

"How old are you?" I asked them.

"I'm twenty-one past," was the boy's answer.

"I'm goin' on twenty," the girl said.

"Good!" I replied. "Neither of you needs parental consent for marrying, then. We can start right away and go to the store down the river. We'll get there in time to catch the mail bus and ride into town to the recorder's office. Then we can get the license and I'll marry you there this morning."

"I'll have to go back to the house and get my boss up to borry 'nuff money fer the license," the boy suggested.

I didn't distrust him but the freedom of the back door might be a temptation.

"No," I said, "let's not do that. I'll get the license and you can pay me some other time." I insisted that we start at once.

We walked the six miles to the little crossroads store and post office and had to wait only a few minutes on the mail truck bound for the county seat. It took us an hour to jolt the rough eighteen miles to the courthouse.

"Shore hope our married life hain't as rough as thet ride," the boy laughed as we climbed from the rear of the canvas-covered truck.

I bought the license with my last dollar and a half and married my charges in the recorder's office with the clerk and his deputy as witnesses. When I had made proper report of the ceremony and filed it with the license, I turned to the newlyweds. "Folks," I grinned, "it took the last cent I had for that license so there isn't any money to hire a jitney to take us home. I guess we'd better light out and walk the twenty-four miles back home."

And it wasn't too glum a wedding processional for all the untoward circumstances. We made a few practical plans for the young folks' future and parted hopefully at the fork of the trail.

These were busy days.

The day after the county seat trip, I received a post card from the superintendent of the Sunday school at Bethel inviting me to preach at the Benton County Singing School on the following Sunday. "Bring some representatives from your part of the woods, too," he wrote.

It had been a long time since I had had a good visit with Jake and Mandy Hillcroft so I went over to their place to discuss the advisability of Mulberry district sending an entry to the singing school. Moreover, I hadn't told Mandy Hillcroft about the charming new teacher at Owsley.

When I walked over the mountain to Dyers' and told them of the invitation from the Bethel church, they suggested that Owsley be represented at the sing by someone from the Young People's Society and Mary Louise as a whistling soloist.

"Brother Howard, I don't believe that old saying holds true of Miss Gordon," Mrs. Dyer said with a twinkle in her eyes. "You know—'A whistling woman and a crowing hen are sure to come to some bad end.' Stay for supper with us," she urged, "and you two can go to the young people's meeting together. If they want to furnish a solo or duet for the sing at Bethel we'll take the contestants over Sunday morning. It's about fifteen miles and that's too far for Miss Gordon to walk. We can start about six o'clock and that'll get us there in time for preaching."

"I'd sure appreciate it if things could be worked out that way," I said. "I want to preach in every community I can and I have never attended an Ozark sing."

Mary Louise came down the trail from school and was pleased when she learned of her invitation to participate in the singing festival. This was to be her initial singing school experience, too.

As I walked home after the young people's meeting I pondered the condition of my wardrobe. I had been seeing Mary Louise rather often and was eager to appear well dressed when in her company. But no matter how hard I tried to evolve a plan to acquire clothes to wear at the Bethel church Sunday, I seemed to find no way of replacing my summer trousers and coat. I should have been grateful for what I had but I found it necessary to struggle with a slight tinge of resentment at this apparent lack.

Like manna from heaven, there came in my mail later

that week a letter of credit from a Springfield clothing store. I thought it merely an advertising circular until I read that fifty dollars had been deposited there for my use toward the purchase of clothing.

I lost no time Saturday morning hitchhiking to Springfield, where I felt rich indeed when I learned that the credit was valid. I selected a new suit, shirt, underwear, shoes and socks. The store manager learned the nature of my work and gave me a ten-per-cent reduction on the cost of my purchases and this consideration enabled me to get a pair of shoes and a shirt for Clayton. I tried to learn my benefactor's name but the manager would not reveal it.

Clayton had loaned me three dollars to be used for bus fare if necessary, but I knew that he was saving for a guitar so I started walking out the highway toward home. Three miles out of Springfield a man gave me a ride that took me only a few miles from the trail that led through the woods to our cabin.

Clayton had not yet come from the neighboring farm where he was working that day, so I gathered the eggs, split the wood for the stove and got supper and had it on the table when he did come in. His precious three dollars was returned to him and his face brightened when I presented him with the new shoes and shirt.

That night both Clayton and I shaved and bathed before going to bed so that come morning we could get an early start on the nineteen-mile hike to the Bethel church. Clayton sensed my elation and my anticipation of the following day and jested, "Dad, you better not wear all those fancy duds tomorrow or that new teacher won't know you."

"I'll take care of that," I returned as I extinguished the light.

It was a rare pleasure to put on my new clothes next morning and I felt that I looked like a magazine advertisement as Clayton and I set off down the trail toward the Bethel sing. Neither of us talked, in deference to my habit of mentally organizing sermons as I hiked along the woodland paths.

The day was bright and beautiful, the air crisp and tangy, and the heavy dew on every blade of grass sparkled against the sun's rays. We saw full-grown squirrels running along the rail fences or scampering high into the hickories in fear lest we follow them to their secret winter storehouses. Birds flew from tree to tree and twittered excitedly as if in realization that their migration time was near.

The singing had not yet started when we reached Bethel church so we stayed outside to watch the gathering crowd. Families came in team-drawn wagons, in Model T's, in rattling old trucks and on shanks' ponies. Many were obviously from outside the immediate community and knew few people there. We, too, were strangers at Bethel but one does not long remain a stranger in an Ozark gathering. We were soon being made to feel at home by the folks all about us. One old-timer proudly related to me that the church had been built upon the site of the old Bethel campground where camp meetings had once been held. The burying ground there had been started in Civil War days as a cemetery for Union soldiers. His memories of those past days were much keener than of things present and evidently he found them much more pleasant.

Mary Louise and Owsley's two entrants in the sing arrived shortly before ten o'clock with the Dyers, in their carriage. I was sure Mary Louise had not been accustomed to riding in that sort of vehicle so I went to the hitch rack to meet them, thinking that perhaps I might be of some assistance in helping her get to the ground. I wasn't too sure that she would like Ozark inconveniences and since I had invited her here I felt responsible for her comfort. But before I could reach the side of the carriage she had hopped nimbly over the wheel and alighted directly in front of me.

"Hello!" she said as she recognized me. Then she motioned to the crowd milling about the church yard. "Where did all these people come from? Why didn't you tell me there would be a big crowd here? I'm scared."

"No need for you to be afraid," I reassured her. "Most of the people here may be able to sing or play an instrument but I'll bet there isn't a one who can whistle as you do."

"Thank you," she returned politely, her gaze full upon me. I had wondered if she would notice my new clothes but, of course, realized that she was too much of a lady to mention them. Nevertheless, I was pleased at what I took to be a look of admiration in her eyes as she smiled at me. When we entered the church building, we found it crowded and only a few seats remaining unoccupied. We found two near a window.

Since the Bethel sing was very popular, both county and district officers were presiding at the table in front of the room. The county president rapped for order and the buzz of talk and laughter subsided; there was an invocation, a short talk about the value of music in the lives of people, and an introduction of the officers of the day.

Each contestant was given a number corresponding to a place on the program and the announcement was made that anyone not in the building when his number was called would forfeit the right to perform. The competitive sing was scheduled for the afternoon program. Congregation singing started when an elderly woman was called to take charge of the pre-devotionals. This lasted an hour before the worship service was turned over to me.

I preached about thirty minutes.

Since it was then nearly noon the presiding officer announced that dinner would be spread in the yard. When the meal was finished and the audience reassembled in the church house, the sing began.

"Folks, let's get started," the presiding officer called above the babel of voices. "We're going to start our sing this afternoon," he continued, "with some of those old Christian Harmony hymns we all love so much." As the room quieted, he beckoned to an elderly man on the front row. "Professor John Frakes here is going to be our leader."

The professor beamed out over the open rectangular book which he balanced on his left forearm. The book's dog-eared pages curved over the crook of his elbow and extended to the palm of his hand.

"Everybody knows number eighty-seven in the Christian Harmony book," he said as he took a tuning fork from his pocket. "You folks with Blessed Hope books'll find it in there, too." He reached between the meager space that separated a couple seated on the front row and tapped the tuning fork on the back of the bench. Once on pitch, the group made the church ring with their song.

The singing continued as members of the audience called out selection after selection of their choice. Finally the presiding officer arose reluctantly and resumed authority. "We could go on singing these good old hymns forever," he said, "but we'll have to get along with the program. Thank you, Professor Frakes," he nodded dismissal to the leader, "you kin still do as good a job as when I went to school to you forty years ago."

"Looks like Mack's Creek community is first on the program," he consulted a sheet of paper in his hand. "They've brought a quartette and are going to sing 'Beautiful Isle of Somewhere.' Come on up and let's hear how you sing at Mack's Creek."

There were more quartettes, solos, duets, trios and other small group singing. An elderly couple, announced as recent celebrants of their sixtieth wedding anniversary, were too feeble to stand, so they sat in chairs on the rostrum and sang a duet.

I saw the afternoon sun dropping into the hills and asked a veteran in the seat near me, "What do you do if they don't get around to all the singers?"

"They'll keep on going 'til they're done," he chuckled. "Why I've listened to good singin' 'til the break of day. Thet war back in the good old days when folks tuk more time fer such doin's."

Mary Louise had been scheduled to appear toward the end of the program when the variety might lend contrast and relief to the long vocal program. When her number was announced, some of the folks appeared displeased that anyone should attempt to whistle at an Ozark sing. But when she took her place at the front of the hall and the first notes poured forth from her lips to fill the place with sweet, clear cadenzas, the audience was entranced. Before the last note had died away a burst broke forth. The handclapping continued until Mary Louise agreed to whistle again. Hers was the only encore of a program that lasted until six o'clock.

"It was splendid," I told her as she climbed into the Dyers' carriage. She nodded an acknowledgment of the compliment.

"Wish there was room to take you and Clayton," Dyer apologized as he snapped the reins over his team.

"So do I, but we may beat you home at that," I laughed. We waved them good-bye and Clayton and I struck out through the woods to our cabin.

CHAPTER 29

Union Church

THE INVESTIGATING COMMITTEE WHICH HAD BEEN appointed by the Owsley church group reported that the community wanted a union church.

"We dug up a few families who'd druther have a denominational church," Dave Cox, spokesman for the committee, stated in Sunday school one morning. "But most of 'em thinks a union house of worship'd be all right. Now, we figgered if we'uns raised a church house of logs, native stone and dressed-lumber an' put on oak shakes, hit'd not take much cash money. I reckon hit wouldn't take more'n a hundred dollars to do the job if we all pitch in an' holped."

There was much enthusiasm evinced over the project that morning so we asked the original committee to proceed with plans for organizing and building a permanent union church. Another group would consider how to raise the necessary money.

It was John and Lela Owen who set us on the path that led to our financial goal. They suggested that we raise the funds by giving a play. *Deacon Dubbs* did the job. This old three-act rural farce was selected because the stage settings and lines were simple and the script so old as to be royalty free. The only objection raised against it was that its fourteen character parts might give us more people on the stage than there would be in the audience. But we went ahead with it and, after six weeks of rehearsing, felt that we were finally ready to present *Deacon Dubbs* to Hickory County.

The Ozark premier of this rustic side-splitter was presented in the Jordan schoolhouse with the assistance of four hill musicians who were admitted free for furnishing olio numbers. We cleared twenty-seven dollars and, flushed by such success in a one-night stand, decided to move to greener pastures.

Cross Timbers furnished a larger hall, so we added forty dollars to our treasury when we played there. The circuit courtroom in the county courthouse in Hermitage was rent free and our net there was twenty-four dollars. Showing at Climax Springs and Mack's Creek netted us thirty-nine dollars more and, as we had exceeded our goal and most of the members of the cast were tiring of a trouper's life, we put *Deacon Dubbs* in our memory books and went back to our normal routine of living.

Now we had both the interest in the union church project and the funds with which to carry out our plans. Mrs. Dyers' mother donated an acre of ground along the road near the high ridge for the church site. The building committee had the lumber sawed and hauled to the building site; an ample supply of shingles was rived and stacked nearby. By the time the stone foundation had been laid the committee had completed the drafting of a set of by-laws and had it checked by the circuit judge. And so we called a meeting to formally organize our union church.

I envisioned this characterful Ozark hilltop church as the first of a great chain of edifices within easy access of the hill folks. They would stand where any who cared might come and worship. It would be the proof that men of good will could work and build together for a united religious kingdom of peace on earth. But I had not considered Self.

It makes no difference now (and I'm not sure I'd care to remember if I could) who it was that injected Self into the discussions at our organization meeting, but as soon as one person expressed a selfish desire there was another with an opposing desire. In less time than it takes to sing a doxology our little band of Christian workers had turned into a pack of snarling mercenaries. And the contention centered around the affiliation of our yet unbuilt church with some "recognized" church.

There was no malice in my heart as I quieted the group long enough to speak to them—only a hurt—a hurt more deep than any I had felt since the day I had followed Madge's casket through the little Iowa cemetery.

"The Church—Christ's Bride—is not an edifice," I began. "Neither is it any given pattern of dogmatic ritual. It is a common blending of a great and undying love that is God's gift to us. The highest pinnacle that love was ever known to reach was when the Redeemer cried from the depths of His broken heart, 'Forgive them, Father, for they know not what they do.'" I looked into each upturned face. They were the faces of hard-earned friends. Finally I continued, "Paul's words apply to us— to individuals and to memberships. 'Though I speak with the tongues of men and of angels, and have not love, I am become as sounding brass or a tinkling cymbal.'"

I looked out over the little group to find one who would take the leadership in restoring harmony to the organization here met to found a church. I saw the faces of bewildered children: Some were hopeful and sympathetic, desiring leadership; some were resentful or willful; a few were hostile. Only one appeared to express full understanding. That one was Mary Louise. There was no doubt of where she stood, but as the district school-teacher and a newcomer into the community she dared not speak one word lest she fan the flame of natural resentment of hill folks to outlanders into fire that would consume our remnant of hope.

"You people have made a splendid start and have done much good work," I continued. I had made a decision.

"When you are ready to forget Self, ready to put aside your petty jealousies and willfulness, I will hope to return and lead you in the glorious enterprise to which we all had pledged ourselves."

With bowed head and heavy heart I walked out of that graveyard of selfishness where the fine people of Owsley community had just buried a great and beautiful vision.

If you will drive over the road that crosses the highest point in Hickory County between Cross Timbers and Edwards, you may see, in a briar patch on the right slope, the unfinished foundation and the rotting timbers that (except for selfishness) might have been raised into a union church.

CHAPTER 30

"Whither Thou Goest..."

FOLKLORIST MAY KENNEDY MCCORD HAD ONCE SUGgested that I keep records of my work in the Ozark backhills, and when, shortly after the Owsley union church fiasco, Ann Fair of the Springfield *News-Leader* came to my Hickory County cabin for an interview, I had figures to show for my missionary efforts. They showed that in one year I had walked 3,363 miles, preached 252 times to audiences totaling 31,000 persons. As may be supposed, many of the persons were counted several times as I had twenty-three mission points where I preached at least one night each month. I never asked for an offering from any of these regular appointments and received one hundred seventy-two dollars and thirty-five cents; an income of fourteen dollars and thirty-six cents a month!

Miss Fair's story dubbed me "The Walkin' Preacher of the Ozarks," which was a virtual invitation to Ozark churches everywhere that they invite me to preach. The requests poured in but I attempted to fill only those from churches within fifteen miles of my cabin. Ozark church audiences are just as large on a weekday night as on Sunday and I maintained a full schedule. Generally I walked home after services but if the weather was bad I would spend the night with the first family that asked me. Then I devoted the following day to visiting as many people as I could. Those on the sick list were visited first.

Once I went to call on an elderly woman who had

been confined to her bed many years and found more sickness than I had anticipated. Granny Fawcett lived with her son and his family in a two-room dressed-lumber cabin and was confined to one of the four beds which, with a smoky King heater, virtually filled the cabin's main room. Her seventeen-year-old granddaughter tossed restlessly in one of the other beds.

I visited with the old woman a few minutes, said a prayer for her and turned toward the disquieted figure in the other bed. "Could I be of help to you, sister?"

"Don't reckon so," spoke up the grandmother. "She's havin' a baby."

I gave the girl a gentle pat on the head. "God bless you, daughter, a birth is a wonderful thing."

The grandmother sniffed, "Hain't nothin' wonderful 'bout hit if hit's a wood's colt."

I turned to leave. The hillman who had followed me into the cabin motioned for me to enter the lean-to kitchen.

"Kin ye stay to dinner, Brother Howard? Howard's yore name, ain't it?" he asked. I nodded. "Hain't no need of running off jist account of a bornin'. Tilly's been powerful sick since last night. We done sent fer Aunt Lizzie Smith—she's good when a baby's comin'." He shook his head mournfully. "I'm shore afraid fer Tilly, she's been so porely of late." His great frame trembled as he talked.

I sensed that he wanted me to stay because he feared for the life of his daughter, so I sat down at the table with him.

The parents of an unwed mother regard this tragedy in the lives of their children differently from the way residents of most urban areas do. Hill people feel that the birth of a child to an unwed mother is a terrible sin, but when a daughter of the hills "gets in trouble" her parents are not so much concerned with the disgrace brought upon the family as they are with the sin of the couple involved. They feel that the disgrace is the natural punishment for having transgressed God's law and therefore must be borne without complaint or any attempt at justification.

The man across the table from me seemed to think of me not as a stranger but as one whose work it is to guide the sinner, the weak, the erring, to the straight and narrow way that leads to an everlasting life. Perhaps I could somehow allay his fear that because Tilly had sinned she was more likely to die in childbirth.

As I watched his nervousness I thought, "What is more helpless than man's strength in woman's hour of pain?"

We had just finished eating and had stepped out into the yard when the man nodded toward the road, "Thar's Aunt Lizzie now," and went to let her through the gate. She was riding a small mule. Two much-worn carpet bags hung across the saddle in front of her. In remote mountain areas where the nearest practicing physician is often forty miles away there is always some elderly woman who officiates at nearly every accouchement. While much superstition and many unusual nostrums are a part of their practice, the granny doctors are often experienced practical nurses.

"How's Tilly comin'?" the woman questioned as she handed the rope halter to the man and slid off the mule.

"She's havin' a rough time," the father answered as he sadly shook his head.

"How long's she bin ahavin' the misery?" Aunt Lizzie asked.

"Hit come on her yesterday. She's been punishin' turrible since."

"If ye'll put my mule in the shed I'll fetch these here two satchels." She lifted the bags. I trailed behind the man as he led the mule away. The midwife walked briskly to the cabin, pulled the latchstring and entered.

"Tilly hain't a bad girl, Brother Howard," the man said as we walked the mule to shelter. "But she shore hankered after that Larkin boy. They'd been sparkin' fer a year 'fore he got drowned anettin'. Hit was 'fore I knowed Tilly war in th' family way. Reckon hit war my doin' that Tilly didn't tell me and Maw. Reckon I been too hard on my young'uns, Brother Howard. Meant to fetch 'em up right—and now she's havin' a wood's colt."

We returned to the kitchen and were listening to the clamor from the front room. Through the half-opened door I could see only Granny's bed but all the sounds came through the entry.

"Oh, oh, hit hurts! Hit hurts!" the girl screamed.

"Now, now, Tilly hit'll soon be here," Aunt Lizzie consoled.

"Oh! Oh!" moaned the girl.

I saw Granny raise up in her bed. "Shet up," she yelled in the direction of the girl's bed. "Lay down thar and shuck out thet young'un. Ye orta bin athinkin' 'bout the hurtin' when ye war slippin' out in the bresh huntin' it."

The father got to his feet. "Maw," he called through the door, "you lay down thar and shet up yoreself." His voice was stern.

Suddenly there was the sound of a resounding smack and a lusty cry came from behind the door. Tilly's child was born.

"Hit's a boy," the midwife called.

"How's Tilly doin'," the father called back.

"She's doin' all right," the girl's mother said as she came into the kitchen and took a steaming kettle of water from the squat iron cookstove and returned with it.

It was some minutes before anyone came into the kitchen again. Finally Aunt Lizzie entered. She carried the baby well wrapped in outing flannel. The child's maternal grandfather smiled faintly at the puffed red face that was almost buried in the swaddling clothes. Then the child's grandmother entered and the bundle was handed to her.

"Don't feed him none fer ten hours," the granny said. "Tilly needs rest and sleep and the little feller'll be better off. Iffen he gits colicky, make some weak catnip or pennyroyal tea an' give him a spoonful 'thout no sweet-enin'." She turned to the wash basin in the corner of the room. "Hank," she said over her shoulder, "you'uns got sheep, hain't ye?"

"Got forty ewes and one old buck," he answered.

"Wish't ye'd git me some dry sheep droppin's." She had finished washing her hands and was straightening her hair. "Pick 'em up on the hard ground er on rocks whar they ain't drawed no damp. I'm goin' to fetch them Davis young'uns some swallers of sheep-nanny tea. All them young'uns got measles and hain't broke out yet."

Hank rose to do Aunt Lizzie's bidding and I stepped into the next room to bid the little mother and the great-grandmother good-bye.

I rejoined the new grandfather outside the cabin. He was setting out with a fruit jar to collect the measle medicine and I bade him well as I took my leave and struck out on a short cut which would take me past the Owsley school. Mary Louise was locking the schoolhouse door when I arrived.

"How about letting me walk as far as Dyers' with you?" I asked.

"I'll be delighted to have you," she said as she turned the key in the lock. "You're so different from any person I've known. It's refreshing to catch a glimpse of you. I suppose you are just returning from some errand of serv-ice."

We left the schoolhouse and headed down the trail toward Mary Louise's boarding place.

"I preached at Hardscrabble last night and spent the

night there," I said without mention of the day's events. "I'm just on my way home. Tomorrow night is my regular preaching appointment at the Turney Ridge brush arbor—it's only four miles from here. Would you care to walk over there with me?"

"Why, yes, I'd like to go if the weather's fit," she replied. "These people are so interesting in spite of their prejudices that I enjoy getting to know them. I love to see you work with them and your sermons are an inspiration to me as well as to them."

Next day the time to call for Mary Louise seemed always to be far away but at last my impatience was rewarded and she was again at my side. I had noticed that the evening chill descended early that evening but I hadn't been much concerned with the lowering of the temperature as we hiked along. Yet when I rose to speak in the brush arbor I realized that fall was truly upon us and that this would have to be my last meeting of the year in an outdoor church.

My text was from the Book of Ruth where Boaz instructed his reapers to purposely leave gleanings for Ruth. In my sermon I spoke of the older Christian's duty to give the young workers parts to perform in church activities, to leave grain in the form of good examples.

The four-mile trail back through the wooded hills was illuminated by a rich harvest moon. The night was almost as light as day. At the crest of Childer's Ridge we paused and stood in silent admiration of the scene that stretched below us.

"I don't wonder that you love these hills and the people here," Mary Louise said softly, "and I can see why they love you. Every day you leave handfuls of the grain of truth, unselfishness and devotion to God where these people can and do glean."

"Thank you," I replied. "That means a great deal to me." I hesitated, and then turned to her. "Mary Louise,

I've been thinking that we both have come to realize just how much we mean to each other." I took her in my arms and whispered, "Mary Louise, will you share these hills, these people and this work with me?"

She was silent, and I was afraid. But when she finally raised her head from my shoulder she quoted softly, " 'Whither thou goest, I will go; thy people shall be my people and thy God my God.' "

CHAPTER 31

A New Life

WE STARTED THE NEW YEAR BY BECOMING MR. AND Mrs. Guy Howard in a simple ceremony at the Dyer home. My father, who had come from Iowa, Albert, Clayton and the Dyers were the only wedding guests. Brother Waisner, a neighboring pastor, read the vows.

We knew that a charivari would inevitably follow so instead of remaining at the Dyers' a second day, in deference to Mrs. Dyer's invalid mother we went to a neighbor's home. I omitted the usual cigar treat but, knowing that even the men never turned down a sweet, I bought six dollars' worth of candy for the event.

The merrymakers came at ten o'clock tooting fox horns, ringing cowbells and firing shotguns; they pounded on pans and hammered on the house with the palms of their hands. The deafening din persisted until we went to the door and bade them enter and partake of the treat which we had piled into a dishpan and set upon the table.

Fiddles and guitars appeared as if from nowhere and the leader of the group led off with a song that eventually evolved into a funny little folk ballad about an old maid and a bachelor "gettin' hitched." As they sang, Mary Louise and I had to stand in the center of the circle which they had formed. The charivari lasted two hours before the celebrants drifted away over the hill trails.

It would have been too far for Mary Louise to walk from our cabin every school day so she continued to board at Dyers' during the week. She had gotten along splendidly with the school. She made no attempt to revolutionize the district but by patient work with the children had been able to convince them and their parents of her love and sincerity. Sometimes the response to her gentleness assumed what to outsiders might appear to be very strange forms. That was the case with the Gulleys, who had come into the district under a clouded reputation. The children had never played with other youngsters and until they came to Owsley had never attended school anywhere. They had a fear of strangers and "the law" that was as keen and alert as any animal instinct. They seemed oblivious of property rights, believing that "if ye kin snuck hit, ye kin have hit."

"I had a terrible time with them when they first came to school," Mary Louise told me, "but finally thought they were beginning to respond. Then the other day the twelve-year-old girl put her arm around me at recess.

" 'I shore like you,' she said. I smiled at her, a little proudly, I fear. 'I'm agoin' to ask Gran'paw to snuck you a pair of slippers when he goes to town,' she said seriously.

" 'Oh no, dear, you mustn't...' I started to protest.

" 'Oh, hit's all right, Miz Howard. Gran'paw won't keer and we shore hain't agoin' to tell.' "

Owsley term ended in April and then Mary Louise took up permanent residence in our little cabin. We decided that she should give up teaching and that I would apply to teach at Owsley. The board granted me the contract and we rented a cabin about a mile and a quarter from the school. Clayton didn't move with us since he had taken a job working out for the summer and was to board at the home of his employer.

Several of the mission points where I preached held pound parties and showers for us and we raised a fine garden that assured us of food for the winter.

The winter was a busy one. Nearly every evening after

school I hiked to week-night appointments for preaching. I usually remained home on Saturday night but had
two Sunday services. There were many funerals that
winter and as invitations to preach came from towns
many miles away we were kept busy. My wife frequently
accompanied me on these preaching trips.

Mary Louise was a member of the Disciples of Christ
(commonly called the Christian Church, or Campbellites).
I had never joined any church in the hills. Since there
were no Friends in the Ozarks I decided, as my parents
had, that a "house divided against itself" would not stand,
so one Sunday we walked into Cross Timbers for morning worship and placed our membership in the Christian
Church there.

Once each month during the two years past I had
preached in the Methodist Church at Cross Timbers, but
after my affiliation with another church, a letter from the
Methodist pastor explained that I was no longer welcome
there. I knew that many members of that church would
be hurt and that a church squabble might result if they
knew of the letter, so I merely told them, when asked,
that I was unavailable.

Shortly after that I was ordained as a pastor in the
Christian Church by Brother J. H. Jones at a Fifth Sunday meeting in Wheatland. He gave the charge as I knelt
on the church platform and the elders stood around me
with their right hands on my bowed head.

Brother Jones asked: "Will you stand ready to answer
the call of service irrespective of personal feelings or
weather conditions?" I replied: "God helping me, I will."
Through my years of preaching I have kept that pledge
and on only four occasions have I been compelled to send
a substitute.

The first wedding I performed after being ordained was
Albert's. He came home from the Civilian Conservation
Corps camp and brought Viola Creason with him. They

were married in our cabin and when it came time for them to return to the forest area, Mary Louise and I rode along in the mail truck. That trip was to be Mary Louise's last for a while as she was soon to become a mother. A few weeks later Louise Ann was born in a Sedalia hospital.

During the two weeks that Mary Louise was away I kept the house and filled my usual preaching appointments at night. One evening at Cedar Ridge a very sad thing happened. A neighbor brought a death message to Ollie Hunt's where I was having supper. He reported that the only child of a young couple of newcomers in the community was dead. They had no kinfolks or acquaintances in the neighborhood and apparently were in sorry circumstances.

"Maw, you and the young'uns walk up to the church and let everybody know Brother Howard's come," my host directed his family. Then he spoke to me. "You and me'll go over and see what we kin do."

We were soon at the cabin and Ollie knocked on the door.

"Come in" was the faint response so I opened the door and we stepped inside the almost bare room. It was illuminated only by the glow from a crack in the stove and a faint streak of light that came through the door at our right.

"I'm the minister," I said as I walked across the room to a corner where a forlorn young man and woman sat on blocks of wood behind a dilapidated King heater.

"We're glad you come," the man said as he rose from his seat. "Reckon the baby'll have to be buried but I sure don't see how we're goin' to do it. We don't know nobody and ain't got a penny." The dismayed mother clung to his frayed denim jacket.

"Where is the baby?" I asked.

"In there," he said and nodded to the door across the room.

We followed the yellow trail of light and pushed open the bedroom door. A smoky kerosene lantern hung from the ceiling in the center of the room and cast its mushy rays over the room's scant furnishings. The light encircled a battered iron bed. A great round shadow from the bottom of the lantern fell across the bed's straw tick and threadbare quilt. The dead child lay almost hidden in the ghostly shadow.

The child must have been almost three years old and apparently lay just as he had died. He had been a beautiful child with long curly hair that came to the neck of his short flour-sack gown. I pulled the thin quilt up over his head and Ollie and I went back to the living room.

"Hasn't anyone been here?' I asked the couple.

"We just come in a week ago," the man replied.

"Where did you live before coming here?" I asked again, trying not to sound too much like a case worker.

"We come from Jeff City," the bereaved father explained. "I worked on W.P.A. 'til a month ago. Boss came around one day and asked us all to sign up for the guys he told us to vote for. Most of the men signed up because they was afraid of losin' their job if they didn't but I don't hold to that stuff. I'll be damned if I vote Democrat. So they fired me. Couldn't get work, so we come to the Ozarks."

"You folks had anything to eat?" asked Ollie. His was the hillman's practical approach to alleviating either physical or spiritual suffering.

"They's a couple cans of milk and a few eggs and a half-box of crackers," the young woman offered. "We bin savin' them fer Jimmie."

"My God!" the hillman exclaimed. "Shore sorry us folks around here didn't know about this. We's allers slow to git knowin' folks but we'uns woulda helped you out."

"You stay here with these people," I suggested, "and

I'll go on to church and send some other folks down. I'm sure we can get something done to help a little."

I arrived at the meeting almost an hour late and the congregation had filled in the time by singing hymns. Without further delays I read from the Bible Christ's rule for serving God as recorded by St. Matthew, 25:40: "Inasmuch as ye have done it unto one of the least of these my brethren, ye have done it unto me."

After the prayer, instead of a homily on the text I told my audience of the sad condition in the neighboring cabin and suggested that we organize to do God's will in an active service. Everyone wanted to help.

Watchers were dispatched to sit up for the bereaved couple, a collection was taken to buy coffin materials and a food and bedding shower was planned. I sent out word via grapevine that there would be no school on the morrow.

The young couple was amply cared for by the good people of the community but it was too late to give anything more than a decent burial to their child.

The months of that year were never dull ones. When Mary Louise and Louise Ann came home from the hospital, the household duties increased and it was my desire to help with them that I might in part justify my happiness. My day was rounded almost to the bursting with activity. I taught, preached, listened by the light of an Ozark moon to the confession of a wife murderer, baptized in winter-cold streams, conducted funerals and performed a few weddings.

In April I permitted my name to be placed on the primary ballot for a county office. The salary from this source would have relieved some of our economic pinch and still allowed me ample time for missionary work. But I wasn't a politician. I did keep my word to the county committee and spent twenty-nine days of weary walking to make my canvass of the voting precincts. Just before the primary election a woman at a missionary point (which also was a voting precinct) asked me for a five-dollar contribution to her aid society.

"You and one other candidate air the only ones that haven't donated and one feller give twenty-five dollars," she told me.

I was irate. "I'm not in favor of such things," I told her, "and I'm ashamed of any ladies' aid society that has to get its funds that way."

My opponents made capital of my refusal to contribute and the tale was repeated and elaborated upon at each telling until it grew into a canard. I was defeated.

"Ye've found Christianity don't need no politics, didn't ye?" consoled Uncle Dick Barnes. "But politics sure needs some Christianity, don't it?"

School was soon to end and I needs must prepare for the summer months when school district treasurers do not write warrants. I was offered the pastorate of the Christian Church at Houston, county seat of Texas County. A parsonage was furnished and I was to have two free Sundays each month for missionary work. I had little choice but to accept the call.

CHAPTER 32

Our Gethsemane

THE PARSONAGE AT HOUSTON WASN'T IMMEDIATELY available, for it had been rented, so we had to take temporary residence at a tourist camp.

Houston was a wealthy little town with considerable social grouping based upon material wealth. Naturally this created social problems and engendered religious problems as well. Just as some people could be catalogued according to the façade of their houses they might also be classed by the church which they attended.

The Baptist and Methodist churches had larger memberships than the Christian church, so one of my first tasks in the new appointment was to conduct a two-weeks revival. The harvest was small. There were only two new members as the result of this initial work in Houston and had it not been for the prospects of successful mission endeavor in the hills surrounding the town, I would have been very discouraged. But the fields were wide and fertile in the backhills and I walked again: Prescott ... Elk Creek ... Oak Hill ... Cantril.

We were finally able to move into the parsonage; and, as Louise Ann was soon to have a playmate and Mary Louise was ill, I spent more and more time close to Houston working with Boy Scouts, Christian Endeavor societies and other young people's groups.

At Oak Hill, which was a nearby community, we raised enough money at a pie supper to buy a linen table-cloth from a mail-order house. In this we embroidered "friendship" names with blue crochet thread, at twenty-five cents a name, and thus earned forty dollars which we used for building a cabin at Bennett Spring where a young people's Christian Service Camp was held annually.

I did missionary work between inmates of penitentiaries and their parents; for some seemingly worthy I obtained paroles. I helped procure medical aid for a number of children whose parents were unable to pay hospital bills and didn't know of the available help of charitable organizations. There were times when I longed to be a medical missionary. So many little backhills people needed so much help and I often wondered if adequate medical care would ever be provided for middle-class, independent and self-supporting people.

We had hoped our second child would be born on Christmas but Freida Helen arrived ahead of schedule. Then life under the parsonage eaves was further complicated when Louise Ann developed pneumonia while Freida Helen was getting her start in life and Mary Louise was still ill from a sickness that had had its beginning three months earlier. Finally, after weeks made bearable only by the kind ministrations of Mrs. Sarah Johnson and the practical nurse whom she brought and help from some of our faithful flock, my family was out of danger and I again had more time to devote to preaching.

Houston was not a wide-open town in the usual sense of the term, but it had within it and on the highways outside of the city limits many of the wrong kind of doors that swung ajar. Beer parlors and honky-tonks caused the townspeople considerable annoyance and I caused these joints some trouble in return. With the help of the Methodist minister I led a campaign to prevent the opening of more of such places and completely blocked the opening of a pool hall.

The two beer places which were able to keep their permits were on my beat and I made a regular practice of dropping in on them sometime between nine o'clock and midnight. Whenever I walked in the dancing couples glided to their seats, juke boxes became silent, beer bottles were whisked out of sight and the women hid their cigarettes. Boisterous laughter and profanity quieted. I would order a cup of coffee and take thirty minutes or more to drink it. Thus I became known as the "weekly nuisance."

One Saturday night as I left a beer joint I picked up a young man from where he lay dead drunk in the near-by alley, carried him home and put him to bed. Later I took him fishing and I guess I disappointed him by not delivering a personal sermon. The nearest I came to reminding him of his folly was when I invited him to "come to church Sunday," which he did.

Another pastor and I compiled a list of dry drugstores and restaurants in Texas County and had the list published weekly in the county newspapers. This publicity campaign began to show its effects when several restaurants gave up their beer permits and asked to be listed in our "dry" advertisement.

We carried our clean-up campaign to the county officials, too. They had grown lax with law enforcement, which was a factor in the flourishing roadhouse business. These men also resented our activity, but after two young people had been killed following brawls which had their beginnings in one particularly notorious place, the sheriff came and invited me to accompany him and the county prosecutor on a visit to the hellhole.

"I'll go if you'll let me take two of my Boy Scouts and get enough evidence to close the place," I said. "Everyone knows Boy Scouts are under eighteen and there's not many in a court who would doubt the word of one of the boys in my troop. I'll take two whose parents will give their consent," I promised.

The sheriff was dubious at first, but he finally agreed

to the idea and took the three of us and the county prosecutor to Happy Hollow Tavern. I went in first and
ordered a cup of coffee. There were more than a hundred
people in the place; men from seventeen to seventy;
women from fourteen to forty-five. This was my initial
visit here and no one paid any attention to me as I
walked through the well-filled room and sat down at a
side table.

The two uniformed Boy Scouts soon entered and acted
as per their instructions. They walked up to the bar and
inquired for the proprietor.

"I'm it," the man near the cash register said. "What
for you boys?"

"Two bottles of beer," they replied.

"Want to drink it here?" I heard the man ask.

"No, put it in a sack," one of the boys requested.

The proprietor took two bottles from the ice chest, put
them in a sack, accepted the boys' quarter and delivered
his ware over the counter to them. The boys walked outside and rejoined the sheriff and prosecuting attorney,
who had watched the proceedings through the window.
Almost immediately the two officials walked into the
place and the sheriff carried the sack of evidence to the
bar, where he arrested the proprietor. Soon this notorious
place was closed.

Mary Louise had a relapse and her condition grew
steadily worse through the spring months. Household
bills pyramided and the weight of it all pressed heavily
upon my shoulders. I worried lest we would never be
able to pay the doctor bill and started to apologize to Dr.
Herron for my negligence.

He smiled at me. "Brother Howard," he said, "never in
my life have I charged a minister a penny for my services
and I'm not going to start on you. Just remember to

tell the folks in a sermon some day that there are tithers who don't go to church. You're doing a fine work here but don't let them nail you to a cross."

Despite the doctor's continued attention to her, Mary Louise seemed to grow weaker and weaker and he recommended that she be taken to a good hospital for thorough examination and diagnosis. But our two babies were a big problem. I couldn't afford a competent nurse for them and I hadn't been able to supply them with adequate food. I was broke.

The income from my work had dwindled to almost nothing in the lean years that were upon the land. I tried to get a school but couldn't. During one period of four days a quart of milk was the daily fare for my family.

Famine and desperation made me abandon my pride and determine to take Mary Louise to St. Louis immediately and somehow see that the right kind of care was provided for the two babies. Several people offered to adopt the little girls, but such requests, even when they came from fine Christian people, hurt us to the quick.

We accepted the invitation of a neighbor to take us to St. Louis in her car after I had made preliminary arrangements for Mary Louise to enter Barnes Hospital. On our way to the hospital I took our little girls to the Christian orphanage. It was a dark hour when I left my family in the city and returned alone to the hills.

Funds were urgently needed to pay local bills; more money would be required for hospital bills. I went to work as a janitor and clerk in a Houston department store but I continued to fill my church appointments. One day I fainted in the store and Dr. Herron was summoned.

"Not a thing wrong but overwork and lack of food," I heard him say as I regained consciousness.

Mary Louise was able to return to Houston after six weeks in the hospital. Our creditors were pressing us so we decided there was only one honest course left open to us. We took it when we held a public sale and sadly parted with everything we possessed excepting a few books and Mary Louise's keepsakes. We paid our local bills and walked out of Houston with each other, a longing for our babies, our faith in God and sixty-three cents.

CHAPTER 33

Return to the Hills

WE WALKED DOWN HIGHWAY NO. 8 TOWARD SPRING-field and the heart of the hill country beyond. Mary Louise was still very weak and we had to travel slowly. All the garments we possessed were on our backs and the little bag I carried was very light for it held only our night clothes and our two Bibles. But the weight we carried in our hearts was great, for even with our faith, the way seemed very long—every step we took carried us farther from our babies.

We knew Louise Ann and Freida Helen would have the best of care in the orphanage until we could claim them, but that knowledge was an ineffectual antidote for the sickness that came from longing for our children. Baby ways and baby smiles weave themselves into one's heart. When they are parents' hearts, the warp and woof of sentiments may weave strange patterns—usually strong ones.

Mary Louise was crying when we stopped to rest under a great oak that spread its sheltering branches above the highway's right-of-way. She made no sound but the hot, salty tears flowed down her face. I was too low in spirit to offer much audible consolation—I could only put my arm around her that her back might not feel the rough-ness of the oak against which she leaned.

It is the hours of deep sorrow that draw husband and wife to a common plane of selfless love and mutual under-standing. We each knew the other's feelings and had not lost faith in our God or each other. That was something to be grateful for. We believed there was a field of service open to us with brighter days ahead when we could have a home and our babies with us again. That was the hope that sustained us in our dark hour and gave us strength to arise and continue walking down the highway accepting rides when they were offered.

Our last ride carried us into Springfield and was with an insurance salesman who asked us why we were on the road. We told him the reason but explained that we knew we'd be taken care of if we kept trying.

"And you still believe in God!" the salesman exclaimed. "Well, Mr. Howard, such living faith is a better sermon to me than many a high-salaried pastor has preached." As he started to drive into the Square he turned and said, "Will you folks eat lunch with me? I'd sincerely like to be that much help."

Naturally, with only sixty-three cents in my pocket, I'd worried a little about our next meal. We gladly accepted his kind invitation and when we said good-bye to this friend, he insisted that we accept ten dollars "because of the good we had done him."

We headed south out of Springfield toward the Arkansas border and by suppertime had progressed as far as Hollister. The comforts of Ye English Inn were a temptation but we compromised on a good evening meal and kept most of our ten dollars. A truck driver who sat at the counter in the Marathon Café where we ate offered to let us ride with him to Harrison, Arkansas. It was night when we arrived there so we went to Ozark Christian College, where Thomas Elmore Lucy, world traveler and elocutionist, with whom we had corresponded, was dean.

We remained there a few days while Mary Louise rested and our mail could catch up with us. I planned a revival itinerary. Then Mary Louise and I struck out across northern Arkansas and southern Missouri on a preaching junket that took us as weary stragglers into Yellville, Cotter and Three Brothers, Arkansas, and back up into Missouri, finally to Gainesville, a quiet inland town that has as its greatest asset a human dynamo called John Harlin. He was one of the first persons we met there because one can hardly turn in the place without encountering him. He is president of the bank, chairman of the White River R.E.A. co-operative, county treasurer, auctioneer and civic wheel horse. He had for many years preached most of the funeral sermons in the county.

"Brother Howard," Harlin said as we finished our visit and he was buying bus tickets to West Plains for us, "why don't you come to Gainesville some time and help me out? I need your help here."

I didn't realize then just how serious Mr. Harlin was about his invitation but before Mary Louise and I departed on the bus, I did agree to return some time and conduct a revival. "Just write when you're ready," I said.

From West Plains we worked southeastward. One beautiful fall day we walked into Naylor, a hard little town in the black bootheel country of Missouri. A three-weeks revival there yielded only one convert. We decided then to leave the lowlands and return to the Ozark hills. Mary Louise was terribly lonely without the babies and we finally decided to go into the city and claim them. She accepted her parents' invitation to bring the little girls to their home in Milo, Missouri, so I left my family in loving hands and continued on the road, walking from place to place, preaching and holding revivals.

Everywhere times were hard that winter. Several two- and three-week revivals each paid me less than fifteen dollars. Yet another Ozark spring finally blossomed into being, and with it came the hope and rise of spirit which always follows the bleakness of winter. Revivals at Roscoe and Schell City netted me sufficient funds to take my family to the latter village where I was given the pastorate of the Christian church there. Berea and Rinehart were added to my quarter-time appointments and the Rinehart church was a joy.

It was a country church in a truly rural setting and the congregation was proud of it. Men came to church there and accepted leadership responsibilities. As there were many tithers in the congregation there was always enough money in the treasury to pay all the church expenses for a year. Almost every family in that farming community had a God's Acre and the revenue from that acre, usually the highest-producing piece of ground on their place, went to the church.

God had rewarded our faith and we rejoiced over the good fortune that permitted our little family to reassemble under one roof. We headquartered at Schell City for it was a point most convenient for missionary work. I even got a short-term teaching job in a rural school near by. Daily I tramped over the Ozark hills to the school, to preaching services or to visit the sick. Often as a diversion as I hiked along the highways I counted things—birds, animals, and stock—killed by motorists. I soon noticed that empty liquor bottles lay in considerable numbers along the grassy highway shoulders. During one period I counted an average of forty-three empty bottles for each mile of highway! This seemed a shocking indication.

One Saturday night after preaching in an outlying community I was walking past a honky-tonk about midnight when I had a sudden desire to enter the place. I turned and walked into the Bucket of Blood Tavern.

"What's for you, Shorty?" the proprietor shouted above the din of the dancing and rowdiness.

"Seems like everybody's having quite a time here tonight," I said. "I suppose anything goes?"

"Sky's the limit, Shorty, sky's the limit," he laughed drunkenly.

I strode to the center of the dance floor just as the juke box ceased playing and before anyone could start it again I clapped my hands for attention and shouted, "Let us all bow our heads reverently while we pray."

Then I prayed as I had never prayed before and the place was silent as a tomb.

The "amen" said, I thanked the proprietor and walked out of the door. A truck driver followed me out and instead of offering to fight, as I expected, he offered me a ride that took me almost home. That evening's experience taught me that no matter how far in sin human beings may go they usually retain some respect for Christianity.

John Harlin was becoming insistent about my coming to Gainesville and finally I promised to go as soon as school was out.

At the invitation of May Kennedy McCord I attended a meeting of the Ozarkian Hillcrofters on Lake Taneycomo and there made the acquaintance of several writers. One of them did an illustrated feature about my work. Publicity came rapidly...*News-Week*, the *American*, We, the People...speaking engagements...the Missouri Press Association. Gordon Huddleson, editor of the *Kansas City Star*'s Missouri Notes, offered me fifteen dollars for a story. It was my first writing money. But I didn't let the illusions of my initial writing success fool me about the fickleness of the craft. I stuck to preaching.

In the meantime our older children became happily located. Albert, who had applied himself to his work in his quiet, industrious way, was soon promoted to the rangers' station at Houston, Missouri, and placed under the Forestry Department. Viola and he have three little children—two boys and a baby girl.

Clayton and Aileen Gates married and live contentedly on a little farm adjoining the place where he and I set up our first home in the Ozarks. They have a boy and a girl.

Virginia married Rolland Hess, a fine boy and a superior farmer. They live at Corwith, Iowa, with their two little girls and baby boy.

Mary Louise and I longed for a permanent home in the hills where we could settle with our own family and have the older children and grand-babies home to visit with us often. Besides there was John Harlin again insisting that I come to Gainesville as soon as possible.

"I'll cry the sales—you do the preaching," he wrote.

We moved to Gainesville in February, 1943. John Harlin had rented for us a beautiful little home tucked away in the cedars high on a hilltop overlooking the town. Later, with the help of kind friends, we bought the place. It was promptly and fittingly named "Cedar Crest Lodge."

Often Mary Louise and I sit before our fireplace as the sun goes down behind the rocky crest of Bald Jess. Thus secure and happy we breathe a prayer of thanks for God's goodness to us.

Our work increases steadily, but God gives us strength and grace to meet each new day's challenge and we are grateful that we are numbered among the workers who strive to carry out the Great Commission.

EPILOGUE

THAT'S THE FRAGRANCE OF YELLOW HONEYSUCKLE you smell. A dreamy sort of fragrance, isn't it? Always comes in on the evening breeze like that, comes from the vines over the woodshed. And that's an indigo bunting you hear warbling near by. Here, just step out upon the porch of our Cedar Crest Lodge a moment and I'll show it to you.... Mind that toy by the screen—it belongs to Louise Ann and Freida Helen's baby brother.

There, did you ever see anywhere a lovelier mass of honeysuckle? Against the blue haze of the Ozark hills, it's a perfect picture.

Have I quit walking? Oh, no! Never. But we feel settled here. We have a dream, and right over there past that fence is where we hope to see that dream become a reality. We are planning toward a self-help Bible school where boys and girls of the Ozarks can be trained in leadership and service for the benefit of themselves and their own Ozark communities. Of course we'll have to move our garden from where it is now, but we'll need a bigger one with our school anyway. It may have to be a regular farm, but it will be one where we'll have time for native craft work; time to sing and play and enjoy the bounties of nature as the Creator intended.

Doubtless God could have made a better country, but doubtless God never did. And when I'm called to leave it and walk down the lonesome road, I hope to go wearin' my walkin' shoes.